CHURCHILL COUNTY LIBRARY

3 1427 80058 2924

811.54
New

D1505086

Churchill County Library
553 S. Maine Street
F DISCARD 9406
(702) 423-7581

Charles Dickens Revisited

Twayne's English Authors Series

Herbert Sussman, Editor

Northeastern University

TEAS 558

CHARLES DICKENS
After a photograph by John Watkins (1861).

Charles Dickens Revisited

Robert Newsom

University of California, Irvine

Twayne Publishers
New York

Twayne's English Authors Series No. 558

Charles Dickens Revisited
Robert Newsom

Copyright © 2000 by Twayne Publishers

All rights reserved. No part of this book may be reproduced or transmitted in any form or by any means, electronic or mechanical, including photocopying, recording, or by any information storage and retrieval system, without permission in writing from the Publisher.

Twayne Publishers
1633 Broadway
New York, NY 10019

Library of Congress Cataloging-in-Publication Data

Newsom, Robert, 1944 –
    Charles Dickens revisited / Robert Newsom.
      p. cm. — (Twayne's English authors series ; TEAS 558)
    Includes bibliographical references (p.) and index.
    ISBN 0-8057-1630-0 (alk. paper)
    1. Dickens, Charles, 1812–1870—Criticism and interpretation.   I. Title.
II. Series.

PR4588 .N45 2000
823'.8 21—dc21

                                           99-046317

This paper meets the requirements of ANSI/NISO Z3948-1992 (Permanence of Paper).

10 9 8 7 6 5 4 3 2 1

Printed in the United States of America

For Cat and Andy

Contents

Acknowledgments

The general challenge of a volume in a series such as this is to pack as much useful knowledge and opinion as one can into a smallish book while still telling a readable story. One would like to be original enough to engage the professional while being conventional enough to serve the novice. Whether I shall turn out to have aptly struck that balance, these pages must show. My first great hope—that I would be able here to dispense the accumulated wisdom I have gained in almost three decades of teaching and writing about Dickens—has in the end given way to the sober realization that I know—or at least I have read—a bit more than I at first thought. Partly, of course, this is because so much can be and has been said about this the greatest novelist in English. Deciding what to leave out among the vast secondary literature has been the most painful part of the process. Deciding what among things included not explicitly to trace to all their various scholarly sources has created another large category of things left out and has been the next most difficult part of the process. I have therefore to acknowledge here that my debts of course go way beyond my endnotes and bibliography. Dickens is so rich that it is hard to write about him badly—or at least hard to write about without saying many true things. Geniuses are people who make criticism easy. I am mindful that for every curious article in an old *Dickensian* from which I *have* learned, there is also much that I never did get around to reading, as well as much from which I was probably just not capable of learning—and much too that I have simply forgotten. As Newman Noggs would say, please "Excuse errors."

My greatest pleasure is in acknowledging personal debts. Steven Marcus started me thinking seriously about Dickens in 1963, and his influence has never abated. A few years after, the late Florian Stuber gathered Linda Georgianna, Barbara Fisher, Monica Raymond, Joanna Cole, Henry Shapiro, Jane Meltzer, Mary Lamb, and myself into a Dickens reading group in New York City that is still going strong, and whose conversations remain lively for me, though Linda and I left it more than 20 years ago to find our fortunes out west. Not long before that move, Laura Ehrgott and the members of the New York branch of the Dickens Fellowship chose me as their leader and taught me to understand and value the perspective of the amateur. I am grateful also to the many undergraduates and graduate students who have endured my excruciatingly close, but loving, readings of Dickens.

Murray Baumgarten, Ed Eigner, and John Jordan changed my life, and the lives of a great many Dickens critics and Victorianists—and amateurs—by founding the University of California's Dickens Project at UC Santa Cruz. To them and especially to John, who now keeps all that marvelous company going, I am deeply grateful. The many faculty who have participated and from whose lectures and conversation I have benefited have included the Bobs Tracy and Patten, Rob Polhemus, Fred Kaplan, Jim Kincaid, David Miller, the late George Ford, Jack Hall, John Glavin, Sandy Welsh, Patrick McCarthy, Cathy Gallagher, Sylvère Monod, Paul Schlicke, Michal Ginsburg, Ruth Yeazell, Philip Collins, Garrett Stewart, Bill Daleski, Helena Michie, Gerhard Joseph, Annie Sadrin, David Parker, Joss Marsh, Michael Slater, Joe Childers, Catherine Robson, Betsy Gitter, Janice Carlisle, and Anne Humphreys. I am especially beholden to Hilary Schor. We have been talking Dickens for over 15 years, and I do not believe I have had a good idea about him in that time that she has not made better. My series editor, Herbert Sussman, has been unfailingly attentive, prompt, and helpful, and I am enormously grateful to him for approaching me with the idea of this project. But my deepest debts, as always, are to Linda Georgianna, who still loves me after all these years.

A Note on References and Editions

There are so many editions of Dickens's works in use that the most useful citations are simply parenthetical references to chapter number (e.g., *Pickwick*, 24), or book and chapter numbers in the case of *Hard Times, Little Dorrit, A Tale of Two Cities,* and *Our Mutual Friend* (e.g., *Tale*, 2.3), or chapter title in the case of some minor writings (e.g., "The Steam Excursion," *Boz*). Titles and chapters are not included where the context makes them clear. The first published edition of each novel usually provides the best text (the many subsequent editions even in Dickens's lifetime tended to introduce more errors than they corrected; the major exception is *Oliver Twist,* which Dickens carefully revised for publication in parts in 1846). The best modern texts of Dickens's works are generally those of the Clarendon edition of the novels (Oxford: Oxford University Press, 1966–). These also appear (without textual notes) in the more recent volumes in the World's Classics editions (also published by Oxford). The Norton Critical Editions of *Oliver Twist, Hard Times, Bleak House,* and *Great Expectations* are excellent, and the Penguin editions are usually the next best, though these are being challenged by a new series of Everymans (published by J. M. Dent) and volumes published by Bedford/St. Martin's and Broadview that, like Norton Criticals, include much supplementary material. My practice in quoting the novels and Christmas Books is to use Clarendons and Nortons as available, then first editions.

For most minor works I have used the texts of the New Oxford Illustrated Dickens (Oxford: Oxford University Press, 1947–1958; reprinted after 1966 as the Oxford Illustrated Dickens) and the two volumes of *Miscellaneous Papers* (which includes poems and plays) in the *National Edition* (ed. B. W. Matz [London: Chapman and Hall, 1906–1908]), which are being superseded in part by *The Dent Uniform Edition of Dickens's Journalism* (ed. Michael Slater [London: J. M. Dent, 1994–]). I use Philip Collins's edition of the public readings (Oxford: Clarendon Press, 1975, cited as *Readings*) and K. J. Fielding's edition of the speeches (Oxford: Clarendon Press, 1960, cited as *Speeches*), both published by Clarendon.

The definitive edition of the letters is *The Pilgrim Edition* (Oxford: Clarendon Press, 1965–), which now covers all but the last half decade or so of Dickens's life. I use this where possible and cite by date (British format, as in Pilgrim) and, if necessary, correspondent all letters directly quoted so that quotations may be checked against Pilgrim as it is completed. I have used various collections for late letters, notably that in the very rare Nonesuch edition (ed. Walter Dexter [Bloomsbury: Nonesuch Press, 1938]), which is the most complete before Pilgrim, and the first major collection, edited by Georgina Hogarth and Mamie Dickens (London: Chapman and Hall, 1880–1882), which is generally more accessible.

In the endnotes and selected bibliography I use the following abbreviations for the major works:

AN	*American Notes*
AYR	*All the Year Round*
BH	*Bleak House*
BL	*The Battle of Life*
BR	*Barnaby Rudge*
C	*The Chimes*
CC	*A Christmas Carol*
CH	*The Cricket on the Hearth*
CHE	*A Child's History of England*
CS	*Christmas Stories*
DC	*David Copperfield*
DS	*Dombey and Son*
GE	*Great Expectations*
HM	*The Haunted Man*
HT	*Hard Times*
HW	*Household Words*
LD	*Little Dorrit*
MC	*Martin Chuzzlewit*
MED	*The Mystery of Edwin Drood*
MHC	*Master Humphrey's Clock*
MP	*Miscellaneous Papers*
NN	*Nicholas Nickleby*
OCS	*The Old Curiosity Shop*
OMF	*Our Mutual Friend*

OT	*Oliver Twist*
PI	*Pictures from Italy*
PP	*The Pickwick Papers*
RP	*Reprinted Pieces*
SB	*Sketches by Boz*
TTC	*A Tale of Two Cities*
UT	*Uncommercial Traveller*

Although there have been many recent biographies, the two most useful continue to be John Forster's *The Life of Charles Dickens* (London: Chapman and Hall, 1872–1874; the best editions are those by J. W. T. Ley [London: Cecil Palmer, 1928] and A. J. Hoppé [London: J. M. Dent, 1966]) and Edgar Johnson's *Charles Dickens: His Tragedy and Triumph* (Boston: Little, Brown and Company, 1952; revised and abridged, New York: The Viking Press, 1977). I shall refer to these simply as "Forster" and "Johnson" and cite book or part and chapter (of the unabridged edition in the case of Johnson).

Chronology

1812   Charles John Huffam born 7 February in Mile End Terrace, Portsmouth, to Elizabeth and John Dickens, a clerk in the Navy Pay Office (married 1809, parents of Frances ["Fanny"], born 1810). Family moves to Hawke Street in June.

1813   Family moves to Southsea.

1814   Family moves to London when John Dickens is transferred to Somerset House.

1816   Letitia Dickens born. Family moves to Sheerness.

1817   Family moves to Ordnance Terrace, Chatham.

1819   Harriet Dickens born (dies in infancy).

1820   Frederick Dickens born.

1821   Family moves to St. Mary's Place, Chatham. Dickens attends William Giles's school.

1822   Alfred Dickens born. Family moves to Bayham Street, Camden Town, when John Dickens is again transferred to London. Dickens's schooling interrupted.

1823   Fanny Dickens a boarding pupil at the Royal Academy of Music. Family moves to Gower Street.

1824   Dickens begins work at Warren's Blacking, and his father is arrested for debt shortly after. Family moves (except for Charles and Fanny) with him into the Marshalsea prison. Dickens lives in Camden Town and later Lant Street, closer to the prison. Family moves to Somers Town after John Dickens's release in late May.

1825   John Dickens retires with a small pension. Charles leaves Warren's and becomes a pupil at Wellington House Academy.

1826   John Dickens begins a second career as a Parliamentary reporter.

1827   Another family move after their failure to pay rent. Dickens becomes a clerk for the solicitor Charles Molloy and then Ellis & Blackmore. Augustus, Dickens's youngest sibling, born.

1828   Dickens begins freelance reporting after learning shorthand. Another family move.

1830   Meets and falls in love with Maria Beadnell. They will part in 1833.

1832   Parliamentary reporting (in the year of the first Reform Bill) for *The Mirror of Parliament* and *The True Sun*.

1833   Dickens's first publication, "A Dinner at Poplar Walk," appears anonymously in the *Monthly Magazine*.

1834   Reporter for the *Morning Chronicle*. Several more sketches published. Moves into lodgings in Furnival's Inn with his brother Frederick. Meets Catherine Hogarth.

1835   More sketches published in various magazines. Engaged to Catherine.

1836   *Sketches by Boz,* first series, published February. Marries Catherine 2 April. *Pickwick Papers* begins publication May (and continues through October 1837). *Sunday Under Three Heads* published in June. A play, *The Village Coquettes,* produced in November. Resigns from *Morning Chronicle. Sketches by Boz,* second series, published December.

1837   First child, Charles Culliford Boz Dickens ("Charley"), born in January. *Oliver Twist* begins publication January in *Bentley's Miscellany* under Dickens's editorship (through April 1839). Move to Doughty Street (now the Dickens House Museum). Death of Catherine's sister Mary Hogarth 7 May.

1838   Mary Dickens ("Mamie") born in March. *Nicholas Nickleby* begins publication March (through October 1839).

1839   Resigns editorship of *Bentley's*. Kate Macready Dickens ("Katey") born. Move to Devonshire Terrace, Regent's Park.

1840   *Sketches of Young Couples* published. *Master Humphrey's Clock* begins weekly publication, including *The Old Curiosity Shop* April (through February 1841).

1841   Walter Landor Dickens born in February. *Barnaby Rudge* begins in *Master Humphrey's Clock* February (through November).

1842   Trip to North America (January through June). *American Notes* published October.

1843   *Martin Chuzzlewit* begins January (through July 1844). *A Christmas Carol*, the first of the Christmas Books, published December.

1844   Francis Jeffrey Dickens ("Frank") born in January. Trip to Italy begun in July. *The Chimes* published December.

1845   Trip to Italy concluded July. First amateur theatricals. Alfred D'Orsay Tennyson Dickens born in October. *The Cricket on the Hearth* published December.

1846   Editor of *The Daily News* (through early February). Living in Switzerland and France. *Pictures from Italy* published. Begins to write a version of the life of Jesus for his children (completed 1849; published posthumously as *The Life of Our Lord*.) *Dombey and Son* begins publication September (through April 1848). *The Battle of Life* published December.

1847   In Paris (through February). Sydney Smith Haldimand Dickens born April. Amateur theatricals. Opening of Miss Coutts's "Home for Homeless Women" (Urania Cottage) in November. Catherine miscarries in late December.

1848   Amateur theatricals spring and summer. Sister Fanny dies from tuberculosis September. *The Haunted Man*, last of the Christmas Books, published December.

1849   Henry Fielding Dickens ("Harry") born in January. *David Copperfield* begins publication April (through November 1850).

1850   *Household Words* begins weekly publication under Dickens's editorship March (through May 1859). Dora Annie Dickens born in August. Amateur theatricals in the fall.

1851   *A Child's History of England* begins publication in *Household Words* (through December 1853). Amateur theatricals. John Dickens dies 31 March. Dora Annie dies two weeks later. Move to Tavistock House, Tavistock Square, in November.

1852 Amateur theatricals (through September). *Bleak House* begins publication March (through September 1853). Last child, Edward Bulwer Lytton Dickens ("Plorn"), born in March.

1853 Living in France June through September. European tour October through mid-December. First public (charitable) reading (*A Christmas Carol* and *The Cricket on the Hearth*) in December.

1854 *Hard Times* begins weekly publication in *Household Words* April (through August). Living in France June (through October). Public readings in December.

1855 Reacquainted with Maria Beadnell (now Mrs. Winter). Public readings. Amateur theatricals. Living in Paris (through May 1856). *Little Dorrit* begins publication December (through June 1857). Commutes between England and France for public readings in December.

1856 Purchases Gad's Hill Place, Rochester. Living in France June (through early September). Amateur theatricals (Wilkie Collins's *The Frozen Deep*) in fall.

1857 Move to Gad's Hill in May. Walter Dickens leaves for India as an infantry cadet. *The Frozen Deep* performed before the Queen. Meets Ellen Ternan.

1858 First for-profit public readings begin in April (through early February 1859). Separation from Catherine in May. *Reprinted Pieces* published.

1859 *All the Year Round* begins weekly publication under Dickens's editorship April. *A Tale of Two Cities* begins weekly publication in first number of *All the Year Round* (through November). Public readings in fall.

1860 Essays that will become *Uncommercial Traveller* begin publication in *All the Year Round* January. Kate Dickens marries Wilkie Collins's brother Charles and brother Alfred dies in July. Sydney Dickens in training as naval cadet beginning September. *Great Expectations* begins weekly publication in *All the Year Round* December (through August 1860).

1861   Public readings begin March (through April). Public readings again October (through June 1862). Charles Dickens Jr. married in November.

1862   Living chiefly in France in the fall.

1863   Charitable public readings in January. Public readings begin March (through June). Elizabeth Dickens dies in September.

1864   Frank Dickens leaves for India in January. Dickens learns in February of Walter's death in India the previous December. *Our Mutual Friend* begins publication April (through November 1865).

1865   His foot frostbitten after a walk in February, the first of several illnesses that will mark his final years. Alfred Dickens sails for Australia in May. Staplehurst railway accident in June.

1866   Public readings begin April (through June). Brother Augustus dies in Chicago in October.

1867   Public readings begin January (through May). Second trip to the United States to perform public readings begins November (through April 1868).

1868   Returns to England in May. "Plorn," his youngest child, sails for Australia in September. Harry enters Cambridge University and brother Frederick dies in October. "Farewell" readings begin in October (through April 1869, when they are interrupted by illness).

1869   First performance of the reading "Sikes and Nancy" in January.

1870   "Farewell" readings resume in January (through March). *The Mystery of Edwin Drood* begins publication April (through September). Felled by a stroke 8 June at Gad's Hill, Dickens dies the following evening without regaining consciousness. Buried in Westminster Abbey 19 June.

Chapter One

Introduction: Dickens and the Problem of the Author

So enduringly popular is Dickens that there scarcely seems a need to justify another book about him. No other writer in English except Shakespeare has established so secure a place in cultural history. Tremendously popular with readers of all classes in his own day, he also exerted a uniquely powerful influence on other writers in English and many other languages. He was revered and imitated in widely varying ways by writers as different as Fedor Dostoevskii, Edgar Allan Poe, Leo Tolstoy, Marcel Proust, George Bernard Shaw, Joseph Conrad, and Franz Kafka. Even writers who stopped short of reverence, like Henry James or James Joyce, could scarcely step out from under his shadow. He shaped the subsequent history not only of the novel but of film as well through his influence on such pioneer filmmakers as D. W. Griffith, Charlie Chaplin, and Sergei Eizenshtein.

But the very idea of the "author" has come under such close critical scrutiny that we may at the outset ask whether even so prominent a figure as Dickens can safely escape the critical phenomenon known as "the death of the author." The French critic Roland Barthes coined this phrase in 1969, and the theme was elaborated shortly after by his countryman Michel Foucault in an essay whose very title asked, "What Is an Author?" Foucault answered, in effect, that an author ought to be regarded not as the autonomous creator of literature, the figure traditionally celebrated by criticism in the nineteenth and much of the twentieth century. He argued, rather, for seeing the author as the product or function of the "discourse" of an age—and by "discourse" he meant not just language abstractly conceived, but the whole range of human communication and interchange, even the range of knowledge, possible at a given time.[1]

Barthes's striking phrase was meant to turn critical attention away from the writer and towards the reader. He celebrated the active and

1

imaginative reader's power as a virtual collaborator in the creation of reading, or what he elsewhere called "the pleasure of the text."[2] Foucault pointed rather to the power of discourse itself, especially discourse as realized at particular places and times, to generate literature and, indeed, even in some real sense the very notion of the "author." In his account, it is more useful to think of the ruling culture (embodied in discourse) as writing *through* authors than the other way around, and he therefore stresses literature as a reflection or realization of culture more than as an individual creative act; in the process, he also transfers onto discourse much of the character (and even personality) previously associated with the writer. It is almost, for him, as though discourse has a mind of its own.

Both Barthes and Foucault saw clearly that interest in authors and authorship was a historical (and therefore limited) phenomenon, tied very much to the rise of individualism, and they regarded themselves as heralding a new era that would somehow get us beyond individualism and the often ahistorical adoration of genius associated with it. The recent turn in criticism to cultural studies seems to be impelled by much the same tide. Ironically, however, both Barthes and Foucault have proven interesting enough themselves as highly individualized "authors" to have elicited engaging biographies and biographical criticism, even if these seem to resist the drift of their own work and to suggest that we are a long way from having transcended individualism. Their views usefully challenge conventional wisdom and some bad critical habits, such as the veneration of "great" writers in ways that ultimately block criticism and turn readers into the merely passive consumers of the "masterpiece." They help remind us that the ideal reading does not exist, that literature emerges out of very specific historical moments that may in important ways be quite different from our own, that the values embodied in "masterpieces" are themselves historical and therefore subject to considerable changes with time, and that, once they are published, literary works actually have life only through the actions of real readers reading them. Because all reading takes place in time, even authors themselves are never perfect readers of their own works, for authors reading their own work are always different, even if only slightly so, from the persons they themselves were when they wrote.

Dickens tests the death-of-the-author proposition in fascinating ways. Precisely because he was so huge a presence in his own time and remains so pervasively influential in ours, his significance as "author" would be foolish to deny. But for the same reason, too, it proves an extremely demanding task to separate Dickens from Victorian culture—or, for that matter, even from nineteenth-century culture generally (beyond Great Britain, that is, to include the United States, Europe, Russia, and Asia; for Dickens's popularity was truly a global phenomenon, and he was read worldwide, in his own time as well as in ours). The study of Dickens's career thus returns no simple answer to the question whether authors write their cultures or are written by them. It might on the one side be argued that the person Charles Dickens was a classic example of someone who enters history by being at the right place at the right time, and that, no great systematic thinker himself, he just happened to combine attitudes and dispositions—many of which were a rather jumbled mix of liberal and conservative—that were characteristic of the rising middle class to which he belonged and which was coming to dominate literary and popular culture as well as political culture exactly when Victoria came to the throne and when the generation that would, years later, be named after her was eager for a bright new voice it could call its own. (As we shall see, a darker version of this argument, perhaps more in tune with the delicious sensitivity to the sinister so often registered in recent theory and most insistently by Foucault, would have it that bourgeois society ventriloquized through Dickens its profoundly repressive ideology in the guise of popular and liberal entertainment.) It might on the other side be argued that it was the Victorians who happened to be in the right place at the right time and that the person Charles Dickens was possessed of a singular and singularly powerful voice and imagination that impressed themselves indelibly upon his contemporaries as well as, indeed, upon the institution of the novel or literature generally.

Our dilemma could be evaded simply by granting that writers and their ages are mutually and hopelessly entangled and declaring that questions about who or what "wrote" the other are pointless, therefore—much less important than the question of what exactly it was that ended up being written, by whom or by what. But the current debates about authorship are interesting and important, and "Dickens" and the "Victorians" (or Victorian "discourse") have such powerful personalities that it proves exceedingly difficult to put either aside. Certainly that has proved largely impossible throughout the history of Dickens criticism, which has from its beginnings been fascinated (and often confused) by just such questions as continue to be turned over in present debates about the author. In 1844, when Dickens's career had not yet reached its zenith, R. H. Horne wrote in *A New Spirit of the Age* a long tribute to

Dickens (the leading essay among some two dozen) and concluded by remarking that "Mr. Dickens is manifestly the product of his age. He is a genuine emanation from its aggregate and entire spirit." Yet he asserts immediately after what seems to contradict this very claim: "He is not an imitator of any one" and, Horne adds, a few lines further down, "His influence upon his age is extensive—pleasurable, instructive, healthy, reformatory."[3] Given such inconsistency on the question of who the real agent is, it may well be said that the distinction between the author and his age has in the case of Dickens been problematic from the very beginning.

Dickens's authorship was very markedly bound up with his personality, which was strong and vividly projected into his writing, not just through his inventive style and marked characterizations, but through the personal, even theatrical note sounded by so many of his narrators, especially his third-person omniscient narrators.[4] At the very end of his career the *Times* noted in its obituary that the loss of Dickens "will be felt by millions as nothing less than a personal bereavement," for he had become so pervasive a figure as to be "the intimate of every household."[5] The appearance of John Forster's biography, the first volume of which was published just a couple of years after Dickens's death, with its appalling revelations about Dickens's boyhood (that he had been obliged by his father's imprisonment for debt to labor in degrading circumstances as a mere 12-year-old boy living in London quite on his own) only heightened interest in the life of a man who had always been so visible—not just as author, but as reader, speaker, actor, editor, philanthropist, and even as a figure of some scandal at the time of a painful and rather public separation from his wife. Part of what Forster revealed, too, was how much of the most familiar of Dickens's writing was in fact based on the most private aspects of the life, most notably the early chapters of *David Copperfield,* in which Dickens incorporated with only slight revision long passages from an autobiography on which he had been working; these passages poignantly described exactly those months during his father's imprisonment that he had kept secret from his public and all but two of his friends and family (Forster and his own wife).[6]

This very intimacy between author and readers was of course mutual and obscures not only distinctions between the "author" and his "age," but also the closely related distinction, so characteristic of the Victorians, between private and public. As a legacy of a large set of interrelated phenomena that had been gathering force since the Early Modern period and even the late Middle Ages—the rise of the middle class, the development of capitalism and industrialism, and (again) the attendant turn to individualism—this split was in the nineteenth century most apparent in the dramatic separation between, on the one hand, the home and, on the other, public places of work and play, as well as striking contrasts in character between these realms. Medieval households were typically both dwelling places and workplaces (even if much of the work was household work, such as the production of soap and candles and other provisions) in which women and men and grown-ups and children were thrown together, often in their sleeping as well as in their waking arrangements. But by the nineteenth century, at least among the more prosperous, a typical home both clearly distinguished itself from the world of work and divided itself up in complex ways that tended to keep both grown-ups and children apart (through the invention of the nursery and children's playrooms), as well as unmarried women and men apart (in individual bedrooms), and even, in the daytime, married men and women apart (through the proliferation of parlors, libraries, studies, dressing rooms, and assorted nooks). It also found new ways to keep servants and masters apart through the celebrated division of "upstairs" and "downstairs." Thus the Victorian home itself represented privacy and repeated the marking off of private spaces within itself.

The nineteenth-century home, moreover, separated itself from the public by championing values assumed to be antagonistic to those of the outside world. The realm of the public and of work was imagined as masculine, competitive, aggressive, and bordering on the amoral, always threatening to dissolve into the lawless. The home by contrast was figured as a comfortable refuge, ruled at least morally by feminine values, safe for children, and a place to which its masculine and legal head might retreat for refreshment in both body and spirit. If the Elizabethans coined the notion that a man's home is his castle, the Victorians saw to it that the castle was, in addition to being safe and secure, cozy and warm. Hence its favorite emblem was, once the door was securely locked, the hearth.[7]

This is the context that informs Dickens's peculiar and peculiarly two-sided intimacy with his readers. If readers felt they knew Dickens well (though perhaps little guessing until Forster's revelations just how *very* well), Dickens also clearly knew his readers well in turn. He knew both what they liked and what they were like. He knew their insides and he knew their outsides, and as much as the history of Dickens scholarship shows how difficult it is to escape Dickens's life, it also shows how equally inescapable were those external features that characterized his era. His works remain among the very best documents of Victorian social history—private and public—that we have. If one wants to know about the Victorian legal scene or the world of the small tradesman, about the impact of the building of the railways in the late forties or about Victorian philanthropy, about bureaucracy or prisons or newspapers or workhouses or schools or countless other institutions, about just how filthy a slum might be or what was done with rubbish, the novels of Dickens are a uniquely rich primary source. This intense curiosity about the minutiae of daily life was recognized already by his contemporaries; in 1858 Walter Bagehot remarked in a wonderful phrase that Dickens "describes London like a special correspondent for posterity."[8] Indeed, in such large areas as the law, crime, and education, the novels of Dickens remain essential reading for anyone interested in Victorian social history. But it is hardly reading of the detached, objective sort one may associate with history. Dickens, good journalist as well as good novelist that he was, aggressively invaded many a private as well as public space. If he was felt to be "the intimate of every household," it was not simply because his works were in virtually any house in which books were to be found, but because he himself penetrated as an active observer into the life of so many homes and workplaces. In the earliest planning stages of his periodical *Household Words,* he imagined the journal as being presided over and unified by

> a certain Shadow, which may go into any place, by sunlight, moonlight, starlight, firelight, candlelight, and be in all homes, and all nooks and corners, and be supposed to be cognisant of everything, and go everywhere, without the least difficulty. Which shall be in the Theatre, the Palace, the House of Commons, the Prisons, the Unions [workhouses], the Churches, on the Railroad, on the Sea, abroad and at home: a kind of semi-omniscient, omnipresent, intangible creature.... I want him to loom as a fanciful thing all over London; and to get up a general notion of 'What will the Shadow say about this, I wonder? ... Is the Shadow here?' (Forster, 6.4)

Striking here is the wish to become not only a magically invisible presence but one whose presence is nonetheless constantly imagined. Striking too is that Dickens seems to have recognized nothing sinister in such a being, whom he also describes as "cheerful, useful, and always welcome."

The tension between public and private is apparent as well in Dickens's ambivalence about secrets—his own as well as others. As I have noted, he kept secret the facts of his boyhood humiliations from everybody except his wife and one friend—who just happened to be the man to whom he had entrusted the writing of his biography. Even his children, therefore, joined in the general surprise when Forster's life appeared, though they could recall hints dropped by their father here and there, almost as if he had dared them to find him out or as if he was toying with the possibility of confession or gloating in the control that comes with secret knowledge. His son Henry records one such occasion just a year before Dickens's death:

> We had been playing a game that evening known as "The Memory Game," in which, after a while, my father joined, throwing all his energy into it, as he always did in anything he put his hand to. One of the party started by giving a name, such as, for instance, Napoleon. The next person had to repeat this and add something of his own, such as Napoleon, Blackbeetle, and so on, until the string of names began to get long and difficult to remember. My father, after many turns, had successfully gone through the long string of words, and finished up with his own contribution, "Warren's Blacking, 30, Strand." He gave this with an odd twinkle in his eye and a strange inflection in his voice which at once forcibly arrested my attention and left a vivid impression on my mind for some time afterwards. Why, I could not, for the life of me, understand. When, however, his tragic history appeared in Forster's Life, this game . . . flashed across my mind with extraordinary force, and the mystery was explained [for Warren's Blacking was the site of his degradation as a child].[9]

The anecdote is worth quoting in full because it is so very characteristic of Dickens's ambivalence about *telling*, which is for him as often a matter of withholding something as it is of a release. As in his imagining himself as the invisible Shadow, telling entails both the possession of secret knowledge and the power that comes when one is known to possess secret knowledge, here registered in the "odd twinkle of his eye," "strange inflection in his voice," and the "arrest" of his son's attention.

Dickens likewise loved secrets as a novelist, which is again to say that he loved first keeping them and then springing them upon his readers. Long before "mystery" was a genre, Dickens was writing mysteries and delighting not so much in their solution through elaborate processes of detection and deduction as in their almost explosive revelation (as, for example, in *Martin Chuzzlewit* the supposed poisoning of Anthony Chuzzlewit, investigated by Nadgett; or in *Bleak House* the murder of Mr. Tulkinghorn, unraveled by Inspector Bucket; or in *The Mystery of Edwin Drood* the murder of Edwin, probably to have been solved by Dick Datchery). The plots of many of his novels are structured by secrets (as, for example, *Nicholas Nickleby, Oliver Twist, Bleak House,* and *Little Dorrit,* and the respective secrets of Smike's, Oliver's, Esther Summerson's, and Arthur Clennam's births, or *Great Expectations* and the secret of Pip's benefactor, or *Our Mutual Friend* and the secret of John Harmon's return from the dead), and from the middle of his career on a fairly predictable pattern of proliferating secrets had become usual, especially in the larger works.

Many of these works begin by presenting a fairly explicit mystery about someone or something (in *Bleak House* we wonder who Esther's parents might be; in *Our Mutual Friend* we wonder who the mysterious John Rokesmith might be). This initial mystery is resolved about halfway through in a not very surprising way, the narrator and his extensive cast of characters often having dropped so many hints and clues that even less alert readers will have not so much solved the mystery as simply seen the revelation coming (in *Bleak House* we learn halfway through that Lady Dedlock is Esther's mother—Guppy figures it out, but so do most readers; in *Our Mutual Friend* we learn halfway through that Rokesmith is the supposedly drowned John Harmon— indeed he tells us so himself). But just as readers begin to congratulate themselves on their acuity, the novel develops a secondary mystery, which may at first not even clearly be identified *as* a mystery and turns out to be a good deal more resistant to solution than the first, or a good deal more dramatic in its solution. (In *Bleak House* there are actually two subsequent mysteries: who killed Tulkinghorn and where did Lady Dedlock flee to? Likewise, in *Our Mutual Friend* there is the mystery of Mr. Boffin's remarkable change of personality and the mystery of a new Harmon will discovered by Silas Wegg buried in the dust mounds.) Moreover, these larger secrets are themselves often hubs around which revolve whole constellations of lesser but interconnected secrets (thus in solving the mystery of Tulkinghorn's murder we also discover through the ancillary detection of Mrs. Bagnet that Trooper George is Mrs. Rouncewell's long-lost son). That is, the novels are not only structured by secrecy, but they are frequently explicitly and self-consciously *about* secrecy.[10]

Dickens's fascination with his own and others' secrets shows us one way in which his authorship was bound up with his personality and negotiated the split between public and private. The constraints he set for himself within which to publish show us another two-way bridge to his audience peculiarly characteristic of his mode of authorship.

All of his novels were published originally in serial parts, either in weekly numbers in journals (edited by Dickens himself) or, more usually, separately and by themselves.[11] The larger novels—the ones that run to 800 or 900 pages in modern editions—follow a consistent format that Dickens arrived at somewhat haphazardly in *The Pickwick Papers,* but that he and his public together liked so well that it became their favorite. In this model, a novel was published in parts that sold for a shilling each and were published at the beginning of every month for 19 months. Except for the last, so-called double number (labeled "Nos. XIX–XX" and priced at two shillings), each number consisted of 32 pages of text, two etched illustrations, and several pages of advertisements front and back, the whole being bound in distinctively colored greenish blue paper bearing an elaborate woodcut design and the novel's title. The final number had 48 pages of text and four illustrations. It also included front matter, usually consisting of a preface, table of contents, and list of illustrations with the pages they were to face. The two additional illustrations were a frontispiece and etched title page.[12]

The provision of front matter allowed buyers to have sets of parts bound up in book form after ads and wrappers had been removed and the plates rearranged using the list of illustrations as a guide. Individual parts remained on sale even after publication of the whole novel was complete so that buyers might obtain missing numbers to complete their sets, and simultaneously with the completion of the monthly numbers the publisher would also bring out the novel in volume form in bindings of various qualities and sometimes made up from unsold parts, sometimes from pages newly printed from stereotyped plates (plates cast from molds made from the original hand-set type). Twenty-one shillings—a guinea (a pound and a shilling)—was a large sum to spend on a single book at a time when an unmarried man might lead a modest but gentlemanly life on a few hundred pounds a year. But stretched out over more than a year and a half, the expense became affordable to many thousands.

Dickens (and his publishers) clearly profited from making his books affordable—in the middle of his career runs of 35,000 were not unusual—but it is not at all certain that economic motives were primary, for the novel in monthly parts imposed terrific limitations on the writer, especially one who, like Dickens, chose to publish as he wrote. When he undertook to write *Pickwick* in parts, serial publication was by no means a new thing, but in the later eighteenth and early nineteenth centuries it had been usual only for very long and expensive works (like dictionaries) or cheap reprints. It was not at all common for the first appearances of novels, which most often were published in three smaller volumes (the so-called three-decker) intended chiefly to be bought by private lending libraries whose subscribers paid a modest annual fee for borrowing privileges. In spite of Dickens's success, the three-volume format remained the most common for novels almost to the end of the nineteenth century. Many novelists published some of their works serially in monthly parts or, more commonly, in journals, but for none was it their favorite mode. Only Thackeray and Trollope among Dickens's major rivals regularly imitated his format.

And it is easy to see why. For the duration of each of the longer novels' publication, Dickens entered a rigorous monthly routine, for he was rarely more than a very few numbers ahead when publication actually began, and by the midpoint of most novels he was writing just one number ahead of his readers. This imposed certainly the most difficult constraint: the writer could not revise a number once published and had therefore to be unerring in judgments about even the tiniest details. The size of the task notwithstanding, the evidence indicates that Dickens did most of his planning in his head. From *Dombey and Son* on, he kept track of each number by folding a sheet of paper in half and noting on the left-hand side items he wanted to attend to in the course of the number and on the right-hand side the chapter titles and particulars to be handled therein. These number plans sometimes provide fascinating clues as to the workings of his mind.[13] But they also are quite spare, considering the density of the novels and that the notations on the memoranda are often nothing more detailed or revealing than, for example, "Miss Murdstone comes on a donkey" or "Aunt ruined?—Next time." As much as they represent Dickens's planning, that is, they also seem to have served as a simple way to keep track of business done and still to be done; the master plan, pretty clearly, was simply in Dickens's head.

An additional constraint was that each part had to come out to exactly 32 pages of print or just a few lines less, and since Dickens wrote in longhand (and of a gradually diminishing size throughout his career), his estimates were frequently wrong, requiring him to make many last-minute cuts or additions. Because a whole month elapsed between numbers, each part had to be reasonably self-contained. Suspense might be necessary and even desirable, but readers still wanted and got some sense of closure, even if only temporary, in each number. Thus number 14 of *Dombey* ends with both Florence's flight from her home after her father strikes her and hints that her childhood sweetheart, Walter Gay, has returned after having been supposed to have drowned in a shipwreck. Indeed, Dickens altered his original plan, which was to end with Florence's flight, by inserting another chapter in which she finds refuge with Captain Cuttle (who knows of Walter's return), "to leave a pleasanter impression on the reader," as he writes in his number plan (Stone, 90–91).

Dickens's monthly routine as a rule blocked off the first half of the month for writing and the last half for corrections. Type was set by hand from Dickens's close and difficult manuscript (often made even less legible thanks to Dickens's fondness for writing with quill pens rather than steel nibs, which were just coming into widespread use, and many deletions and insertions, strangely spelled names, and renderings of characters' idiosyncratic pronunciations). Sometimes two or more sets of proofs might be struck before publication day. Dickens always made numerous changes on the proofs, and throughout his career he relied at this stage on Forster, who served unofficially as editor. Moreover, since each number was accompanied by two illustrations, Dickens had to leave adequate time for his illustrator to prepare designs for plates, to revise the design if Dickens should wish it, and then to etch the plates themselves (in duplicate and even triplicate, on occasion, because the steel plates could stand only so many impressions before they wore down). As we shall see in chapter 4, interactions between writer and illustrator could be very difficult. Often Dickens had to choose subjects for plates before he had actually written the passages describing them, and this could cause delays should he later change his mind about details that might have seemed trivial until they showed up—or failed to show up—in an illustration.[14]

Already it should be clear that the business of writing was for Dickens a less private affair than we are likely to imagine for authors of novels—indeed he styled himself as a "conductor" when he came to edit *Household Words,* was director and stage manager in numerous amateur theatricals, and would surely have relished the job of film director had film been invented. Forster and the illustrators were privy to Dickens's plans and therefore in a position themselves to effect changes. And

Dickens on occasion shared proofs with other friends as well. The most famous such instance, because it led to a complete rewriting of the end of a novel, involved his showing the proofs of the last chapter of *Great Expectations* to his old friend Bulwer Lytton (also a novelist), who persuaded Dickens that the ending as written was far too somber. But then many authors show unpublished work to trusted friends and agents. What is truly extraordinary about Dickens's situation is again the fact of serial publication, which put the whole of his reading public in a situation only slightly less immediate than that of Forster or the illustrators. Not only might a close friend urge Dickens to handle his fictional creations in such and such a way, but *anybody* following the course of a story was in a position to throw in an opinion or request. A famous example of a change of this kind occurs in *David Copperfield,* into which Dickens had introduced the character of Miss Mowcher, a dwarf manicurist who, it was hinted, was of doubtful morals and might even be a pander. Dickens drew from life in at least some details; he had often seen such a figure in his own neighborhood. When the woman after whom Miss Mowcher was modeled read number 8 of *Copperfield,* she recognized herself and promptly wrote to Dickens to complain of the hurt he had done her. He quickly returned an apology and vowed to "alter the whole design of the character" (to Mrs. Jane Seymour Hill, 18 December 1849), and he made good on his promise in subsequent numbers, turning her indeed into something of a heroine.

It was not only private parties who could hope to sway the author's design. For the early numbers of the novels were regularly and heavily reviewed in journals and newspapers, and it frequently happened that reviewers—normally under cover of anonymity—would venture guesses as to outcomes of plot and would also make plain their own preferences.[15] Questions about how the plots were to turn out therefore provided convenient topics for general conversation, and Dickens heard about them and could read about them in almost any newspaper he cared to pick up. Like many writers, he claimed to pay reviews small mind and even declared in 1843 to have gone for five years without reading any for himself, but even so he allowed himself the loophole of hearing about reviews from acquaintances, and the claim is in any case clearly belied by fairly frequent references to "notices" in his letters.[16]

But in many ways the most powerful—because public—pressures came via plagiarisms and stage adaptations mounted without his permission often before the novels were finished, so as both to capitalize on public interest and to beat potential competitors. The lack of an international copyright agreement meant that the novels were regularly pirated abroad, especially in the United States. The general lack of enforcement of copyright law at home meant that, unless authors or publishers were willing to engage in very costly and uncertain litigation, they were easy targets for imitators and adapters.[17] The plagiarisms in book form tended either to be such flagrant copies or to be so badly written as to attract negligible notice, however much they may have drawn off sales. But the popularity of the theater and the dramatic (even melodramatic) nature of the novels themselves meant that stage adaptations could be successful and of some merit in their own right. In our own day, the popularity of Dickens as a source for stage and film adaptations continues so forcefully that it is easy to imagine what must have been the temptations on Victorian producers to satisfy the public appetite for Dickens, especially while a novel was still unfolding. A successful stage adaptation that was clever in its completion of plot lines could put Dickens in the somewhat awkward position of having to assert his own preeminent authority without appearing to have been forced into any given move by good guesses on the part of a plagiarist-adapter. One successful adapter of *Pickwick* even claimed, however implausibly, actually to have increased that novel's popularity and to have improved upon the original in his *Sam Weller, or the Pickwickians:*

> Some apology is due to Mr. Dickens for the liberty taken with him in fin-ishing his work before its time; but the great increase of popularity which it must have received from my putting it on the stage, will, I think, more than excuse a step to which I was urged rather by circumstances than desire. . . . Every wretched mongrel can, I am aware, dramatise *The Pick-wick Papers* now that I have shown them how . . . but even the original author will admit that he had never contemplated his matter could have been so compressed and his incidents put in so connected a form as they assume in "Sam Weller."[18]

Infuriating as such bold exploitation was, Dickens nonetheless throughout his life preferred serial publication and loved the compli-cated relations with his public that it entailed, because, for all its many inconveniences, hardships, and even injustices—as in the instance above—it created a peculiar closeness and even mutuality between author and reader not otherwise possible. In preface after preface (always the last piece of each novel to be written), Dickens sounds the theme of that closeness and refers to what in the preface to *Little Dorrit* he calls "the affection and confidence between us." He hated finishing his novels, both because ending meant "dismissing" his imaginary creatures and even "some portion of himself into the shadowy world" (as he writes in the preface to *Copperfield*) and because it meant a break with his public, whom he felt as much a friendly presence in his own life as they felt him in theirs.

It seems self-evident that this almost collaborative relationship between author and reader ended for all time when Dickens died. The literal, biological "death of the author" surely precluded the public's having any further say about how Dickens's writing might turn out. Or did it? In the narrowest sense this is a truism, for after the ninth of June, 1870, there was no more Dickens to make *anything* turn out. But "Dickens" rightly names not just the person Dickens who became on that date a corpse; it also names the corpus, the body of his work. And insofar as that work "lives," it may be said (varying a point already made), there has to be an audience to animate it, readers who become cocreators, who necessarily revise the original in the process. This collaborative revising occurs whenever a deceased writer is read, whether or not the writer is one who has become an institution, a legend, one of the "greats." But the collaboration and revising are more apparent still when the corpus is one that has been reanimated time and time again by generations of readers, critics, and adapters. *Mickey's Christmas Carol* may not look so very much like Dickens's because it has all those Disney characters playing the parts and letting their personalities get in the way. And Frank Capra's *It's a Wonderful Life* may not look like *A Christmas Carol* at all until an especially alert reviewer makes the connection.[19] But in a real way the process of "Dickens's" writing goes on through such works. And "Dickens" goes on writing us too, insofar as his work continues to shape our very culture, to define our possibilities for imagining something as inescapable as "Christmas," for example, or for imagining what a miser is supposed to look like. A large part of the fun of *Mickey's Christmas Carol* is in seeing how the traditional Dickens roles are played by characters from the Disney stock company who have their own well-developed personalities and in considering their appropriateness (the mild-mannered Mickey as Bob Cratchit, Pinocchio's conscience Jimminy Cricket as the Ghost of Christmas Past) or inappropriateness (Goofy as Marley, Donald as nephew Fred). That fun is given an unexpected twist when we realize that Fred's uncle Scrooge is played by Uncle Scrooge—that Uncle Scrooge is actually getting to pretend to be the character after whom he is named: his own original, as it were. An adaptation that may strike us as notably farfetched thus turns out to be surprisingly authentic.

There is an odd fact about Dickens's death that may be relevant to the unusual mutuality between Dickens and his readers and the question of the persistence of his writing. He died in the very middle of composing *The Mystery of Edwin Drood,* which duly appeared in its monthly installments until September 1870, when the pipeline of completed parts ran dry. Immediately there began to appear attempts at completions, at least one of which claimed to have been dictated to a medium by Dickens's spirit, and there has continued a steady trickle of these in many media—including, most improbably, a musical—down to the present day. The timing of his death has therefore left us in a singularly interminable relationship with him. Just as he was never able to put "The End" to a final novel, so too has he kept us perpetually in suspense. Does this make us even more fully his collaborators? Or does it point out to us once and for all how fictitious that collaboration has always been?

Before leaving the topic of authorship, let us return to "What Is an Author?" for one last turn, this time considering differences mentioned there among various *kinds* of authors. Foucault makes a curious distinction between writers of literature and writers of more overtly intellectual fare, to whom he grants a grander status:

> in the course of the nineteenth century there appeared in Europe another, more uncommon kind of author, whom one should confuse with neither the "great" literary authors, nor the authors of religious texts, nor the founders of science. . . . They are unique in that they are not just the authors of their own works. They have produced something else: the possibilities and the rules for the formation of other texts. In this sense they are very different, for example, from a novelist, who is, in fact, nothing more than the author of his own text. Freud is not just the author of *The Interpretation of Dreams* or *Jokes and Their Relation to the Unconscious;* Marx is not just the author of the *Communist Manifesto* or *Capital:* they both have established an endless possibility of discourse. (Foucault, 153–54)

In inventing elaborate theoretical structures complete with technical vocabularies, such "founders of discursivity," as Foucault calls them, have certainly provided the rest of us with endless possibilities for discourse. And Marx and Freud have undoubtedly been dominant thinkers for literary criticism and theory throughout the twentieth century, having even more lasting importance here, perhaps, than in their nominal disciplines. But it is not clear (apart from the fact that Foucault's kind of writing is much more like Marx's and Freud's than it is like a novelist's) why he makes so invidious a distinction, nor why novelists may not make the same impressive claim to having invented "the possibilities and the rules for the formation of other texts." For "discourse" is not limited to explicit theory or jargon; it includes ways of seeing and knowing and expressing, and novels are as likely to be the media through which discourse marks changes in its current as are works of economics or psychology.

Freud certainly gives us lots of new ways of talking about anxiety, for example. But then so does Dickens, who is masterful in his evocations of anxiety and makes his own enduring contribution to the vocabulary of anxiety via Mrs. Gummidge's marvelous—and now indispensable—term, "the creeps" (*Copperfield*, 3). Foucault unaccountably fails to imagine the influence novelists have not only on their immediate audience but on other novelists and, indeed, on his esteemed "founders of discursivity" themselves. Freud's favorite novel, as it happens, was *David Copperfield*, a copy of which he gave to his future wife not long after they met. And he gave the protagonist of one of his most important case histories the name of David's first love, "Dora." Like Dickens (and like David), he was auspiciously born with a caul—a membrane surrounding the fetus that occasionally still covers its head at birth and has been supposed sometimes to protect a child from death by drowning and sometimes more generally to be an omen of good things to come for its owner.[20] Freud was always among the first to credit poets with being ahead of psychoanalysis in its insights into the unconscious; he regularly points to the ancient Greeks, to Shakespeare, and to Goethe to familiarize his readers with otherwise difficult and disagreeable psychological truths. That he never leans on Dickens in similar circumstances has suggested to at least one critic that it was Freud's very closeness to Dickens that may have blinded him to Dickens's importance.

Psychoanalytic critics have always had a field day with Dickens. The critical essay that more than any other turned Dickens's reputation around among intellectuals in the United States in the middle of the twentieth century, Edmund Wilson's "Dickens: The Two Scrooges," was centrally informed by Freud.[21] But Ned Lukacher makes a sustained and intricate argument for Dickens as himself the deepest, most powerful influence on "the most fundamental aspects of Freud's thinking. . . . the problem of memory and . . . the necessity, indeed the compulsion, to construct alternate scenes in those instances where memory has become unreliable or somehow suspicious."[22] After showing how markedly the plot of Freud's case history of "The Rat-Man" follows that of *Copperfield*, he concludes that "In the culture of psychoanalysis, Dickens has always been the figure of both its prehistory and its future" (Lukacher, 336). This is a majestic claim indeed, for, without detracting anything from Freud, it nonetheless envelops him, so to speak, in a Dickensian caul. It gives Dickens a kind of active immortality, living not just through later readers and writers, but virtually continuing to write through them, so that it might even be said again that we have yet to put "The End" to Dickens's last work.

We have seen how complicated is the answer returned to the question of whether Dickens writes the Victorians, the Victorians write Dickens, Dickens writes us, or we write Dickens, for in important ways the answer turns out to be "all of the above." Less than almost any other literary figure, Dickens the "author" will not go quietly into the anonymity of "discourse." More than most other writers, he presents an uncommonly vivid self through his narrations, and more than most, too, he bases fictions upon his own life, though often in secret ways while thematizing secrecy itself. He liked to think of himself as knowledgeable about the secrets of others and imagined himself as an invisible presence throughout Britain, as though he would like actually to have the kind of magical power imagined for omniscient narrators—the ability to move through walls, to read minds. Nor will the figure of Dickens easily let itself be eclipsed by his era, which we are as likely to figure as "Dickensian" as "Victorian." His chosen mode of publication created a peculiarly intense relationship that felt to him almost like collaboration between himself and his public, and here again the line between public and private was intentionally blurred or crossed, though it was in the end not the fact of serial publication so much as the extraordinary fit between the writer and his readers that has made Dickens so literally and lastingly impressive.

In the course of considering the many complications surrounding Dickens and authorship, we have encountered a number of issues, many of which involve a family of related conflicts that can perhaps best and most generally be understood under the rubric of the conflict between public and private. Individualism, secrecy, the Victorian home, gender, authorship itself—these all entail tensions between public and private, which, in the case of Dickens, are markedly unstable and active. Just when we think we have pinned him down in a solidly private moment, he reveals himself most publicly; just when he seems to be speaking most publicly, he turns out to be protecting some deep secret. I will argue that such tensions are characteristic of Dickens and, moreover, that they are characteristic of his age—that the wonderfully, uncannily intimate fit between Dickens and the Victorians is more a matter of shared tensions and ambivalences than of simple characteristics or beliefs. And I will suggest that these continue to be of interest to us because they remain to a large extent conflicts still unresolved. Our innovation, indeed, may be more in having recognized their essential irresolvability than in having made progress towards their resolution.

Although this study aims to do justice to Dickens's career as an evolving whole and therefore to attend to almost all the major works and several of the lesser ones, it is arranged thematically around a series of tensions characteristic of Dickens and the Victorians. The particular tensions I have chosen figure more or less prominently at various stages of his career, and I have arranged these roughly chronologically, so that while reference will be made to works from every period of the career in each chapter, each chapter will nevertheless be centered on particular periods. Readers I hope will find that reading the chapters of the present study consecutively gives them a sense of Dickens's development.

Chapters 2 and 3 are more biographical than the rest in showing how the various competing pulls on and within Dickens personally resulted in a multiplicity of lives and careers. The pulls between private and public will continue to be of central interest and raise a related topic of lifelong concern to Dickens and the Victorians, very appropriate when lives begin to multiply—the problem of integrity. Integrity as a moral value was of course a central Victorian virtue, and integrity means wholeness, being consistently the same person in all situations, having no sides, and presenting an outer self the same as one's inner self. The Victorians were not only sensitive to hypocrisy but also adept at it, and hypocrisy may be said to mark one of the first stages down the road whose end is marked by an actual multiplication of selves, or the kind of divided self that is typified by Robert Louis Stevenson's *Dr. Jekyll and Mr. Hyde*, or, for that matter, Dickens's John Jasper, the protagonist of the unfinished *Mystery of Edwin Drood*. Criticism and theory, especially as informed by psychoanalysis, have in the twentieth century had much to say about the problem of the integrity of the self, and we shall see not only how Dickens's work lays important groundwork in this area, but also how his life proves paradigmatic. The very idea that people possess discrete and autonomous "selves" has come under skeptical questioning (related too to the problem of the "death of the author"), and Dickens's handling of his own self marks some important milestones on the way towards that questioning. In the following two chapters we will look at

Dickens's various selves and at his relations with women—the most significant category among his various "others."

Chapter 4 shifts attention to the works and takes up some explicit ethical and religious considerations that intersect with problems of self and integrity. These manifest themselves in a conflict between sentiment and skepticism, and I argue here that Dickens early in his career is deeply influenced by competing legacies of the Enlightenment: on the one hand a very secular tradition well on its way to denying any authority beyond the human, very antagonistic to traditional moral authority vested in ecclesiastical power, and on the other a pronounced sentimentalism that clothes the figures of children and females especially in conventionally religious imagery, replete with all the trappings of heaven, the divine, and the angelic. This particular split is connected in the purely secular realm with Dickens's political ambivalence, for the skeptical side aligns itself most often with an almost violent spirit of reform while the sentimental side fears change and seeks the security of the status quo.

We shall concentrate in chapter 5 on the central third of Dickens's career and its turn to an apparently (if *only* apparently) more "realistic" engagement with the domestic—marriage and the home. We shall see that even the most seemingly ordinary Dickensian home is beset by dangers internal as well as external and that chief among these is that bane of the housewife's existence, dirt. Dirt threatens not just neatness and the orderly arrangement of lives, but also life itself when it becomes the agent of disease, physical as well as moral. And dirt thus proves not just a domestic but a large-scale social problem as well, threatening all of London—indeed the whole nation and the very Empire. Dirt calls not only for the attention of the woman of the house, but also of the police.[23] And once again we shall see that Dickens does not come down cleanly, so to speak, on one side or the other, but that he continues to be characteristically divided. Not that he actually savors dirt in the way that he savors skepticism as well as sentiment, perhaps, but that he is at least drawn to the disorderliness that dirt signifies. Dirt, we might say, is never something he can simply leave alone or simply clean up.

Chapter 6 will bring us to the last phase of Dickens's career, and the competing concerns we shall centrally examine here are love and death. Neither, of course, is a simple opposite of the other, and in many situations the one is closely associated with the other while being itself unstable and threatening to erupt into its more obvious opposites, hate and life. In the later Dickens, powerful loves are always near neighbors to powerful hates, in a world at once pervaded by death and bursting with life—a world in which everything is dying, yet nothing dead stays dead for very long.

Our conclusion will return to some of the concerns already touched on here—the relations between the author and his culture and how the various conflicts that have structured our study relate to questions of class and specifically the peculiar nature of the middle class in the nineteenth century. We will attend here also to some larger questions about why it is especially the novel that is the dominant form, not just in literature but in Victorian culture more generally (in the way, say, that film comes to dominate the mid-twentieth century and television the latter twentieth century), and also revisit the question of Dickens's remarkable and, indeed, uniquely close fit with his era. What is it about the middle class, we shall ask, that produces a literary form so fraught with conflicts and ambivalence? And what makes Dickens the dominant novelistic voice for the middle third of the nineteenth century?

These final questions are important ones because ours remains a middle-class culture and even world. The values and beliefs associated with the middle class and the contradictions, inconsistencies, and problems associated with them have, since Dickens's day, become much more widespread and powerful across the globe, in spite of the decline of Britain and the Empire and, perhaps, the West in general. Even if the heyday of the novel is past, it remains a very important form that arguably persists as the chief cultural tool for articulating thinking, especially critical thinking, about class as class manifests itself in the daily life of home and workplace. And in parts of the world in which film and television are dominated by the productions of the United States, the novel still has a kind of cultural primacy it has not enjoyed in Europe or the United States for some while. If we in the United States and Britain look to Hollywood or the BBC for the latest incarnation of Dickens, in many parts of the world, notably Asia, it is still within the novel that his presence is most lively. (The question of Dickens's reception in the British Empire, the uses to which he and other Victorian writers were put by the ruling colonial classes in, for example, India, is a fascinating story in its own right.) Reading Dickens thus may help us understand not just the Victorians, not just the Victorians and ourselves, not just middle-class culture, but some of our contemporaries very different from ourselves and in some very distant reaches of the planet.

Chapter Two

Dickens's Lives (I): Selves

People who become international celebrities at the age of 25 are bound to lead eventful and complicated lives. Even before he became famous at that young age, Dickens's life was complicated enough for us to speak of it as already amounting to many lives. And, as already suggested, Dickens's writing was very much tied up with his own capitalizing upon those earlier lives. But his life was multiple, we shall see, in much more than in the fact that he did so many different things.

A very quick outline of Dickens's life has to list several episodes and crises that have achieved a quasi-legendary status among "Dickensians."[1] There is his happy childhood in seaside country towns where his father is a minor civil servant working in the Navy Pay Office—a childhood full of soldiers and sailors and theaters, toys, and fun; many moves (14 in as many years), climaxing in a move to London, where he experiences misery, trauma, and shame as his improvident father, John, who affects gentility, is imprisoned for debt and the 12-year-old Charles pawns the family possessions (including the little set of his father's books that he had avidly read and that had become his chief companions); working in a blacking factory (where shoe polish is made) and spending such free time as he has visiting the Marshalsea prison and desolately wandering the streets, despairing of the distinguished career he had, even at that young age, already imagined for himself; bitterness about his parents' apparent complacency, and jealousy of his older sister, Fanny, who, during all this unhappy time, is a boarding pupil on partial scholarship at the Royal Academy of Music and well on the road to a musical career; return to something like normal boyhood (and schooling) upon his father's release; brief employment as an attorney's clerk trying out the law; passionate infatuation with Maria Beadnell and, after three or four years, failure of his courtship; after a period intensely studying the mysteries of shorthand, working as a reporter recording parliamentary debates alongside his father, whose retirement from the civil service has allowed him to take up a second career; an aborted move towards professional acting; first efforts at writing (a moderately successful series of sketches of London life); marriage to Catherine Hogarth, the eldest of three daughters by whom Dickens has been charmed not long after his rejection by Maria; the smashing success of *The Pickwick Papers,* making him almost overnight the English-speaking world's favorite novelist and very soon thereafter virtually the whole world's favorite novelist; the sudden, tragic death in his arms of his beloved teenage sister-in-law, Mary, who frequently paid extended visits to the young married couple (her younger sister Georgina supplied her place a few years after by actually moving into the household); a quick succession of continuously popular works *(Oliver Twist, Nicholas Nickleby, The Old Curiosity Shop, Barnaby Rudge);* quarrels with publishers; lots of babies; a whirlwind tour of the United States, where he is as popular as in England (though he manages to make himself unpopular with some by denouncing slavery and complaining publicly about the lack of an international agreement on copyrights); more novelistic successes *(Martin Chuzzlewit, Dombey and Son)* and the inauguration of a series of small annual Christmas books (of which *A Christmas Carol* is the first); travels in Italy; experiments in therapeutic mesmerism with Mme. de la Rue, an emotionally unstable married woman, leading to Catherine's jealousy; forays into journalism, beginning with the brief editorship of *The Daily News,* and then founding his very own weekly periodical, *Household Words,* which he edits and writes for; forays into philanthropy, including becoming in effect private secretary and chief advisor to the Baroness Angela Burdett-Coutts, an immensely rich heiress devoted to good works, such as the reformation of prostitutes in Urania Cottage, a home for "fallen" women zealously overseen by Dickens on her behalf; forays into amateur theatricals (elaborate benefit productions that Dickens acts in, directs, produces, stage-manages, and sometimes writes); more novelistic successes *(Bleak House, Hard Times);* buying Gad's Hill Place, a house that he had admired as a very small boy in Rochester, and that his father had long ago told him he might one day attain if he persevered and worked very hard; strains upon the marriage that come to bursting when Dickens becomes infatuated with yet another woman in her teens, Ellen Ternan (or Nelly as she was "almost always known," according to her biographer, Claire Tomalin),[2] an actress whom he has come to know through the theatricals; painful and public separation from Catherine and setting up Nelly secretly in her own establishment, frequently visited by Dickens; more quarrels with publishers, leading to a new weekly edited by Dickens, *All the Year Round;* more successful novels *(Little Dorrit, A Tale of Two Cities, Great Expectations, Our Mutual Friend),* and a whole new career as a public reader of his own works, initially for charity, and then for (considerable) profit; heroism in a dreadful railway accident at Staplehurst that leaves him seriously unnerved; a very successful second visit to the United States with a frenzied reading tour; ominous signs that the readings are literally killing him, but he is unable to leave them alone and becomes morbidly attached to the most demanding and violent of the performances, "The Murder of Nancy" from *Oliver Twist;* after a final farewell round of readings, sudden death at only 58 from stroke in the middle of writing *Edwin Drood;* burial in Westminster Abbey after thousands visit the open grave, and the world mourns his loss—it will be months before the site is not daily marked by mounds of flowers left by a steady train of mourners.

And quite apart from the novels, Dickens had a full career as a writer in other genres. The early trips to America and Italy each led to a book about those travels, and the novels are rounded out in the works that Dickens thought well enough of to include in "The Charles Dickens Edition" of his works (completed shortly before his death) by two volumes of collected essays, a volume of short Christmas stories (in addition to the five Christmas Books), and *A Child's History of England.* Subsequent editions of the works have frequently been supplemented by additional journalism (some of it collaborations with his stable of writers for *Household Words* and *All the Year Round*), a volume of speeches, a volume of plays and poems, a volume of public readings (as well, of course, as several volumes of letters). Many nineteenth-century novelists wrote more than Dickens, but Dickens's work is unique in that the novels have all managed to hold the interest of scholars and students, and a great many of even the shorter minor writings remain in print and continue to be taught.

Packed though it is, such a sketch still neglects activities that almost amount to careers in themselves. The Pilgrim Edition of the letters will when complete contain about 12,000 letters, and these of course are only those whose texts survive. Given Dickens's early fame, many or even most correspondents were likely to have made some attempt at keeping letters from him, but still many thousands more have perished, and we know that Dickens on average wrote many letters a day. He had a very large circle of friends with whom he stayed in touch through letters (many he had met during his frequent travels, and his busy schedule often made it difficult to see even those in London), but of course his roles as editor and philanthropist attracted many letter writers who might otherwise not have approached the novelist. He loved to entertain children as well as grown-ups and was an extremely accomplished

magician; his conjuring, like his acting, was of professional caliber. He
was also a daily walker, and never more energetically so than when in
the middle of writing a novel. A walk of 8 or 9 miles was quite usual (he
had had to walk more than 5 miles a day when working at the blacking
factory, and about 12 miles on Sundays, when he visited his parents in
the Marshalsea and accompanied Fanny to the Royal Academy of
Music).[3] A walk might be especially useful when preparing an after-din-
ner speech (another of his careers); he would compose while walking and
use features of the landscape as mnemonic prompts, for he never spoke
from notes and would recall what he had composed by remembering his
route and the things he had encountered while on it, each of them associated with some point or heading.[4] Walks were also important during
several prolonged periods of insomnia when he was beset by unpleasant
imaginings and recollections, which he would flee by abandoning his
bed and prowling the streets. Walking relieved a certain restlessness
that manifested itself in frequent moves, lots of long and short journeys,
and working vacations in England and abroad.[5]

Restlessness, indeed, is a theme noticed by all his biographers and
amply attested to by Dickens himself. During the writing of *Barnaby
Rudge,* for example, he tells Forster, "I am in ecstatic restlessness" (2.5).
It is a curious expression, because the last thing we expect restlessness to
be is ecstatic. But it is characteristic too of Dickens's apparently unlim-
ited capacity for ambivalence—itself perhaps the sign of a restlessness so
deep that it might be said to lay within his very character.

Elsewhere Forster quotes Dickens as saying, "Assumption has charms
for me so delightful—I hardly know for how many wild reasons—that I
feel a loss of Oh I can't say what exquisite foolery, when I lose a chance
of being someone not in the remotest degree like myself" (11.3). Dickens's special brand of restlessness, that is, often entailed not just wanting
to be some*place* else, but to be some*body* else. The love of "assumption"—taking on the part of somebody not like oneself—and being a
restless mass of contradictory impulses are obviously related; both traits
suggest not only lots of internal conflicts, but also an acute self-consciousness moving towards a realization of what would be recognized in
the next century as the problem of selfhood. And both traits are evident
too in this remarkable description by one of his children of Dickens
actually in the process of writing:

> It was at Tavistock House [the house Dickens occupied in London
> through most of the fifties] that one of his daughters, after an illness, was

taken, at his request, to lie on the sofa in the study while he was at work. Of course this was considered a great honour, and of course she lay as quiet as a mouse. For a long time there was no sound but the rapid moving of his pen on the paper, then suddenly he jumped up, looked at himself in the glass, rushed back to his desk, then to the glass again, when presently he turned round and faced his daughter, staring at her, but not seeing her, and talking rapidly to himself, then once more back to his desk, where he remained writing until luncheon time. It was a most curious experience, and it was wonderful to see how completely he threw himself into the character his own imagination had made, his face, indeed his whole body changing, and he himself being lost entirely in working out his own ideas.[6]

It is no wonder that he loved to act, and his acting was certainly of a piece with the writing of his novels. His public readings, that is, simply let in on the spectacle of his creative "assumption" an audience much wider than his ill daughter.

In a similar vein, Dickens also reported that "every word said by his characters was distinctly *heard* by him" (Forster, 9.1), and, not surprisingly, that account has led to questions about hallucinations and even Dickens's sanity, though there is no reason to believe that he was ever close to being mad in fact. For while he may have "heard" voices and acted most peculiarly in front of mirrors, he always understood perfectly well what the insane do not—the difference between the fictional, or pretending, and the real. This is, however, emphatically not to deny that he was fascinated by insanity, fictionality, the problematic nature of the "real," or that he was in a meaningful sense possessed of or by multiple selves.[7] But Dickens's fascinations were not simply with the pathological so much as with the ways in which the pathological connects with the normal and the ways the pathological, indeed, reveals the normal. During one of his walks taken to ease a spell of insomnia, he wanders by Bethlehem Hospital—the London hospital for the insane whose corrupted name gives us the word *Bedlam*—and he asks himself, outside its walls,

Are not the sane and insane equal at night as the sane lie a dreaming? Are not all of us outside this hospital, who dream, more or less in the condition of those inside it, every night of our lives? . . . Said an afflicted man to me, when I was last in a hospital like this, "Sir, I can frequently fly." I was half ashamed to reflect that so could I—by night. . . . I wonder that the great master who knew everything, when he called Sleep the

> death of each day's life [i.e., Shakespeare, in *Macbeth*], did not call
> Dreams the insanity of each day's sanity. ("Night Walks," *Uncommercial*)

The anticipation of Freud is striking, and nowhere more so than in the
recognition of the close relationship between normal dreaming and
abnormal delusion. There is an unusually strong sympathy with the
mad in Dickens as in Freud, but it is a sympathy made possible by an
unusually confident sense of the real and of the self.

Taking a cue from Dickens and Forster themselves, many critics have
sought a sort of master narrative explaining Dickens's restlessness—
indeed, virtually every aspect of his adult personality and career—in the
"Hard Experiences in Boyhood" first revealed by Forster (1.2) and based
upon the autobiographical fragment that Dickens wrote sometime in
the forties, around the time a chance remark made to Forster by a friend
of John Dickens's prompted the sharing of the secret.[8] The friend
remembered long ago having seen the young Charles at work in the
blacking factory, and the recollection was mentioned in turn by Forster
to Dickens, who fell silent in obvious discomfort, as though Forster "had
touched a painful place in his memory." Shortly after, Dickens told
Forster the full story and showed him the autobiographical fragment,
which he later gave to him, after having already designated Forster as
his official biographer. He seems to have abandoned the project of writing his autobiography after having incorporated much of what had been
written into *David Copperfield,* with only very slight alterations.[9]

Dickens and Forster together make much of these experiences,
although exactly *what* they make of them is hard to say. "In what way
those strange experiences of his boyhood affected him afterwards, the
narrative of his life must show," Forster tells us. And he quotes as typical
a letter of 1862 in which Dickens seems to be asking allowance for some
transgression (no doubt in the long unhappy wake of his separation
from his wife, though Forster does not specify the context):

> I must entreat you . . . to pause for an instant, and go back to what you
> know of my childish days, and to ask yourself whether it is natural that
> something of the character formed in me then, and lost under happier
> circumstances, should have reappeared in the last five years. The never-
> to-be-forgotten misery of that old time bred a certain shrinking sensi-
> tiveness in a certain ill-clad, ill-fed child, that I have found come back in
> the never-to-be-forgotten misery of this later time. (1.3)

In the fragment itself, written during that time of "happier circumstances," Dickens confides "that even now, famous and caressed and

happy, I often forget in my dreams that I have a dear wife and children; even that I am a man; and wander desolately back to that time of my life."

Short though it is, the fragment is too long to quote at length here, but, given all the attention it has received from Forster on, it is important nevertheless for any serious student of Dickens to read it closely. It records the family's steady decline after moving to London and the crisis at which it arrived when John Dickens's lifelong tendency to spend a good deal more than he could afford caught up with him, and he was imprisoned for failure to pay a baker's bill of some £40—actually quite a considerable sum, and evidently a bill that had been accumulating for some time.[10] The logic behind imprisonment for debt assumed debtors would pay up once they were imprisoned, and an imprisoned debtor could get out of jail only by paying the debt, declaring insolvency (which could bring with it some bad consequences), or dying. A surprising number of debtors followed that last path, so the young Dickens's despair when his father was arrested was from one perspective perfectly understandable.

The shame he felt at being sent to work at the blacking warehouse is perhaps another matter. Only just turned 12, Dickens was, through the intercession of a family relative and friend (a young man who had been a frequent companion of Dickens in earlier and happier days), put to work at Warren's Blacking, a business where shoe polish was made and sold and where the relative himself worked in a managerial capacity. The young Charles's job was to tie onto the little blacking jars oil-paper tops, trim them, and paste on a printed label. Although just off a fashionable street—the Strand—the establishment was in a decaying and rat-infested old building abutting on the muddy shore of the river Thames, which in the early nineteenth century had no paved embankment. But most painful for Dickens seems to have been the shameful consciousness that the work threw him into the company of working men and boys and his bitterness about his parents' apparent abandonment of him and complacency about his lot. They had no plans for his further schooling, and they arranged for him to live in lodgings at some distance from both Warren's and the Marshalsea (into which the whole family, except for Charles and Fanny, moved shortly after his father's arrest). Two passages of the fragment are frequently quoted as conveying the depth of Dickens's hurt:

> It is wonderful to me how I could have been so easily cast away at such an age. It is wonderful to me, that, even after my descent into the

poor little drudge I had been since we came to London, no one had compassion enough on me—a child of singular abilities, quick, eager, delicate, and soon hurt, bodily or mentally—to suggest that something might have been spared, as certainly it might have been, to place me at any common school. Our friends, I take it, were tired out. No one made any sign. My father and mother were quite satisfied. They could hardly have been more so, if I had been twenty years of age, distinguished at a grammar-school, and going to Cambridge. . . .

No words can express the secret agony of my soul as I sunk into this companionship; compared these everyday associates with those of my happier childhood; and felt my early hopes of growing up to be a learned and distinguished man, crushed in my breast. The deep remembrance of the sense I had of being utterly neglected and hopeless; of the shame I felt in my position; of the misery it was to my young heart to believe that, day by day, what I had learned, and thought, and delighted in, and raised my fancy and my emulation up by, was passing away from me, never to be brought back any more; cannot be written.

The period at Warren's may have lasted as little as six or seven months, but the most informed estimate puts it at a bit more than a year (Allen, 102–4). And that is a very long time in the life of a 12-year-old.

But was Dickens "right" to be so traumatized by this episode, and have he and Forster and countless subsequent critics been "right" to see in it a key to his character and writings? These are questions that have occupied a good deal of attention among Dickens scholars. Is there not a fairly loud note of self-pity sounded throughout the fragment and in that letter to Forster with its mawkish and oddly indirect third-person reference to "a certain shrinking sensitiveness in a certain ill-clad, ill-fed child"? Could the year or so spent at Warren's really have been so terrible as to have left its mark on virtually everything Dickens wrote? The quotation marks around "right" are meant to question the validity of such judgments, but still they are hard to keep from making. Master narratives can be awfully attractive and convenient and, like charity, cover a multitude of sins.

There is much to be said on both sides of these questions. The conditions Dickens worked under were far better than many a child laborer's, and there were of course in this period many children who labored. What Dickens records as his chief pains were feelings of shame and abandonment. The shame of associating with working-class men and boys was compounded by the even more shameful—and secret—fact of his father's imprisonment. Because of his association with the relative who worked in Warren's office and had secured his employment, he was accorded some special status and referred to as "the young gentleman." The pretense must have been that he hardly needed the six or seven shillings a week that he earned, and, as we shall see, he went to great lengths to conceal his family's real distress and protect the fiction of his own respectability.

It is no doubt hard for us to understand and empathize with such strong class feeling, which may look today like simple snobbery. The sense of class divisions as properly unbridgeable is hard for us to recover, even if we liken it to the more intense feelings unfortunately still aroused today by race and gender. Twelve-year-olds under the best of circumstances can be awfully snobbish, but the nasty conformism of adolescents scarcely accounts for what Dickens's "secret agony" was all about. He felt utterly degraded, without hope, and abandoned to a shameful yet undeserved hell.

Shame is a peculiarly deep emotion that speaks to our very sense of self, unlike guilt, which attaches to deeds.[11] Guilty deeds can be forgiven or paid for in punishment or money; shame, however, exposes us to the painful gaze of others who are let in on the secrets of our being, and our being is something that can hardly be paid for or undone. Of course shame and guilt often go hand in hand: a guilty deed may reveal a shameful character, and we may, rightly or not, feel a guilty responsibility for things of which we are ashamed. But shame is also produced by things over which we have no control at all. And feelings of shame, reflecting our identity, can be touched off simply by virtue of our identifications with others, especially our families. We feel guilty for things we as individuals have done or even just thought about doing; we may be ashamed of ourselves, but also potentially of our parents, siblings, children, friends, and so on. *Their* bad deeds can readily produce *our* shame.

Shame is always a confusing emotion, both in that it makes a problem of our identity and in that it actually produces feelings of confusion, sometimes profound and uncanny. In Dickens's case, shame seems to have been made especially painful and confusing by the fact that his parents refused to some considerable degree to share it. It is bad enough to feel ashamed because your father is in prison. It is far worse to believe that he is blind to his own shame and that nobody else is doing anything to protect the family's honor. Shame shared can bring a family together; shame denied can likewise break it apart. John Dickens's talent for denial, his ability to maintain the fiction of gentility amid the extreme shabbiness of the debtor's prison (certainly reflected in Mr. Micawber in

Copperfield and Mr. Dorrit in *Little Dorrit* and their respective imprison-
ments for debt), must have put the young Charles in a peculiarly unsettled state that at once intensified and threatened his identification with
his family.

One episode in the autobiographical fragment is particularly telling
on this score. Among the workers at Warren's was an older boy, Bob
Fagin, whose name, Dickens casually remarks, he "took the liberty of
using . . . , long afterwards, in *Oliver Twist*." Bob Fagin first taught the
young Charles the tricks of pasting labels and tying covers on the blacking jars, and he evidently took a kindly interest in the boy, once defending his special status against complaints from other boys about the custom of referring to him as "the young gentleman." Dickens from early
childhood on had occasionally suffered agonizingly painful attacks in his
back—perhaps renal colic (spasms in small tubules of the kidney)—that
would incapacitate him for hours, and he relates that

> Bob Fagin was very good to me on the occasion of a bad attack of my
> old disorder. I suffered such excruciating pain that time, that they made
> a temporary bed of straw in my old recess in the counting-house, and I
> rolled about on the floor, and Bob filled empty blacking-bottles with hot
> water, and applied relays of them to my side, half the day. I got better,
> and quite easy towards evening; but Bob (who was much bigger and
> older than I) did not like the idea of my going home alone, and took me
> under his protection. I was too proud to let him know about the prison;
> and after making several efforts to get rid of him, to all of which Bob
> Fagin in his goodness was deaf, shook hands with him on the steps of a
> house near Southwark Bridge on the Surrey side, making believe that I
> lived there. As a finishing piece of reality in case of his looking back, I
> knocked at the door, I recollect, and asked, when the woman opened it, if
> that was Mr. Robert Fagin's house.

Steven Marcus in a brilliant essay has explored this episode and asked
the obvious question: why would Dickens turn his young champion and
nurse into the villainous old monster who personifies evil in *Oliver
Twist*?—a novel that is I believe inescapable in any consideration of
Dickens's life and, thanks to the clue of the two Fagins, offers a unique
view into Dickens during the period at the blacking factory.[12] A simplified version of Marcus's answer is that Bob Fagin's kindness actually
posed the most serious threat to "the young gentleman," for his insistence on accompanying him home could easily have led to the exposure
of his greatest secret. Ironically, it was Bob Fagin's very protectiveness

that was most liable to lead to Dickens's exposure, and in the novel it is this threat that is expressed in the transformation of Fagin into a satanic figure—though he interestingly retains some of Bob Fagin's nurturing aspect as well; it is Fagin who gives Oliver his first substantial meal (8).

We shall return to the relation between Warren's and *Oliver Twist* in due course, but for the moment may note how complex already are the relationships not only between young Charles and Bob Fagin, but also, so to speak, between Dickens and himself. For there is the unsettledness not only of Dickens's ambivalence towards Bob, but of Dickens's fiction about his own identity. So great is his shame (though he significantly figures it here as shame's necessary companion and opposite—"I was too proud to let him know about the prison") that he invents a whole new identity for himself, and then, "as a finishing piece of reality," doubles the lie by asking if the house he is pretending is his own is "Mr. Robert Fagin's." Marcus notes how much the young Dickens here, as well as in several other moments recorded in the fragment, resembles not the passive and utterly innocent Oliver Twist, but his opposite, that most resourceful of street children, the Artful Dodger (Marcus, 368).

Here then is another way in which the lives of Dickens may strike us as multiple. For while the grown-up Dickens clearly looks back on his younger self as "delicate, and soon hurt, bodily or mentally" and marked by "a certain shrinking sensitiveness"—all quite Oliver-like traits—he was by his own account at the same time "a child of singular abilities, quick, eager," sufficiently agile when it came to tying up those blacking jars that a small crowd would gather to admire him and Bob Fagin when they were put to work near a window on the street for the light's sake after Warren's had moved into new quarters, and sufficiently an inventive survivor to come up with the scheme to fool Bob Fagin as to his family's real circumstances. How many times he may have had to show similar resourcefulness when walking the streets alone and beset by very different dangers we can only guess.

Another result of asking whether he was "right" to regard his life at Warren's as so traumatic and pathetic might therefore be to note, in addition to his capacity for self-pity, his tendency to underplay some pronounced virtues—agility, wit, resourcefulness, pluck—and his reluctance to tell, even to himself, what would seem an equally plausible tale of proud survival and the triumph of bravery over adversity. In *Hard Times* he will mercilessly parody such narratives through Mr. Bounderby, the "Bully of humility" who boasts (quite untruthfully, as it turns out) of having been abandoned by his mother and having been born in a ditch

(1.4). Although he is in so many ways the perfect representative of the rising Victorian middle class, Dickens nowhere allows either himself or any of his sympathetic characters to show straightforward, legitimate pride in a rise in their class, though he and they can easily enough praise such rises in others, at least when they follow upon earnest and hard work. He has David Copperfield say this, rather priggishly, of the time when he first enjoys literary success (closely based of course upon facts well and widely known of Dickens's own career by his contemporaries):

> I laboured hard at my book, without allowing it to interfere with the punctual discharge of my newspaper duties; and it came out and was very successful. I was not stunned by the praise which sounded in my ears, notwithstanding that I was keenly alive to it, and thought better of my own performance, I have little doubt, than anybody else did. It has always been in my observation of human nature, that a man who has any good reason to believe in himself never flourishes himself before the faces of other people in order that they may believe in him. For this reason, I retained my modesty in very self-respect; and the more praise I got, the more I tried to deserve. (48)

First-person accounts written by the very successful necessarily struggle with the rhetorical problem of achieving an attractive balance between modesty (a virtuous sort of shame) and pride. Dickens has David Copperfield up the ante at the very outset with his famous first sentence: "Whether I shall turn out to be the hero of my own life, or whether that station will be held by anybody else, these pages must show" (1). It isn't just success that is at stake, in other words, but out-and-out heroism, though here too there is already and again a marked unsettledness surrounding the protagonist, whose life, it is strangely suggested, may turn out to have an entirely different hero than himself.

Every life must have a hero, David implies, and heroism, moreover, names not just a virtue, but a station—a rank or class. It would be an odd and probably unworkable theory both of life and of society, if made explicit, but it does faithfully record an entanglement of class and moral categories we shall encounter again and again as well as a profound discomfort with heroism—an uncertainty about its legitimacy, perhaps, together with an inability to leave it aside. It is the same uncertainty evident when we consider how much the young Dickens of the autobiographical fragment at moments looks like no one so much as the Artful Dodger.

Dickens thinks back upon himself as an innocent, forlorn and fragile little waif—there was, he writes, "No advice, no counsel, no encourage-

ment, no consolation, no support, from any one that I can call to mind,
so help me God"—but the child he actually portrays is a courageous and
aloof survivor who apparently neither needed advice nor sought it.
Dickens can't imagine why no one took pity on him, yet he daily
demonstrated his ability to cope, and he systematically set out to keep
his distance:

> But I held some station at the blacking warehouse too. Besides that
> my relative at the counting-house did what a man so occupied, and deal-
> ing with a thing so anomalous, could, to treat me as one upon a different
> footing from the rest, I never said, to man or boy, how it was that I came
> to be there, or gave the least indication of being sorry that I was there.
> That I suffered in secret, and that I suffered exquisitely, no one ever knew
> but I. How much I suffered, it is, as I have said already, utterly beyond
> my power to tell. No man's imagination can overstep the reality. But I
> kept my own counsel, and I did my work. I knew from the first, that if I
> could not do my work as well as any of the rest, I could not hold myself
> above slight and contempt. I soon became at least as expeditious and as
> skilful with my hands, as either of the other boys. Though perfectly
> familiar with them, my conduct and manners were different enough
> from theirs to place a space between us. They, and the men, always spoke
> of me as "the young gentleman."

The special status he enjoyed, it is implicit, came not just from the fact
that his "relative at the counting-house" treated him "upon a different
footing," but from his own steady effort to maintain that different footing himself. If the theme of this passage is "suffering," it is also the
strength that allowed him always to keep his suffering a perfect secret.

The fragment is full, moreover, of episodes that belie in other ways
the portrait of the miserable waif. He would entertain the men and boys
with stories derived from his readings in his father's little library. Wait-
ing for the gates of the Marshalsea to open in the mornings, he would
sometimes meet the workhouse orphan who served his imprisoned family within its walls (for one could not only house one's family within the
prison, but even employ servants there) and similarly regale her with
"quite astonishing fictions about the wharves and the tower." To Forster
he used to describe "Saturday night as his great treat. It was a grand
thing to walk home with six shillings in his pocket, and to look in at the
shop windows, and think what he would buy." He remembered sneak-
ing a piece of his own bread into "the best dining-room in Johnson's
alamode beef-house [where scraps of beef were boiled down into a thick,

soupy stew] . . . and magnificently ordering a small plate of alamode beef to eat with it." In an episode made use of in *Copperfield,* he visited a public-house and placed a similarly magnificent order for the "very best—the very *best*—ale." The landlord and his wife, he relates, "asked me a good many questions. . . . To all of which, that I might commit nobody, I invented appropriate answers" (Forster, 1.2).

The fictional David and, we may presume, the real Charles were brave and resourceful, but perfectly respectable, their talent for telling whopping big fictions aside. In the fragment, among the ways in which Dickens expresses his abandoned but innocent state is by referring to himself as a "small Cain . . . , except that I had never done harm to anyone," and he later remarks that "I know that, but for the mercy of God, I might easily have been, for any care that was taken of me, a little robber or a little vagabond." The Artful Dodger is, by contrast, a criminal who exits his novel by being transported for life to Australia while grandly demonstrating his "pride" in his "profession" and rising to new heights of cheekiness before the magistrate who is to sentence him. His exit takes up almost a whole chapter spun around the joke of this ironic pride in crime. One of Fagin's boys is grieved to discover that the Artful has been arrested for a petty theft and bemoans the fact that his real distinction will thus never be properly acknowledged in court proceedings (as it would have been had he been arrested for a worthier, i.e., more serious crime), but his leader consoles him:

> "Never mind, Charley," said Fagin, soothingly; "it'll come out, it'll be sure to come out. They'll all know what a clever fellow he was; he'll show it himself, and not disgrace his old pals and teachers. Think how young he is too! What a distinction, Charley, to be lagged [transported] at his time of life!" (43)

And in his final appearance, the Artful is full of class airs: "my attorney is a-breakfasting this morning with the Wice President of the House of Commons," he announces to the court, just before he is escorted out. Can one imagine *him* ever demanding anything less than the "very best—the very *best*—ale"?

We have complicated the question whether Dickens was "right" to be so shamed and traumatized by his time at Warren's by asking whether he really was so shamed in fact. In the Artful Dodger we have found a sort of double for Dickens, who, like all good doubles, is at once strikingly like and unlike his original. He shares with the young Dickens

bravado, ingenuity, resourcefulness, agility, self-reliance—all the qualities one wants to see in a hero of Romance, except that he happens to be
an outlaw. And he takes pride in these very qualities—unlike the young
Charles, but, again like any good hero of Romance (I think of Odysseus
as the classic example)—though his pride is comic and ironic, given his
criminality. The Dodger helps us see traits in the real Dickens that are
evident in the fragment, but at the same time strenuously played down,
masked by the emphasis on suffering, and even at times simply denied.

One inference is that Dickens was sufficiently unsettled about his self
to split off characteristics of that self into quite opposite fictional characters, like Oliver and the Artful, although it is important to keep in mind
that such psychological splits are never simple or clean. Thinking about
the Artful as a *piece* of Dickens, for example, does not exhaust his character. His real name is "Jack Dawkins," which surely resonates with "John
Dickens," and the resonance, we may say, is appropriate in that the
Dodger looks in various lights *both* like Charles *and* his father. For John
Dickens may not have been so resourceful a survivor as either the Artful
or Charles, but, like both the Artful and another character bound for
Australia—Mr. Micawber—he was a great, theatrical talker, flamboyant
and proud in spite of his poverty, and, of course, on the wrong side of
the law. That Dickens put both himself and his father into the Dodger is
perhaps connected to thoughts he had expressed to Forster about inher-
iting his father's worst traits—anxieties that also help us understand his
mania for maintaining his (and Oliver's) respectability and his motivation for denying his own Artfulness.[13]

The process of splitting himself into Oliver and the Artful would be
analogous to what he would do in turning the real Bob Fagin into his fictional counterpart, who is both very like and unlike his original, and the
motivation in both cases could well have been the same, at once to protect a certain innocence while dramatizing just how very seriously threatened it was. In the novel, the threats are entirely external, which is consistent with Oliver's thoroughgoing passivity and goodness. In the
fragment, the threats are also internal, and young Charles is seriously
threatened not just by the external dangers of the life of the streets, but
by his own ambition and temptations, by what Forster elsewhere calls his
"profound attraction of repulsion" to London streets and slums (1.1).[14]

We can only speculate about the nature of these temptations and
attractions. The preoccupations of the fragment suggest they were frequently connected with food and Dickens's perpetual hunger, but that
hardly accounts for the extreme ambivalence of an "attraction of repul-

sion" and its implication of something almost perverse. Dickens also refers to his having been, "seduced more than once . . . by a show-van" to see "the Fat Pig, the Wild Indian, and the Little Lady," and he must have encountered displays of a more conventionally seductive kind in a city by all accounts overrun with prostitutes of every manner of description. Very likely, as a 12-year-old thrown for the first time among working-class men and boys, he was at Warren's initiated into sexual mysteries too, and if that initiation was shocking, as well it might have been to a sensitive and hitherto sheltered boy, that might help account also for the intensity of the shame he experienced and for his writing about the fragment that "it does not seem a tithe of what I might have written, or of what I meant to write." But this, again, is merely speculation.[15]

Steven Marcus offers a psychoanalytic reading—also necessarily speculative—of the months at Warren's that supposes beyond and prior to both *Oliver* and Warren's a "primal scene" in Dickens's childhood. Freud believed that these scenes, real or fantasized, were virtually universal in boys' early-childhood experiences. In a primal scene, a child sees or overhears his parents' lovemaking and interprets it as an act of violence against the mother and potentially a threat to himself, especially if his seeing is actually or imagined to be discovered. Primal scenes are important for literary purposes, among many other reasons, because they embody excitement, wonder, horror, and the exposure of secrets, especially the great family secret of sex. So they have an inherent narrative interest relevant to many genres, but especially Romance and its progeny the novel, both of which delight in mysteries dealing with origins. Much sensational fiction—the Gothic especially, with its haunted houses and their uncanny sounds and doings in the middle of the night—seems to borrow most heavily from the material of primal scenes, and Dickens's novels are full of Gothic trappings.

Marcus bases his interpretation on several scenes in *Oliver Twist* and one in the fragment in which people witness others or are themselves witnessed doing something secret and shameful and in which there is often a threat of violence when their seeing is discovered. Whether Freud and Marcus are respectively correct about the universality of the primal scene and its particular manifestation in Dickens, however, there is good evidence that Dickens understood such scenes very well. (It is the kind of evidence that gives Ned Lukacher, as we saw in the previous chapter, cause to see Dickens as not just a marvelous instance of anticipation of psychoanalytic insight, but as positively shaping Freud's imagination.) In a very minor and—except for the fact that it presents in comic form a starkly brutal representation of a classic primal scene—entirely forgettable piece written for the monthly magazine *Bentley's Miscellany* while *Oliver* was being serialized in its pages, Dickens presents an anecdote told by "Robert Bolton, the 'Gentleman Connected with the Press,' " who resembles both himself and his father not just in being connected with the press, but in being as well "a literary character" and "a short-hand reporter."[16] Mr. Bolton amuses his drinking companions (and Dickens, who claims to have overheard him) with the story of a "horrid murder" just committed that morning. It features a baker and his wife, "whom he was frequently in the habit, while in an intoxicated state, of kicking, pummelling, flinging mugs at, knocking down, and half-killing while in bed, by inserting in her mouth a considerable portion of a sheet or blanket," and the baker's son. The evening before, the baker had returned home drunk and was taken off to bed by his long-suffering wife. His son arrived shortly after and proceeded to retire as well:

> Scarcely (gentlemen, conceive his feelings of alarm), scarcely had he taken off his indescribables, when shrieks (to his experienced ear *maternal* shrieks) scared the silence of surrounding night. He put his indescribables on again, and ran down-stairs. He opened the door of the parental bed-chamber. His father was dancing upon his mother. What must have been his feelings! In the agony of the minute he rushed at his male parent as he was about to plunge a knife into the side of his female. The mother shrieked. The father caught the son (who had wrested the knife from the paternal grasp) up in his arms, carried him down-stairs, shoved him into a copper of boiling water among some linen, closed the lid, and jumped upon the top of it, in which position he was found with a ferocious countenance by the mother, who arrived in the melancholy wash-house just as he had so settled himself.
> "Where's my boy?" shrieked the mother.
> "In that copper, boiling," coolly replied the benign father.

It requires only the translation of dancing (which has jokingly been described as "a vertical substitute for a horizontal reality") to complete the picture. The mention of the son's "indescribables"—very curious in itself as no one but the dead son could possibly have known that he had taken them off and put them back on—establishes a comically risqué tone (as well as the need for translation), and the detail of the knife about to be plunged into the mother's side adds a bit of classic phallic symbolism, but they are scarcely necessary to make the point. The cli-

max—the son's being boiled in spite of his success in wresting away the
father's knife—is perhaps the one significant variation on the orthodox
psychoanalytic story, which Freud would expect to end with a threat of
castration, though it certainly satisfies psychoanalysis's taste for elementary fears and, so to speak, gets the job done.

"What must have been his feelings!" exclaims Mr. Bolton, and the
question is a good and perhaps also an unanswerable one, for if there is a
particular "meaning" to Dickens's fascination with the primal scene, as
with his fascination about the period at Warren's more generally, it may
be that it remains, like the son's underclothes, "indescribable." "No
words can express the secret agony of my soul," he had written in the
fragment. Indescribability, like confusion, is among the phenomena
associated with shame. It may for a writer be a sign of failure, for what
cannot be described "cannot be written" (to repeat another phrase from
the fragment). But the indescribable is also the storyteller's friend insofar as it keeps alive the need to keep trying and the need to keep telling.
Rather than trying to identify a "key" to all Dickens in his hard experiences of boyhood, therefore, we might notice in the "master narrative"
such central elements as indescribability and confusion that ensure its
continual retelling and revising and ensure that the lock on the mystery,
so to speak, will never be opened.

Whether they *explain* anything or not, the events surrounding the
blacking factory and Marshalsea reveal and therefore help define issues
that will haunt Dickens and his writings until the end of his life.[17] And
the fragment realizes strategies—"defenses" when considered from the
psychological standpoint, "techniques" from the literary—that he will
adopt again and again, such as the splitting or doubling of himself into a
shrinking, sensitive child on the one hand and a plucky street urchin on
the other. When we move from the life to the work, we see similar
strategies deployed in the transformation, for example, of young Bob
Fagin into Fagin the elderly criminal mastermind, or the young Dickens
into both Oliver and the Artful. In work after work, Dickens presents
neglected and innocent children of often doubtful origin, sometimes
actual orphans, sometimes virtual orphans, whose life project is to attain
respectability, win some affection, establish some identity, reclaim some
inheritance. When these children are protagonists, like Oliver and
David, they are often successful, though especially in the later Dickens
their successes may be seriously qualified (as is Pip's in *Great Expectations*). Neglected children who are secondary characters, however, more
usually have tragic ends—like Smike in *Nicholas Nickleby* or Oliver's

workhouse friend, the notably named "Poor Dick." But even being a protagonist does not protect the neglected child from a tragic end, as the cases of Little Nell in *The Old Curiosity Shop* or Paul Dombey in *Dombey and Son* famously demonstrate.

These neglected children are invariably doubled, sometimes by bad doubles, like Oliver and the Artful, and sometimes by good ones, like Oliver and Poor Dick. The bad doubles are usually the most interesting, like David's double Uriah Heep or Pip's double Orlick. And their parent figures (for even the actual orphans have plenty of people standing in for their parents, no matter how badly) tend likewise to be doubled, again in both good and bad versions. Oliver has Mr. Brownlow and the Maylies on the one hand, the workhouse crew and Fagin on the other. David has his mother, Peggotty and her family, the Micawbers, and Betsey Trotwood and Mr. Dick on the one hand, the Murdstones on the other. Children who die have, not unexpectedly, only bad (or at least impotent) parent figures, generally, though even these may be doubled, as, for example, in the case of Smike, who has only the bad parents Wackford Squeers and Ralph Nickleby.

There is moreover an air of unsettled confusion that hovers about the fragment and is even more insistent in *Oliver Twist* and many of the works, where confusion is both a narrative technique and frequently explicitly thematized, as in *Bleak House*. Confusion, indeed, provides a useful matrix for the techniques of splitting and doubling that can at once promote and hide them. We are less likely to notice that Mr. Brownlow and Fagin are both referred to as "the old gentleman" within a few pages of one another (10, 11) thanks to the dreamlike, nightmarish atmosphere of *Oliver Twist,* for such confusions are, within the context of dreams, quite normal—we may recall here Dickens's own observations about dreams quoted above. Or should we say rather that techniques of doubling and splitting themselves help create that air of confusion?

It is not necessary to describe here most of Dickens's adult lives beyond the summary sketch I offered at the beginning of this chapter. With the important exception of his relations with women—the subject of the next chapter—they are relatively public, straightforward, and uncomplicated, except insofar as they repeat the patterns we have already identified, or except insofar as they are realized through the novels. What is most dramatic in the adult biography, such as the final public readings so ruinous to Dickens's health, likewise reanimates the issues of childhood and the earlier work, as for example through the reading of the murder of Nancy derived from *Oliver Twist*. This is not, emphatically, to deny the importance of Dickens's maturity. Alexander Welsh is one of several writers who have directed biographical attention away from Warren's and towards Dickens's adult development.[18] But, excepting his relations with women, what is significantly new in the adult biography, as Welsh has shown, is best seen through the evolution of the works, to which we shall presently come.

Chapter Three
Dickens's Lives (II): Women

In discussing Dickens's life, it has proved impossible not to talk about the work. That is, we have followed Dickens's own lead when he points us to *David Copperfield* or *Oliver Twist* in narrating the hard experiences of boyhood that "worked together" to produce the person he became—the fragment is indeed full of references to the novels and characters and places from the life that he worked into them. This mutual implication of the life and work, like the mutual implication of the "Dickensian" and the "Victorian," will be a recurring theme for us. In both the life and the work, moreover, we have found splittings and doublings of Dickens himself—as well as of others, like Bob Fagin and Dickens's parents—that repeat, so to speak, the pattern of repetition. When Esther Summerson in *Bleak House* first encounters Lady Dedlock, who is actually her mother, though Esther could hardly have imagined it, she is puzzled to find arising in her mind "innumerable pictures" of herself (18), and Esther's uncanny experience will turn out to be paradigmatic for us in that we will ourselves encounter "innumerable pictures" of Dickens and people important to him throughout our study. But one additional and large aspect of Dickens's lives needs to be introduced and discussed before we shift our view from biography as such, and this is the topic of Dickens and women.[1] For if the techniques of splitting and doubling tend to involve problems of *self*hood, problems of the *other*—that against which the self is defined and with which the self often is in struggle—tend to involve issues of gender. And these will be prominent throughout Dickens's adult life.

Already in the fragment there are signs of trouble, even though it is the relationship of father and son that has attracted chief attention among psychoanalytically inclined critics.[2] There is his resentment that his sister Fanny, only two years older than he, was being provided for as a boarding pupil at the Royal Academy of Music throughout the period that he was at Warren's and his father was in prison, even though her annual premium was a substantial 38 guineas a year—about 10 percent of John Dickens's annual income and almost as much as he spent on lodgings in a typical year (Allen, 110). While Charles was earning his six

or seven shillings a week, Fanny was costing the family more than twice
as much just in her premium.

But Dickens's greatest resentment by far was reserved for his parents
and his mother, Elizabeth Dickens, in particular. After his release from
the Marshalsea, John Dickens quarreled one day by letter with the
cousin who had secured young Charles's employment, perhaps over his
son's working with Bob Fagin near the window where he was virtually
on display to passersby, and young Charles was sent home, "with a relief
so strange it was like oppression."

> My mother set herself to accommodate the quarrel, and did so next
> day. She brought home a request for me to return next morning, and a
> high character of me, which I am very sure I deserved. My father said I
> should go back no more, and should go to school. I do not write resent-
> fully or angrily: for I know how all these things have worked together to
> make me what I am: but I never afterwards forgot, I never shall forget, I
> never can forget, that my mother was warm for my being sent back.

That is very strong language, notable for its deliberateness and even a
certain sinister coolness evident in its ominous repetitions of "I never." If
Dickens was truthfully not passionately or angrily resentful, there seems
little doubt that he was resentful nevertheless, even 20 years after the
fact and, if his declaration here is to be believed, even to the end of his
life.

Not that his resentment seems to have manifested itself in any ostensible behavior. Just as he may have felt himself to be an abandoned waif
while he presented to the rest of the world the picture of a cheerful and
resourceful lad, he may also have experienced himself as bitter and at
least potentially rebellious while masking those feelings to all around
him. By all accounts, he was a very dutiful son, attentive to his mother
throughout her long life (she died in 1863 after a few years' decline into
senility, having outlived her husband by a dozen years). And we know
that the subject of the blacking factory became taboo in the family, his
father and mother both "stricken dumb" about it and Dickens himself
likewise absolutely silent: "From that hour . . . , no word of that part of
my childhood . . . has passed my lips to any human being," he writes at
the very end of the fragment. But young Charles had his revenge nevertheless, and in truth an undying revenge at that.

Several female characters in the works are conventionally recognized
as having some basis in Elizabeth Dickens, most notably the garrulous

and flighty Mrs. Nickleby, a complex character because she is at once a great comic triumph and someone who does much real, if unintended, damage.[3] It is also usually assumed that many of the doting but weak young mothers portrayed in the fiction, like David's mother, Clara, reflect the young Elizabeth Dickens (only in her early twenties when Charles was born). If those assumptions are correct, we can perhaps better understand Dickens's portrayal not only of mothers, but of women generally and his ambivalence about them.

On the one hand there is the powerful relationship between the very young mother and her child—the first son and the only child in the respective cases of Elizabeth Dickens and Clara Copperfield—that is remarkable for a mixture of eroticism and innocence. Mother and child seem almost to be babies together or more like sister and brother than mother and son, and both are idealized and feminized in good Romantic fashion as heavenly beings, and there is much caressing and fondling and baby talk between them. It is as though the idealized mother is so very young that she needs a mother herself. Aunt Betsey repeatedly addresses and refers to David's mother as a "baby," and the curiously named nurse Clara Peggotty—curious because her first name doubles David's mother's—likewise finds herself having to baby both mother and child. These older, surrogate mothers tend to be, moreover, in various ways masculinized. On the other hand, there are a host of bad mothers and mother surrogates. These generally come on the scene when the good, young mother dies prematurely, like David's mother (replaced in effect by Miss Murdstone) or Pip's (replaced in effect by his sister Mrs. Joe). And even when this pattern does not appear to hold, as, for example, in the case of *Little Dorrit*'s Arthur Clennam, who seems to have been simply unfortunate in having a horror of a mother to begin with (another version of the severely evangelical Miss Murdstone), the unraveling of mysterious family plots may well reveal a weak young mother somewhere in the past after all. Good mothers of protagonists by and large just don't survive very long.

Not surprisingly, Dickens and his male protagonists tend to fall in love with women who reproduce features of the idealized young mother: almost childlike and babyish themselves, if angelic and doting. These infatuations are—like all infatuations—in the beginning uncritical, though by the middle of his career there is an explicit effort being made to recognize the problems caused by an "undisciplined heart" (*Copperfield,* 45). Nevertheless, a lack of such discipline is a continuing problem for Dickens and his heroes.

Dickens's first love sets the pattern. The daughter of a banker, Maria Beadnell was a small and very pretty girl almost two years older than Dickens, who was probably 18 when he first met her. She seems to have been an accomplished tease who managed to keep several young men's hopes of winning her alive during the three or four years that Dickens was enamored of her. Michael Slater argues persuasively, and against the previous conventional scholarly opinion, that it was as much Maria herself as her parents who prevented a match (49–76). This leads him to speculate that there is as much or even more of Maria in Pip's Estella than Dickens's presumed mistress at the time he was writing *Great Expectations,* Ellen Ternan (73–75). Maria has long been recognized as laying the basis for *David Copperfield*'s Dora, who, unlike her original, is wholeheartedly devoted to her suitor and whom he does succeed in marrying, only to lose her to the complications of a failed pregnancy in the early years of a marriage that had begun to show how unsuited the pair really were and how ill-adapted she was to life after courtship.[4] And the middle-aged Maria reappears in the fiction as well, for after several years of separation Dickens and Maria became reacquainted after she happened to write just before Dickens was to leave for a week's vacation in Paris. Looking over a pile of letters handed to him while he was reading, and at first recognizing no handwriting among them, he went back to his book. But, as he wrote to Maria the next day,

> I found my mind curiously disturbed, and wandering away through so many years to such early times of my life, that I was quite perplexed to account for it. There was nothing in what I had been reading or immediately thinking about, to awaken such a train of thought, and at last it came into my head that it must have been suggested by something in the look of one of those letters. So I turned them over again,—and suddenly the remembrance of your hand, came upon me with an influence that I cannot express to you. Three or four and twenty years vanished like a dream, and I opened it with the touch of my young friend David Copperfield when he was in love. (10 February 1855)

It was a quintessentially Dickensian moment (and quintessentially Freudian too in its sensitivity to the ways unconscious thought becomes conscious) in which the past reaches out to the present in a "curiously" disturbing, perplexing, and inexpressible way—an uncanny moment of *déjà vu* or something very like it. Dickens gallantly offered to "discharge any little commission" for Maria while in Paris. At her request he bought some jewelry for her and evidently was preoccupied throughout his stay there with thoughts of her. Fervent letters were exchanged (Maria professing really to have loved Dickens after all), and upon his return a meeting was promptly arranged for a Sunday afternoon at Dickens's house when Catherine Dickens was virtually certain to be out. Maria, herself married and a mother, warned him he would find her "toothless, fat, old, and ugly" (he quotes her own words back to her in a letter of 22 February 1855), and no doubt she was right at least in her drift, though in the fictionalized account of the meeting that he wrote only the next year (in *Little Dorrit*), it is not what age has done to the body that breaks the spell. Arthur Clennam encounters his old flame, Flora Finching:

> Flora, always tall, had grown to be very broad too, and short of breath; but that was not much. Flora, whom he had left a lily, had become a peony; but that was not much. Flora, who had seemed enchanting in all she said and thought, was diffuse and silly. That was much. Flora, who had been spoiled and artless long ago, was determined to be spoiled and artless now. That was a fatal blow. (1.13)

After his first meeting with the mature Maria, the tone of Dickens's letters immediately cools, and within scarcely more than a month the theme of the letters becomes that peculiar restlessness, again, that characterizes what Dickens refers to as "the author's mind" and his need to put his work before all merely personal considerations (3 April 1855). In short, he finds excuses to put her off. Subsequent letters were few and far between. After Dickens's death, Maria stayed in touch with Georgina Hogarth (Slater, 76), and there is a sad memoir of Maria in the 1860s published many years later by a former nursemaid who recalled her drinking too much and waxing sentimental over her former lover: "I have seen her, in one of these moods, actually kiss the place on the couch [where Dickens had sat], and recall something that Charles Dickens had said to her" (Slater, 72). Arthur, to his credit, did rather better by Flora, and Flora, for her part, proves in the end not silly at all, however "diffuse," and a true friend to Little Dorrit.

Dickens's relationship with Maria parallels the much more complex and sad relationship with his wife, begun when Dickens was on the rebound from Maria's repulse and ended only a few years after the aborted reunion with his first love. And that relationship is complicated in turn by Dickens's relationships with several other women: his sisters-in-law Mary and Georgina Hogarth, his mistress, Ellen Ternan, and a number of less important but still significant female acquaintances, such as Mme. de la Rue, the English wife of a Swiss banker whom Dickens met while on holiday in Italy in 1844 and whose severe psychological maladies he treated intensively for several months with hypnosis (Slater, 122–25).

Dickens had met Catherine probably in the winter of 1834–35. She was the daughter of a distinguished Scot, a lawyer, music critic, and journalist, a friend and advisor to Sir Walter Scott, the editor of the newly founded *Evening Chronicle,* who had invited Dickens to write a series of sketches for the new paper like those he had already begun to place in other periodicals. Catherine at 19 was the eldest of several pretty daughters (including Mary, age 14, and Georgina, 7), and Dickens seems to have been a frequent guest in the Hogarth household. By May they were engaged. Although even in Dickens's earliest letters to Catherine there are some prickly and priggish moments in which he upbraids his fiancée for minor faults and "cossness" (crossness), he typically looks very much the conventional and sincere young lover. And the overall impression gathered from the letters of an affectionate as well as conscientious husband persists right up until the crisis. (That we have Catherine's letters is because she saved them and on her death-bed directed her daughter Kate to give them to the British Museum, so "that the world may know he loved me once."[5]) The late letters are notable for their straightforwardness; there is little of the somewhat forced jokiness adopted in letters to those with whom he is less close. In difficult moments he can be remarkably tender, as when he prepares Catherine for the news that their baby Dora is dead. Reading through Dickens's letters to Catherine, it is easy to see why she was so bewildered at the breakup.

This is not to say there were no rough spots that might have signaled trouble. Dickens loved to flirt and play at being madly in love, just as he loved to play at having all kinds of powerful emotions, as we saw in his praise of the charms of "assumption." Dickens joined with Forster and their friend the painter Daniel Maclise in sustained joking about their passion for the newly crowned Queen Victoria, who was only 18 at her coronation. Slater quotes a letter extraordinary for its *double entendre* in which Dickens writes in mock agony of the pain it causes him to encounter so many pubs called "The Queen's Arms" and the attendant "visions of Albert in the Queen's arms calling for what he liked and having it. The thought is madness" (Slater, 122 and Pilgrim letters, addendum, 7:812). Even before the marriage, Dickens demonstrated that his appetite for feminine affection was large enough that no one woman could satisfy it. He became during his engagement deeply attached to Catherine's sister Mary, who often chaperoned the young couple before their marriage and was as often as not in their company after the marriage, to the extent that many biographers have assumed that she actually moved into the household.[6] After her sudden death at 17 in Dickens's arms one night after an evening at the theater (probably due to a congenital heart defect), Dickens became obsessed with her memory. For a long time afterward, he dreamed of her nightly and formed the plan of eventually sharing her grave. Until his own death he wore a ring he had taken from her finger just after hers. In novel after novel he celebrated her memory, most notably in the figure of Little Nell. There seems little doubt that Dickens's attachment to Mary was in every important sense "innocent," but little doubt too that its intense emotional charge drew at least unconsciously upon the erotic.

While Dickens visited America with his wife in 1842, their three very young children were left at home and tended to by various friends and family, conspicuous among whom was the 15-year-old Georgina, youngest of the Hogarth sisters. And not long after the Dickenses' return, she moved permanently into their household as companion, housekeeper, and nanny (Pilgrim letters, 3:409 and n.). Clearly she in some sense took Mary's place. As Dickens wrote to his mother-in-law:

> I trace in many respects a strong resemblance between her [Mary's] mental features and Georgina's—so strange a one, at times, that when she and Kate and I are sitting together, I seem to think that what has happened is a melancholy dream from which I am just awakening. The perfect like of what she was, will never be again, but so much of her spirit shines out in this sister, that the old time comes back again at some seasons, and I can hardly separate it from the present. (8 May 1843)

Georgina remained in the household through its several moves, right through the separation, and up until its breakup after his death, after which she took up residence with two of Dickens's children (Storey, 144). She was joint executor of Dickens's will (with Forster) and, not surprisingly, though baselessly, there were rumors at the time of the separation that she was actually its cause.

An 18-year-old woman named Christiana Weller, whom Dickens met a few years after Mary's death, also revived Mary's memory with peculiar intensity. "Good God what a madman I should seem, if the incredible feeling I have conceived for that girl could be made plain to anyone," he wrote to his friend T. J. Thompson (28 February 1844), and he was delighted to learn soon after that Thompson had fallen in love with her. Dickens worked ardently to promote Thompson's courtship, though the married Mrs. Thompson failed to delight so much as the unmarried Miss Weller. "She is a mere spoiled child, I think, and doesn't turn out half as well as I expected," he writes to his friend Emile de la Rue (17 August 1846).

The de la Rues were a couple Dickens had met while spending a year in Italy in 1844. Emile was a prosperous Swiss banker; Augusta was his English-born wife, who reminded Christiana Thompson of Dickens's sister Fanny.[7] She was plagued by a host of hysterical symptoms—involuntary movements, convulsion-like spasms, catalepsy, and even delusions and quasi hallucinations, as well as severe attacks of anxiety—and Dickens, who had for a long while been fascinated by "animal magnetism" or "mesmerism" (as hypnotic phenomena were called in the nineteenth century), decided to use hypnosis to alleviate her symptoms. He followed the example of his own physician, John Elliotson, who was a pioneer in the therapeutic uses of mesmerism and had taught him the technique. In what was surely the most dramatic anticipation of Freud (and Freud's teacher, Jean-Martin Charcot) in Dickens's life (if not in his work), he undertook a course of treatment with Mme. de la Rue that lasted several weeks and involved daily sessions of hypnosis, probing questions, and long talks about her symptoms. And, like the early Freud, Dickens achieved some marked, if temporary, success. He became, characteristically, obsessed with the "case," whose progress he kept track of in lengthy notes and letters. It did not take very long for Catherine to object, though whether this was simply because Dickens was spending so much time with Mme. de la Rue or because Catherine saw in the pretty patient a serious rival is not entirely clear. In any event, the friction was sufficient to be remembered more than 10 years later when Dickens wrote to de la Rue with the news of his marital troubles:

> Between ourselves (I beckon Madame De La Rue nearer with my forefinger, and whisper this with a serio-comic smile), I don't get on better in these later times with a certain poor lady you know of, than I did in earlier . . . days [i.e., in Italy in 1844–45]. Much worse. Much worse! (23 October 1857)

It is significant both that Dickens thinks of a melodramatic stage gesture here and that he feels the need in effect to bring Mme. de la Rue into the conversation on this point.

The story that Dickens came to tell himself and everybody else about the eventual failure of his marriage was that he and Catherine were simply a terrible and unfortunate match, that he had already recognized this only two years after they were married—"What is now befalling me I have seen steadily coming, ever since the days you remember when Mary [Mamie] was born," he writes to Forster (8.2)[8]—and that he had done everything in his power to accommodate her very different personality and had fought against the inevitable through 22 uncomfortable years (and the births of 10 children). In his more temperate statements, he regretted a fundamental incompatibility: Catherine was "amiable and complying," he wrote to Forster, "but nothing on earth could make her understand me, or suit us to each other." Elsewhere, Catherine is presented as unstable, an incompetent mother and manager of her household, lazy, unloving towards her children and unloved by them, and, finally, guilty in the last days before their separation of some terrible but unspecified betrayal that led Dickens to vow never to forgive her and cease virtually all direct communication. As Michael Slater and others have amply demonstrated, however, all the evidence we have, including a very large number of Dickens's letters to Catherine, suggests quite a different picture—or pictures, rather—than the one Dickens has painted. We need therefore to offer here, as in the case of the autobiographical fragment, not one, but several versions of the tale.[9]

The crisis was precipitated by Dickens's falling in love with Ellen (Nelly) Ternan, an 18-year-old actress whom he had met in 1857 through amateur theatricals he was producing for philanthropic causes. She was the youngest of three daughters of Frances Ternan, a widow and herself an actress of some distinction, and she appeared with her mother and her sister Maria in *The Frozen Deep*, a play on which Dickens had collaborated with his young friend Wilkie Collins and in which Dickens took the leading part. Although Dickens evidently fell in love with Nelly very suddenly, it is most likely that their relationship remained platonic throughout the breakup of his marriage (and possibly it remained platonic a good deal longer; there is in fact no conclusive evidence about the extent of its intimacy at any point). Charles and Catherine were said many years later by a confidante of their daughter Kate to have made a promise to one another early on in their marriage that if either should fall in love with someone else there would be a prompt confession. While there is no independent corroboration of this story, it does seem probable that such a promise was made and that the idea was Charles's, not Catherine's, for it accords well with his anxieties in general about secrecy and selfhood. Although fascinated with secrets, as we have seen, he was no good at keeping them himself; he believed that they have a way of their own of coming out; and he was, moreover, appalled by hypocrisy—his greatest villains and his most hilarious objects of satire are furtive schemers and hypocrites. But this raises in turn a large question we shall have to address presently about how he could have tolerated the liaison with Nelly and the secrecy that it entailed.

Whether Dickens immediately confessed to his infatuation with Nelly or not, the fact soon became plain to Catherine, and Charles became positively frantic to end the marriage. His daughter Kate is reported to have said that he was "like a madman" during the breakup, and from the time Dickens first laid eyes on Nelly to Catherine's leaving his household was less than a year. The events of this period occur thus: In August 1857 he acts with Nelly for the first time. By the beginning of September he is telling Forster of his marital problems. In October he writes the letter to de la Rue quoted above and changes the sleeping arrangements at Tavistock House, turning a dressing room that adjoined his and Catherine's bedroom into a little bedroom for himself and walling up the opening between them with shelves. By March of the following year he is telling Collins about his misery and writes to Forster that the marriage is "over." By May rumors are spreading through the men's clubs. The novelist William Makepeace Thackeray hears the story that Georgina is the other woman and tries to quash the more serious charge (sexual relations with a sister-in-law technically amounting to incest) with the correction that the liaison is only with an actress (and therefore a woman presumed to be of loose morals and suitable sexual prey for a gentleman); word of this gets back to Dickens, bringing on a serious break with Thackeray, and there will be several rifts with friends and business associates who fail to come over entirely to Dickens's way of seeing.

Dickens by now is writing to his friends generally about the crisis, and before the month is over he has effected a separation and a settlement, though Catherine has no wish to leave him. By the terms of the settlement, she is to leave his house and be set up in her own establishment in London with her oldest son, Charles Jr., and will receive £600 a year for life. Those of the children still living at home will remain with their father and Georgina at the recently bought and refurbished Gad's Hill Place in Rochester. Catherine's mother and younger sister Helen are coerced by Dickens to sign a statement refuting rumors they have themselves spread about Nelly, whom Dickens refers to as "innocent and pure, and as good as my own dear daughters" in a letter he gives to a friend "to show, to anyone who wishes to do me right" (Pilgrim letters, 8:741, and to Arthur Smith, 25 May 1858). Perhaps misconstruing Dickens's wishes, the friend distributes copies of the letter widely, and it is published in several British and American newspapers. The following month Dickens himself publishes on the first page of his weekly magazine *Household Words* a statement headed "PERSONAL" that alludes to his new domestic "arrangement," without specifying what it is, and also to "misrepresentations, most grossly false, most monstrous, and most cruel . . . involving innocent persons, dear to my heart," but also without specifying what they are, and this statement too is widely republished and arouses the baffled curiosity of thousands beyond the reach of metropolitan gossip who no doubt otherwise would never have heard a word of the marriage's failure (Pilgrim letters, 8:744).

Was it a wonder that none among Dickens's friends and family could deter him from his course or that he should feel himself to be, like King Lear, "more sinned against than sinning"? These are questions perhaps impossible to answer. There can, however, be no other judgment of his behavior than that it was terribly cruel in fact. But throughout her painful banishment, Catherine remained poignantly loyal to Dickens and made no public complaint about him. She kept up an active social life with many friends and was always in close contact with those of her children who had not been shipped off to make their way in distant parts of the Empire. She survived her husband by almost a decade and after his death was able to visit Gad's Hill and achieve a reconciliation of sorts with Georgina. According to Slater (156–57), the only protest she made against Forster's *Life* and its heavy if tactful bias in Dickens's favor (for Forster omitted all mention of Ellen Ternan except the prominent place she had in Dickens's will, which Forster published as an appendix) was to authorize Charley to say, against Forster's implication that he was alone in sharing the secret of Warren's and the Marshalsea, that Dickens had read the autobiographical fragment to her some time before the writing of *Copperfield*. This may seem an insignificant claim, but given the power Charles himself ascribed to that story, it does promote Catherine's poignant hope "that the world may know he loved me once."

The story of Dickens's relationship with Nelly Ternan is necessarily much harder to tell than the story of his marriage because the principals and their friends and family were for obvious reasons almost entirely silent about it, and no letters between Dickens and Nelly have survived.[10] About *this* secret, at least, Dickens seems to have been not at all ambivalent. He went to extraordinary lengths to protect it, even doing business connected with her under an assumed name and communicating with the few associates circumstances required to entrust with the secret, like his subeditor at *All The Year Round,* W. H. Wills, practically in code. He traveled to and from meetings with her at the various homes in which he had established her by rather circuitous routes that may have been chosen to keep his very famous face out of the most public byways, and it is not too far-fetched to imagine him even resorting on occasion to disguise. (One of the villages at which he seems to have alighted in his railway journeys to and from Nelly for much of 1867 is called Datchet; in *The Mystery of Edwin Drood* we meet a character who is rather obviously in disguise called Dick Datchery.)

Claire Tomalin's wonderful biography of Nelly, the most sympathetic and extensive treatment of her, extends Nelly's story well beyond Dickens's death right up to her own in 1913 and is aptly called *The Invisible Woman.* The title evokes what was necessarily the virtual nonexistence of a woman who was the mistress of one of England's most celebrated public men and presumptively a model of decorum. But the *private* man who loved Nelly so powerfully for the last dozen years of his life is in fact almost equally invisible. Critics have worked hard to find clues about Nelly in the later Dickens heroines: Lucie Manette, Estella, Bella Wilfer, Rosa Bud, but these efforts yield little that is not highly speculative. What their life together was really like remains elusive.

Some facts are fairly well established, however, and many of these can be inferred from public records and from a pocket diary that Dickens kept in 1867 and probably lost just at the time of his second trip to the United States.[11] A lease on a house close to Dickens's London home was purchased for Nelly's older sisters, Fanny and Maria, in 1859 and sold in turn to Nelly the following year, when she had attained her majority. As Tomalin points out, there is no proof that Dickens bought the lease, though there are reports that Nelly later said he had done so, and there are no other likely suspects. Moreover, Dickens had only a few weeks before consulted Forster on the possibility of selling the lease of the London house to a particular family, to which idea Forster returned an emphatic negative as a scheme that would prove *"very damaging indeed,"* strongly suggesting that the family in question was the Ternans (Tomalin, 121). Certainly Dickens in these months gradually adopted the role of protector of the Ternan women, having, for example, his subeditor,

Wills, intervene with the police when they became suspicious of the late hours kept by Nelly and Maria and questioned them, assuming them to be prostitutes (Tomalin, 118). Dickens provided letters of introduction for Nelly's mother and sister Fanny when they traveled abroad, and his bank records show payments to both Ellen and her mother (Tomalin, 117, 127).

For the next few years the trail of evidence completely disappears. (Tomalin guesses that Dickens set Nelly up in France, possibly to conceal a pregnancy, which would explain her absence at her sister's marriage and Dickens's very frequent trips across the channel [135 – 45].)[12] The trail emerges again dramatically in a spectacular railway crash in which Dickens, Nelly, and very probably her mother were all involved in 1865. Returning to England from France, they were on a train from Folkestone to London when it was derailed near Staplehurst going over a bridge whose rails had been torn up for repairs; the work crew had failed to give oncoming trains adequate warning, and the whole train except for the final car left the tracks. Several cars were virtually destroyed, many people died, and many others were seriously injured. The wreck was widely reported in the press (one story included an illustration of Dickens valiantly tending to the wounded), and was sufficiently memorable that when Forster wrote his biography seven years later he had merely to allude to "the terrible railway accident at Staplehurst" rather than describe it (8.7). The publicity surrounding the crash and Dickens's prominence at the scene of course threatened to reveal with whom he was traveling, and the danger was compounded by the fact that Nelly lost several pieces of jewelry in the wreck. These Dickens managed successfully to retrieve by writing somewhat disingenuously to a Station Master in London that he had promised a lady who, presumably, just happened to be in his compartment "to make her loss known at headquarters, in case these trinkets should be found." We can be pretty sure that the lady was Nelly because Dickens mentions among these items "a gold seal engraved 'Ellen' " (Johnson, 9.4).

The evidentiary trail would have grown almost completely cold again were it not for the accidental survival of one of the annual pocket diaries that Dickens routinely kept but later destroyed. He seems to have lost his diary for 1867 around the time he left England for a second visit to the United States, where he would continue his wildly successful tour of public readings; it did not turn up again until 1922, when it was offered for sale at auction in New York (Aylmer, 13 –14; Tomalin, 167– 68). Dickens kept detailed but extremely abbreviated daily entries in the diary, whose tiny pages were about the size of a modern business card and each of which covered a whole month, a single line being devoted to every day. Thanks to the efforts of Aylmer and others, it is possible to reconstruct Dickens's daily whereabouts during this period with unusual thoroughness, and presumably the pattern was representative of all Dickens's later years. Heavily involved with public readings and the editing of *All the Year Round,* he nevertheless managed, in Tomalin's words, to spend "one third of his time with, or near Nelly; one third at Gad's Hill; and one third serving his other love, the public" (168).

Dickens must have been one of England's champion railway travelers (in spite of being left by the Staplehurst accident with severe anxiety on trains), for Gad's Hill was an hour and a half's railway journey to London (where the offices of *All the Year Round* were and in which Dickens frequently spent the night in a little apartment he had made for himself), the various houses in which he had established Nelly after 1862 were all short railway commutes from London, and the public readings took him to at least 35 towns throughout Great Britain during this year as well, sometimes more than once. Although such friends and associates as Forster, Wilkie Collins, Wills, Georgina, and some of Dickens's children were necessarily in on the secret of his life with Ellen (Wills in particular being called on occasionally to transact business on her behalf), the fact that Dickens regularly spent nights in the *All the Year Round* offices and at Gad's Hill made it very easy for him to keep even those closest to him in the dark as to where he might actually be. Comparing surviving letters to Georgina with the diary makes clear that he would sometimes pretend to be at the office when in fact he was spending time with Nelly, so that even she may not have known how much time the couple spent together. Even among those he most trusted he remained intensely private.

The contrast with other famous Victorian men who kept mistresses is striking. As Tomalin reminds us, Wilkie Collins kept not one but two mistresses, each of whom regularly presided over gatherings of his male friends, and Dickens's first illustrator, George Cruikshank, likewise maintained two households, virtually around the corner from one another, having no less than 10 children by his mistress (107, 169). Victorian morality strikes us as hypocritical precisely because it "recognized" such relationships through a set of strict but double rules that insulated the respectable relationship from the illegitimate along gendered lines: the mistress was invisible to respectable female society generally while socially accessible to respectable males. And everything was felt to be fine so long as the line between the respectable and illegitimate was securely held. Although uniquely famous and certainly identified with the domestic virtues (in spite of all sorts of competing drives to the contrary, to which the writings amply testify), Dickens could no doubt have managed a love affair with much less fuss had he simply followed those rules himself. But his very ambivalence about double standards and double lives prevented him from such an accommodation. Thus his cruelty in ridding himself of Catherine seems to have resulted from a mania for honesty of a peculiar kind, while his concealment of the relationship with Ellen seems to have resulted from a mania for secrecy of, by Victorian standards, a singularly *dis*honest kind, for it decidedly blurred the line between legitimate and illegitimate, allowing Nelly after Dickens's death to accomplish what no *acknowledged* mistress could have pulled off, a spotlessly respectable subsequent marriage. There was, in short, a proper Victorian way of going about having a mistress, but Dickens would have none of it. As in his childhood, he remained a curious mixture of innocence and artfulness.

Nelly was the last actual woman in Dickens's life, but one imaginary woman deserves discussion here as having played an important part in the real end of it. This is Nancy, the prostitute who towards the very beginning of Dickens's career had rescued Oliver Twist from a life of crime by revealing his whereabouts to his respectable relations and was rewarded for her efforts by being savagely beaten to death by her lover, Bill Sikes, after her secret meeting with Mr. Brownlow and Rose Maylie had been spied upon by a member of Fagin's gang. Nancy returned to Dickens's life in 1863 when he began experimenting with the idea of doing a reading based on her murder, but it was not until five years later that he brought the plan into being and added it to the readings making up the "Farewell" tour, which began shortly after his return from his second visit to America in 1868 and lasted until just under three months before his death.[13]

From the very outset there were signs that this reading had a special significance for Dickens, for his first efforts left him feeling he had produced something so "horrible" that he was "afraid to try it out in public"—or perhaps so horrible that he could not resist doing it in public. The fear was shared by the several others upon whom he tried the piece out. There were predictions of mass hysteria. One among the hundred or so invited guests (including members of the press) to whom Dickens presented the "experiment" of a "trial performance" confessed to "an almost irresistible impulse . . . to *scream*," and a "great ladies' doctor" warned him "that if one woman cries out when you murder the girl, there will be a contagion of hysteria all over this place." His family and friends were afraid that the exertion of the Murder (as he himself generally referred to the reading) would destroy his already poor health, but he wanted, as he said, "to leave behind . . . the recollection of something very passionate and dramatic," suggesting both that he shared their intimations of mortality and that he saw in the murder intimations of immortality as well, a really sensational close to an already sensationally successful public life. As it turned out, the reading was by all accounts a great *tour de force,* though it seems not to have produced quite the dire panics imagined by the great ladies' doctor.

But the performance did have dire consequences for Dickens, whose already poor health was broken by this last series of readings and the Murder in particular. His pulse would race to as much as 124 after some performances, and he would have to lie down for 10 minutes, unable to speak, before returning to his podium (for it was his policy never to end a performance with the Murder). In spite of the obvious damage being done—"I shall tear myself to pieces," he whispered to a friend as he went on the platform just before the last reading of the Murder—he simply could not leave it alone. "Assumption" in this instance seems to have been much more than merely figuratively "charming," but quite literally and fatally entrancing or captivating. It became the most often-performed item of his readings repertoire in 1870. His manager, George Dolby, records that while Dickens recovered from his exhaustion after every performance of the Murder with great rapidity, so that he could present the final more cheerful item on the bill "as blithe and gay as if he were just commencing his evening's work," nevertheless the shocks to his system "invariably recurred later in the evening, either in the form of great hilarity or a desire to be once more on the platform, or in a craving to do the work all over again."

Dickens was drawn to the Murder not simply because of the added sense of power over his public that it gave him, but because it drew upon deeper emotions that even the frequent and obsessive repetitions of the performance did nothing to lessen, as is evident in Dolby's report that a "craving" to do it all again and indulge what Dickens "used jokingly to call his 'murderous instincts' " would return within hours after a performance.[14] Dickens was even said to have been seen doing the Murder all by himself on the grounds at Gad's Hill only a day or so before his death. But what exactly those deeper emotions were is not so easy to say. Dickens's joking about his "murderous instincts" and his fascination with the horrible effects of the reading on his audiences may suggest too simple an answer that overlooks an important fact: that in playing the Murder he of course played *all* the parts, not just Sikes, that is, but Sikes *and Nancy* (as well as Fagin and Noah Claypole and Mr. Brownlow and Rose Maylie). Indeed, many reviewers were most powerfully moved by his portrayal of Nancy and, as one witness described them, "her last gasping, shrieking apostrophes, to 'Bill, dear Bill,' when she sinks, blinded by blood, under the murderous blows dealt upon her upturned face by her brutal paramour."[15]

The return to *Oliver Twist* no doubt signals a return to, or rather the survival of, the childhood fears associated with Warren's and his father's imprisonment, although Nancy's relationship to that material is indirect and complex—her plot effectively takes over the novel at a point when Oliver himself seems to drop out except as a mere counter in other people's games. What deserves notice, however, is that the Murder entailed not only playing at murdering, but being murdered as well; not only acting a brutal male murderer, but his female victim. Just as the Artful and Oliver embody Dickens's various selves, so too do Sikes and Nancy constitute further splittings of Dickensian selves. We have been looking at the women in Dickens's life primarily as "others," but this final episode connects in more ways than one with the material of the previous chapter. "I shall tear myself to pieces," he had said before the final reading of the Murder. What a marvelous statement from a man determined to kill himself by playing all the parts.

Chapter Four
Sentiment and Skepticism

In a famous review titled "Signs of the Times," Thomas Carlyle in 1829 characterized his age as "Mechanical" in every respect. Work, every social institution, national culture, science, philosophy, and even religion for Carlyle had all fallen under the sway of the "Mechanical." Work is no longer done by hand, he complains, but by machine. Everywhere faith is placed solely in the rearrangement of external circumstances or things material, and "men have lost their belief in the Invisible, and believe, and hope, and work only in the Visible."[1] What should be infinite and unspeakable is wrenched into the mechanical, explicit, and skeptical discourse of science and theory and subjected to the calculating logic of self-interest and profit-and-loss. Carlyle strikes themes here that resound through the nineteenth century and on through the twentieth, for in our own age conflicts between the authority of science or reason on the one hand and countless competing epistemologies that might be broadly characterized as "spiritual" on the other are apparent in most contemporary debates of consequence. The conflict is most apparent nowadays in arenas that involve religion, such as reproductive rights and technologies, but it is evident too in such disparate debates as those about education and the so-called culture wars, the rights of indigenous peoples versus the needs of anthropologists to study the living and the dead, animal rights, and more purely academic controversies about whether consciousness itself is merely a byproduct of the specialized computers we call brains or a unique and perhaps ultimately inexplicable phenomenon. It is apparent wherever people argue about the authority that lies behind ethical obligations, wherever people argue whether social goods can be measured in numbers or require qualitative judgments not reducible to quantity, and wherever people argue about whether social or cultural phenomena are reducible to their material conditions.

In Dickens's day as in ours, many thoughtful people felt called upon to identify themselves with Carlyle and what we might call the party of the spirit—which would certainly have included many of the best-remembered literary people of the day: Samuel Taylor Coleridge, William Wordsworth, John Ruskin, John Henry Newman, Matthew Arnold,

Charlotte and Emily Brontë—as against the mechanical or skeptical party (which would have included Charles Darwin, John Stuart Mill, Harriet Martineau, Thomas Henry Huxley, and Herbert Spencer, for example). Dickens always consciously and explicitly identified himself with Carlyle and the party of the spirit. He dedicated *Hard Times,* his most didactic novel, to Carlyle, and once said of him, "I would go at all times farther to see Carlyle than any man alive" (Forster, 11.3).

But then as now the contest between the mechanicals and the spirituals was interesting because, in spite of the party lines, people on both sides were more often than not genuinely, if not always consciously, conflicted about the competing claims of, for example, rationality and traditional beliefs. Then as now, the obvious power of science and its allied technologies to offer not just powerful explanations but powerful tools that make life safer and more comfortable was hard for even the most temperamentally or ideologically conservative to deny. Dickens was no exception in being ambivalent about the mechanical, nor, for that matter was Carlyle, who had been trained as a mathematician at perhaps the most scientifically advanced university in Britain, the University of Edinburgh, and who had, while still in his twenties, lost the orthodox Christian (and Calvinist) faith of his family. Like many another Victorian who experienced a spiritual crisis, Carlyle after his crisis nevertheless still very much resembled the product of an Enlightenment education that he had been before it, and what felt to him a profound break with his past and virtually a second birth—recorded in fictionalized form in his *Sartor Resartus*—left him struggling still with the competing claims of reason and faith, though certainly his understanding of what reason and faith themselves consisted in may have altered radically.

The party of the mechanicals likewise included people whose orthodox Christian faith was surprisingly untouched by the most alarming of scientific theories—no less, for example, than Darwin himself, whose theory of natural selection in best skeptical fashion deprived humankind of the unique and privileged position it enjoyed in the scriptural account of creation when read literally. The rationalist and Utilitarian John Stuart Mill underwent a spiritual crisis very like Carlyle's in that it left the new Mill looking very much like the old, though at its most general level it seemed to carry him away from the rationalism of his father (the philosopher and political economist James Mill, who had educated the little Mill himself in a famously rigorous educational experiment, starting his son on the study of Greek at the age of three), towards a softened and more spiritualized faith in feeling. The subtlety of the distinction between mechanicals and spirituals is perhaps apparent when we consider that while Mill in his autobiography specifically likened his crisis to Carlyle's, nevertheless, there was no doubt in anyone's mind (except perhaps his own) that he remained a leader of the rationalists.

A central figure in this story is the philosopher Jeremy Bentham, whom many among the mechanicals looked to as their guide. His career spans the period from the French Revolution to the passage of the first Reform Bill in 1832, a period of both intense anxiety and hope when the rising middle class in England began to come into significant Parliamentary power and the growing democratic tide became irreversible. Bentham made famous what he called the "Greatest Happiness Principle," which proclaimed that there is no ethical good but pleasure, that the pleasures of all sentient beings are of equal ethical value, and that the only valid measure of any political action or goal is its tendency to promote the greatest happiness of the greatest number. He had enormous confidence, further, in human reason and our ability actually to measure both pleasures and the consequences of our actions, and he firmly believed that ethical and political action would become real sciences. Because his ideas about political, economic, and legal reform tended to sweep away hidebound traditions, they were attractive to democrats and entrepreneurs, and by the early decades of the nineteenth century Bentham was surrounded by a group of younger disciples variously identified as Utilitarians (after his unfortunate and misleading use of the word "utility" to mean simply "pleasure") or Philosophical Radicals, who were in turn leaders of the reformist movement that had its first great success in the bill of 1832 and who also were important in the reform of a greatly expanding civil service and such brand-new areas of social engineering as education and sanitary reform (entailing such innovations as the building of an effective system of drains and sewers for disposing of wastes that had previously simply been dumped into the same bodies that supplied drinking water). But Utilitarians were also the guiding force behind such extremely *un*popular measures as the New Poor Law of 1834 (satirized so effectively by Dickens in *Oliver Twist*). Bentham, more than any other figure, embodied a happy and unconflicted member of the mechanicals, and he is a frequent explicit target and a constant implicit target of polemics by the spirituals throughout the remainder of the century (in those works from Carlyle to Matthew Arnold and beyond that go by the generic or canonical name of "Victorian Prose"). John Stuart Mill took Bentham as one of his subjects in writing a pair of essays about the "two great seminal minds of England in their age" and "the teachers of the teachers"—his contrasting figure being the equally happily unconflicted spiritual or antimechanical, Samuel Taylor Coleridge.[2]

Precisely because he identified himself so explicitly with Carlyle, Dickens's ambivalence about mechanism versus spirit or rationalism versus faith or, as I shall figure the conflict most generally in this chapter, skepticism versus sentiment, is not always easy to see.[3] Dickens scholars, where they have recognized it, have often drawn the split along the lines of practical political alliances on the one hand and roughly philosophical, ethical, psychological beliefs, as manifested in the imaginative writings, on the other. It is often pointed out, for example, that Dickens found himself allied with doctrinaire Utilitarians (like the sanitary reformers Edwin Chadwick, who had been Bentham's private secretary, and Dr. Thomas Southwood Smith, who had been his physician) even as he attacked Utilitarian doctrine through both his journalistic writings and novels like *Hard Times*. I shall argue, however, that the ambivalence runs deeper—that it is evident within the writings and within the very structure of beliefs that they embody, that it is a tremendous source of Dickens's creative energies, and that it is therefore of permanent interest.

It may seem strange to take up such dry and weighty considerations in beginning to look closely at the works of a writer who has so often been characterized as above all an entertainer, who himself decried "philosophy" generally, and who could easily be recognized by his contemporaries in a reference by his rival novelist Anthony Trollope (in chapter 25 of *The Warden*) to "Mr. Popular Sentiment." The charm of his earliest works, the little pieces collected as *Sketches by Boz* and the first novel (which may truly be said to have started its life as scarcely anything so ambitious as a novel at all), *The Pickwick Papers,* exude a spontaneity apparently quite inconsistent with anything very serious, much less the central intellectual debate of the age. Oliver Twist, Nicholas Nickleby and his sister Kate, their adopted brother (and actual cousin) Smike, and, more than any other character, Little Nell all introduce pathos to Dickens's fundamentally comic imagination, but none of these early heroes and heroines has the sort of brain anyone would like to see weigh in on the question of "the spirit of the age."[4]

The early Dickensian narrator, generally a pretty close approximation of Dickens's own voice, though sometimes merely diffident about matters intellectual, has also on occasion a positively anti-intellectual edge. This can certainly be traced, at least in part, to his master, Carlyle, who praises the spontaneous, the unself-conscious, the unconscious, the unsayable, and even the unspeaking; but Carlyle's writing is itself so self-conscious and voluble—above all, so manifestly *learned*—that it would be very hard indeed to mistake it as unthinking. Dickens, however, can throughout his career do a sufficiently convincing impersonation of an anti-intellectual as to give some comfort to readers who are perfectly content to find in him mere fun and entertainment and who have never quite reconciled with the later and more obviously somber and serious works. He had plenty of such readers in his lifetime and has plenty of them even now.

But as even some very early readers appreciated, for all his fun, Dickens is by no means unserious. Halfway through the publication of *Pickwick,* an anonymous reviewer dubbed that work's hero "the legitimate successor to Don Quixote"—the hero, that is, of what is certainly the most important forerunner of the modern novel—and in 1840 Thackeray ventured that "a man who, a hundred years hence, should sit down to write the history of our time, would do wrong to put that great contemporary history of *Pickwick* aside as a frivolous work" (Collins 1971, 31, 38). Another early review (unsigned, though probably written by G. H. Lewes, who was later to become the partner of Marian Evans, better known as George Eliot) in 1837 praised *Sketches, Pickwick,* and *Oliver* as "volumes of human nature, that have a deep and subtle philosophy in them" (Collins 1971, 65). But the "philosophy" referred to here undoubtedly was hardly intended by the writer to signify systematic philosophy. It would be almost a hundred years before an academic philosopher would grant Dickens something like the status of an equal: "I think he was a good philosopher," wrote George Santayana in 1921.[5] And it would not be until the mid-twentieth century that Dickens's name would be routinely matched with those thinkers whom we have seen Foucault call the "founders of discursivity"—even if Foucault himself would not grant any merely literary figure that honor.

The story of how *Pickwick* came to be written is justly famous in literary history and underscores the unlikeliness of its being a text that enters the great intellectual debates of the period.[6] Very briefly, Dickens was approached by the publishers Edward Chapman and William Hall to supply text for a work to be published in parts that would include four illustrations and 26 pages of text each month for about 20 months. This project was the idea of Robert Seymour, an experienced etcher almost as popular as George Cruikshank.[7] Seymour's plan was to follow the comic misadventures of a group of Cockney bachelor sportsmen (that is, Londoners much out of their element in the country), drawing upon a vogue for sporting works. He and his prospective publishers imagined that the plates would be the chief attraction and that the text would be necessary chiefly to show how the bumbling heroes got from one funny situation to the next and thus to introduce the scenes that Seymour would illustrate. Dickens must have seemed an ideal choice. His *Sketches by Boz* had just appeared as a volume and showed him to be a highly talented and energetic young man very knowledgeable about London. It seems not to have occurred to them that he knew nothing about sportsmen. Dickens drew upon his knowledge of Bath for the name of his protagonist, Mr. Samuel Pickwick (a family of that name being innkeepers in the coaching business there) and upon his knowledge of eighteenth-century literature for the conventional types that became the other members of the club. Edward Chapman seems to have supplied ideas for Pickwick's physical traits.

Only a couple of months into the collaboration, and before the second number was in press, Seymour early one morning committed suicide by gunshot. He seems to have been in emotional as well as financial trouble for some time, and this last business venture was perhaps designed to rescue a career he felt to be failing. No doubt it did not help that the youngster hired to supply copy turned out to be ambitious and headstrong and much happier to be the leader than the follower in the enterprise, in spite of his youth and inexperience. Seymour's suicide occurred just as he was reworking a plate. Dickens had written to him rather imperiously that "it is not quite my idea; and as I feel so very solicitous to have it as complete as possible, I shall feel personally obliged, if you will make another drawing. It will give me great pleasure to see you, as well as the drawing, when it is completed" (14 April 1836). No sooner was Seymour dead than a search for his replacement was begun. Initially the choice fell upon a successful portrait painter, Robert William Buss, who proved insufficiently adept with the etcher's needle, and two months later it finally settled upon Hablot Knight Browne, younger even than Dickens, who adopted the sobriquet of "Phiz" (to match Dickens's "Boz") and was his chief illustrator through *A Tale of Two Cities* more than two decades later.

And Dickens also immediately proposed to Chapman and Hall a new format for each number: 32 pages of text and a reduction of illustrations from four to two. As we have seen, this became the standard format for the big Dickens novels, his own favorite format, and one that his popularity led many other novelists rather uncomfortably to follow.

Sales of the first numbers were disappointing, but the new serial slowly attracted some positive notices, and after number 4, which was the first for which Browne was sole illustrator and in which Dickens introduced Sam Weller—the "boots" (polisher of boots and brusher of clothes) at the White Hart Inn, whom Mr. Pickwick engages as his valet, and who subsequently plays Sancho to his Quixote—sales began really to take off. Soon people of every station and generation seemed to be reading the new work. From an initial run of 400 copies per number, by the end of its publication orders had risen to 40,000 copies per number (or about three times the sales for the novels of Sir Walter Scott at his greatest popularity [Ford, 6]).[8] And what had begun as a miscellany had become a novel. In the words of Forster:

> The plan of it was simply to amuse. It was to string together whimsical sketches of the pencil by entertaining sketches of the pen; and, at its beginning, where or how it was to end was as little known to himself as to any of his readers. But genius is a master as well as a servant, and when the laughter and fun were at their highest something graver made its appearance. . . . The book itself, in teaching him what his power was, had made him more conscious of what would be expected from its use; and this never afterwards quitted him. (Forster, 2.1)

In other words, not just the experience actually of writing a long work but the very fact of its success had more a sobering than an intoxicating effect on the young Dickens and left him with a life-long consciousness of a real—that is, ethical—obligation to his public.

What we might call the ethical seriousness of *Pickwick* emerges in a number of ways that by novel's end are clearly related. It emerges with the relationship between the two Sams, master and servant, and the echoes of Cervantes' great novel. It emerges with Mr. Pickwick's legal troubles and eventual imprisonment in the Fleet after he refuses to pay damages to the widow Mrs. Bardell, who has won her suit against him for breach of promise of marriage. It emerges through the celebration of Christmas and the whole ethos of Dingley Dell, where Mr. Pickwick's friend Wardle is squire of Manor Farm. It emerges also through the satire of the Reverend Mr. Stiggins, a hypocritical dissenting minister who preys on credulous women. It emerges through the sufferings of Mr. Jingle, who begins his life in the novel as an adventurer and cad, but who becomes an object of great pity when he and Mr. Pickwick meet up again in the Fleet. And it emerges most of all through the maturation of

Pickwick himself, who begins his life in the novel as a rather cantankerous and self-important bumbler but ends almost as a saint.

We are told as early as the second chapter that "general benevolence was one of the leading features of the Pickwickian theory," and the very fact that the Pickwick club has such a thing as a theory perhaps plants the seed of later seriousness, but that first reference to benevolence is ironic and comic, and there is no real practice to match the theory until the Pickwickians meet Mr. Wardle, the Squire of Manor Farm at Dingley Dell, and learn from him what benevolence is really all about. Dingley Dell, indeed, is the closest thing to paradise on earth in the Pickwickian world and embodies all the classic Dickensian virtues. Significantly, it is the locale not for the very first Christmas celebrations described by Dickens, but certainly the first Dickensian Christmas that rises to mythic proportions, and also the first that very clearly anticipates Scrooge's moral journey in *A Christmas Carol*.[9] Significantly too, Dickens places that Christmas at the literal center of *Pickwick*, in the novel's tenth number, suggesting that it is the novel's thematic or moral center as well. It therefore bears some looking into.

One of the more striking features of Christmas at Dingley Dell, and indeed of Christmases in Dickens generally, is how little of religion there is in them. Dickens in fact was criticized by some Evangelical reviewers for the lack of religion in *Pickwick*, and he defended himself against that charge, not altogether successfully, in the preface to the Cheap Edition of the novel 10 years later:

> Lest there should be any well-intentioned persons who do not perceive the difference . . . between religion and the cant of religion, piety and the pretence of piety, a humble reverence for the great truths of scripture and an audacious and offensive obtrusion of its letter and not its spirit in the commonest dissensions and meanest affairs of life . . . , let them understand that it is always the latter, and never the former, which is satirized here.

Dickens is sounding a note that he will strike again and again, right up to the very end of his career, whenever the piety of his works is questioned. But his invocation of the spirit as against sectarian controversies about the interpretation of the letter is question-begging and altogether too easy (please understand, he says in effect, that he only satirizes *bad* things), and it is somewhat disingenuous as well. It is true that *Pickwick* never satirizes religion, piety, or "the great truths of scripture" *per se*. But it does satirize a number of doctrines dear to Christian enthusiasts: the conviction of sin and corollary importance of the Atonement, the importance of a spiritual rebirth, and the importance of missionary work; and, indeed, it satirizes religious enthusiasm itself.[10] The Rev. Stiggins is undoubtedly satirized because he is a hypocrite, but we are given no counterexamples of what true piety might look like; there are not here—nor indeed anywhere in Dickens—any good Christian enthusiasts, and, as we shall see, the Christianity of Christmas is virtually eclipsed by secular goods.

The goods of Dingley Dell are, most simply, the goods of a really first-rate inn, and Mr. Wardle is above all else the ideal host, though in noting this we should be careful not to belittle these goods: Dickens works very hard indeed to exalt them and to impart them precisely with that mythic status with which he invests his Christmases, and if such goods seem tired to us, this is partly because Dickens has played so large and successful a part in making them part of the dominant culture. Wardle supplies companionship and comfort in a snug setting, warm and safe from the trials of the road, where the Pickwickians invariably get themselves into trouble (for they can rarely get themselves where they mean to go without help). Christmas eve is celebrated with an extended party, including a wedding, card-playing, dancing, and plenty of eating and drinking, and the narrator extols the season as chiefly a time for reunions:

> How many families, whose members have been dispersed and scattered far and wide, in the restless struggles of life, are then reunited, and meet once again in that happy state of companionship and mutual goodwill, which is a source of such pure and unalloyed delight, and one so incompatible with the cares and sorrows of the world, that the religious belief of the most civilized nations, and the rude traditions of the roughest savages, alike number it among the first joys of a future condition of existence, provided for the blest and happy! (28)

There is in this a curious and unthinking association between companionship and the unworldly that leads to thoughts of heaven. But the heaven imagined is the one *all* humans imagine; it is not merely nondenominational but broad enough to admit "the roughest savages," and its "first joys" are the human ones of "companionship and mutual goodwill," not the pleasure of finally seeing God nor even the reward of eternal life in itself. It is significant, too, that such an afterlife, in which one goes to heaven to see friends and family, seems to be reserved for "the

blest and happy," not for the lonely and miserable. The imperative is to
be happy *now*, and if you expect to go to heaven (or at least to enjoy
yourself there), you'd better be sure to make some good friends on earth
first.

This is, indeed, the moral of the ghost story Wardle tells on Christmas eve, "The Story of the Goblins Who Stole a Sexton," which is about
a sexton named Gabriel Grub—an earlier version of Scrooge—who is

> an ill-conditioned, cross-grained, surly fellow—a morose and lonely man,
> who consorted with nobody but himself, and an old wicker bottle which
> fitted into his large deep waistcoat pocket—and who eyed each merry
> face, as it passed him by, with such a deep scowl of malice and ill-humour,
> as it was difficult to meet, without feeling something the worse for. (29)

Gabriel spends one memorable Christmas eve digging a grave and
drinking alone, when he is suddenly interrupted by a goblin king and a
throng of lesser spirits who chastise him for his gloom and threaten to
carry him off into their world. They take him to a goblin cave and show
him a series of visions of real people bearing up under various depriva-
tions and sufferings.

These visions, prefiguring the visits paid to Scrooge by the spirits of
Christmas Past, Present, and Yet To Come, effect a similar conversion,
for Gabriel comes to realize

> that men who worked hard and earned their scanty bread with lives of
> labour, were cheerful and happy; and that to the most ignorant, the
> sweet face of nature was a never-failing source of cheerfulness and joy. He
> saw those who had been delicately nurtured, and tenderly brought up,
> cheerful under privations, and superior to suffering, that would have
> crushed many of a rougher grain, because they bore within their own
> bosoms the materials of happiness. . . . Above all, he saw that men like
> himself, who snarled at the mirth and cheerfulness of others, were the
> foulest weeds on the fair surface of the earth; and setting all the good of
> the world against the evil, he came to the conclusion that it was a very
> decent and respectable sort of world after all. (29)

In an odd juxtaposition, and almost as though to rub our noses in the
secularism of Christmas at Dingley Dell, the novel follows up this tale
by showing us Mr. Pickwick spending Christmas morning itself meeting
the medical students Bob Sawyer and Ben Allen, who entertain themselves by the fire with cigars and brandy, oysters and fowl, and converse
thus:

"Nothing like dissecting to give one an appetite," said Mr. Bob Sawyer, looking round the table. . . .

"By the bye, Bob," said Mr. Allen, "have you finished that leg yet?"

"Nearly," replied Sawyer, helping himself to half a fowl as he spoke. "It's a very muscular one for a child's."

"Is it?" inquired Mr. Allen carelessly.

"Very," said Bob Sawyer, with his mouth full.

"I've put my name down for an arm, at our place," said Mr. Allen. "We're clubbing for a subject, and the list is nearly full, only we can't get hold of any fellow that wants a head. I wish you'd take it." (30)

There is a ghoulishness that haunts *Pickwick,* not just in its several interpolated tales but, as here, in the very body of the work, and that rather undermines its vision of the world as "a very decent and respectable sort of world after all." Such coarseness and even brutality are partially functions of the novel's ethos, which belongs in many ways more to the Regency than to what would, after all, take many years to be identified as the "Victorian"—a world in which "sport" typically means blood sports: hunting and fighting, whether man against animal, man against man, or animal against animal. But even if we take the novel's contemporary context into account, Dickens seems positively to go out of his way to contrast the secular pleasures of Christmas with just those secular horrors—the horrors associated with the physical facts of death—from which Christian doctrine might be supposed to rescue its adherents. In other words, in celebrating the goods of comfort and companionship in the here and now, Dickens does not simply overlook that greatest evil that Christianity centrally promises to undo via the Resurrection but actually flaunts it.

This is a tactic that Dickens will return to in *A Christmas Carol,* which prepares for Scrooge's conversion through his reliving his own past and his being allowed to witness the private domestic happiness and pains of the Cratchits. But in the end the story clinches his conversion by granting him a horrifying vision of his own lonely death, when he will be mourned by no one and preyed upon by undertaker and servants, who will rob his very body and deathbed of his linen, silver, and other belongings. As Scrooge's nephew, Fred, puts it at the *Carol*'s beginning (and he surely expresses Dickens's own views here), the peculiar goodness of Christmas is actually that it renders us kind under the very shadow of death:

I am sure I have always thought of Christmas time, when it has come round—apart from the veneration due to its sacred name and origin, if anything belonging to it can be apart from that—as a good time: a kind, forgiving, charitable, pleasant time: the only time I know of, in the long calendar of the year, when men and women seem by one consent to open their shut-up hearts freely, and to think of people below them as if they really were fellow-passengers to the grave, and not another race of creatures bound on other journeys. (1)

In Fred's statement of the philosophy of Christmas, there is of course a careful equivocation. He both thinks about Christmas "apart from the veneration due to its sacred name and origin" and disingenuously questions whether it *can* be thought about apart from them. He saves himself from the charge of irreligion at the same time that he advances an entirely secular theory about the good that Christmas can do. Quite "apart" from the Christianity in Christmas, that is, it is a season that reminds us that in spite of the vast differences of class, we all belong to the same family or "race" in that we are all mortal and headed for the same end—we are all "fellow-passengers to the grave."

There is, in fact, nothing about Christmas *per se* that brings this particular lesson home. Of all times in the Christian year this is perhaps the only one in which believers might be excused for *not* being mindful of death. It is, rather, Dickens's picking up and exploiting an old secular convention of telling ghost stories on Christmas eve, his taking Gabriel Grub into a graveyard and then into the goblins' cave, his having the Ghost of Christmas Yet To Come show Scrooge his probable death chamber and grave, and his introducing a conversation about dissection and appetite at breakfast on Christmas day, that make the point.

Fred's having it both ways certainly seems to leave room for both religious and secular interpretations of Christmas, especially in that the kindness, forgiveness, and charity of which he speaks so clearly resonate with the spirit of the New Testament. Given Dickens's lifelong aversion to public professions of faith, and given also his awareness that among his audience were people of other faiths as well as people of no particular faith and people who had lost their faith, it is no wonder that he should be scrupulous, even in the works specifically written for the Christmas trade, about expunging all traces of the doctrinal or sectarian. But that he could so entirely do so, without any apparent strain, points out how completely his ethics focus on this world rather than the next, and how easily all the goods that he can imagine reduce to those goods of comfort and companionship embodied by Dingley Dell or Scrooge's nephew Fred or the Fezziwigs' ball.

This is not, I must emphasize, to question the sincerity or depth of Dickens's Christianity, which he does profess at significant moments, such as, for example, in his will, which he closes thus: "I commit my soul to the mercy of God through our Lord and Saviour Jesus Christ, and I exhort my dear children humbly to try to guide themselves by the teaching of the New Testament in its broad spirit, and to put no faith in any man's narrow construction of its letter here or there" (Forster, appendix). In the late forties he wrote for his children a simplified version of the New Testament, and while its theology is far from orthodox, in places approaching a Unitarian position that questions Christ's divinity, it also, if inconsistently, identifies Christ with miracles and the hope of resurrection.[11] In spite of the looseness of Dickens's understanding of or interest in Christian doctrine, he seems never to have come close to a characteristic Victorian crisis of faith like Carlyle's.

Two years before Dickens's death, in a letter written to his youngest son, "Plorn," who at the age of only 16 was being sent off to Australia, Dickens sums up his own religious beliefs in offering his son advice:

Never take a mean advantage of any one in any transaction, and never be hard upon people who are in your power. Try to do to others as you would have them do to you, and do not be discouraged if they fail sometimes. It is much better for you that they should fail in obeying the greatest rule laid down by Our Saviour than that you should. I put a New Testament among your books for the very same reasons, and with the very same hopes, that made me write an easy account of it for you, when you were a little child. Because it is the best book that ever was, or will be, known in the world; and because it teaches you the best lessons by which any human creature, who tries to be truthful and faithful to duty, can possibly be guided. As your brothers have gone away, one by one, I have written to each such words as I am now writing to you, and have entreated them all to guide themselves by this Book, putting aside the interpretations and inventions of Man. You will remember that you have never at home been harassed about religious observances, or mere formalities. I have always been anxious not to weary my children with such things, before they are old enough to form opinions respecting them. You will therefore understand the better that I now most solemnly impress upon you the truth and beauty of the Christian Religion, as it came from Christ Himself, and the impossibility of your going far wrong if you humbly but heartily respect it. Only one thing more on this head. The more we are in earnest as to feeling it, the less we are disposed to hold forth about it. Never abandon the wholesome practice of saying your own private prayers, night and morning. I have never abandoned it myself, and I know the comfort of it. I hope you will always be able to say in after life, that you had a kind father. You cannot show your affection for him so well, or make him so happy, as by doing your duty. (Forster, 11.3)

Dickens here is in the comfortable mainstream of liberal Protestantism, what the Victorians called "Broad Church." Read your Gospels and say your prayers (in private), do your duty, follow the Golden Rule above all, and eschew "mere formalities" and *everybody's* interpretations of what it is the Bible might actually be saying.

It is of course not a particularly coherent position, as both Evangelical Protestants and Roman Catholics were quick to recognize. For it blithely ignores many real difficulties of religious faith and doctrine and the inescapability of problems of interpretation and authority. It is all well and good to say "be truthful and do your duty," but it is not always clear in life exactly where the truth or one's duty actually lie. Duty implies an obligation to some authority or other, but it is precisely authority—notably in its human manifestations—that this brand of Protestantism calls into question by turning away from public formalities and "the interpretations and inventions of Man." Implicitly, moral truth can be known by reading Scripture without the intervention of authoritative interpreters, but that is a very doubtful position in its supposition that reading without interpretation is not only a theoretical possibility but one achievable in practice by any literate person. Or, equally doubtfully, it supposes that the only good interpreter of Scripture is oneself. One can easily see why Roman Catholic and High Church or Anglo-Catholics on the one hand, and Evangelicals and most Low Church Dissenters on the other (not to mention Freethinkers), would consider such a position as scarcely religious at all.

If Dickens's more private professions of faith appear to religious enthusiasts and nonbelievers alike as scarcely religious, his public references in his fiction, and especially his early fiction, must look even less so, for, as we have seen in the instances of Dingley Dell and the *Carol,* he goes to some lengths to dramatically attenuate if not entirely purge his writing of Christian reference. His hostility to questions of doctrine, his profound distrust of people who profess their faith publicly, and his sensitivity to the religious diversity of his audience all worked together to produce an ethical view in the works that is perfectly congenial to an almost entirely secular reading in which the good reduces rather directly to pleasure and most notably the sociable and domestic pleasures of comfort and companionship.

Ironically, the reduction of the good to pleasure puts Dickens's works for all practical purposes into the ethical camp of Bentham and the Utilitarians—precisely that party of the mechanicals against whom Dickens's moral mentor Carlyle had set himself up in such strenuous opposition. There are rather different flavors, it is true, with which Dickensians and Utilitarians imbue the good of pleasure, the latter—thanks to the goal of maximizing the pleasure of the greatest number—tending to aim at large social goods that can be measured and analyzed statistically or through the tools of political economy (which is among the reasons we consider them to belong to the party of the mechanicals). And when such "pleasures" as being employed or having enough food to feed one's family or living in a country rich in natural resources are looked at in the aggregate, they of course may cease to look very much like pleasures at all, especially when the measure of a particular "pleasure" is a statistical average that loses sight of the particular pains and pleasures of the individuals within whatever group is under consideration. This is exactly the problem with Utilitarians and political economists that Dickens later exposes in *Hard Times,* in which the circus girl Sissy Jupe challenges the schoolmaster who proclaims the glorious prosperity of the nation because annually only a tiny proportion of its people starve to death: "it must be just as hard upon those who were starved," Sissy observes, "whether the others were a million, or a million million" (1.9).

Bentham himself generally did much better than his followers, however, in not losing sight of the fact that a statistical measure of aggregate pleasures is only a fiction, of no matter how useful a kind, and that what is of ethical significance are the pleasures and pains of the real individuals who make up the aggregate. Although certainly committed to working towards the happiness of the greatest number, and suspicious therefore of sentimental acts of individual charity that were not well thought out in terms of their actual consequences—that therefore could easily prove wasteful or even harmful (such as handouts to a beggar as likely to buy gin as feed a family)—Bentham was far less scornful than many among his disciples of precisely the pleasures of domesticity and companionability that Dickensians like to celebrate. Less than a year before his death, he penned the following motto:

The way to be comfortable is to make others comfortable.
The way to make others comfortable is to appear to love them.
The way to appear to love them—is to love them in reality.

Probatur ab experientiâ [proved by experience], per Jeremy Bentham, Queen's Square Place, Westminster. Born, 15th February, anno 1748— Written (this copy) 24th October, 1831.[12]

No one, to my knowledge, has ever accused Bentham of being a sentimentalist, but this is as syrupy a formulation of Dickensian ethics—or the Golden Rule—as one could ask for.[13] Indeed, in person Bentham looked and even behaved far more like Mr. Pickwick than Mr. Gradgrind (the implicitly Utilitarian figure satirized in *Hard Times*), and there is even some reason to believe that the portly, jolly, and eminently eccentric figure of Bentham was in Dickens's mind when he dreamed up Mr. Pickwick—whom he resembles, unlikely though it would seem, in many particulars beyond the physical.[14] Thus, while it is, again, tempting to give into the age's own fondness for dividing itself up into the emotional, sentimental, spirituals on the one hand, and the rationalistic, skeptical, mechanicals on the other, even so apparently easy to place a figure as Bentham reminds us how people on both sides of the debate were genuinely, if not always consciously, conflicted.

But it is Dickens's conflicts about sentiment and skepticism, and not Bentham's, that are our subject. And Dickens's ambivalence on this score, we shall see, is even more pronounced in the novels that immediately follow *The Pickwick Papers,* though these conflicts manifest themselves in quite various ways.

Oliver Twist began publication when *Pickwick* was still in midstream. At roughly the same time that Mr. Pickwick goes to jail, Dickens begins his next novel with a satire of the workhouse and the New Poor Law of 1834, an amendment intended to bring rational and centralized reform to a system of providing relief that had become highly inconsistent, inefficient, and corrupt. A major component of the reform was designed to appeal to people's self-interest (as understood by a highly mechanical psychology) by confining relief to the workhouse (eliminating so-called outdoor relief) and quite intentionally making the workhouse second only to the prison in unattractiveness. Make the workhouse sufficiently repulsive, it was reasoned, and at least the able-bodied will quickly figure out it is better to find work. But the reform generally made matters worse and quickly became very widely detested.

In the middle of the workhouse, Dickens places a newborn—a figure of absolute innocence, though illegitimate and an orphan. This looks like a sure recipe for sentimental excess, especially when we see Dickens contrasting again and again his innocent little hero with the cynical and mechanical "philosophy" that lies behind the thinking of both the board that governs the workhouse and the design of the reform of the poor law itself. Their theory assumes that people are rational and selfish and that the only way to motivate them is to appeal to their self-interest. "Although Oliver had been brought up by philosophers," the narrator writes sarcastically, "he was not acquainted with the beautiful axiom that self-preservation is the first law of nature" (10). Against the assumption that humans are essentially selfish and calculating beings, *Oliver Twist* appears to argue for the triumph of an innocence that is notable for its selflessness. The idealization of selflessness helps to account for Oliver's extraordinary passivity, which strikes most readers as a profoundly improbable trait in a boy brought up under the miserable circumstances of the workhouse. It helps to account, too, for the equally improbable and dangling subplot involving Rose Maylie and her eventual marriage to her adopted brother, Harry, a plot that is largely about disinterestedness, both in the Maylie family's attachment to Rose, who is virtually a foundling and presumed (erroneously) to be illegitimate, and in her protracted refusal of Harry's proposal because she believes that his marriage to a woman of doubtful identity would harm his career. Rose's brief, but nearly fatal, illness likewise occasions the celebration of selfless love—and also privately evokes Mary Hogarth's death.

But while Dickens explicitly intended to show "in little Oliver, the principle of Good surviving through every adverse circumstance," as he tells us in the preface to the third edition, that sentimentally satisfying lesson is tempered and even undermined precisely by all those adverse circumstances that the novelist throws in his way, as he says in the same place, "to try him." The more serious the trial, the darker the vision of the world. Ironically, therefore, the world that *Oliver* portrays is rife with selfish folk, in the world of the workhouse, in the world of the board and the parish that governs it, in the world of the criminals into which Oliver falls when he flees to London, and even, we may say, in the respectable world generally, excepting only the Brownlow and Maylie circles, each of which just happens to be closely connected to Oliver's family. And even that family is no safe refuge from selfishness, for in fact Oliver's greatest nemesis, and greatest emblem of greed in the novel— surpassing even Fagin—is his own half-brother, Monks.

Ironically, too, it is the criminal Fagin who most clearly articulates the theory of selfishness that Dickens ascribes to the "philosophers."

Towards the end of *Oliver*, Fagin gives a new recruit into his band of
pickpockets, Noah Claypole, alias Morris Bolter, a pithy lesson in social
theory:

> "In a little community like ours, my dear," said Fagin, . . . we have a
> general number one; that is, you can't consider yourself as number one,
> without considering me too as the same, and all the other young peo-
> ple. . . . You see, . . . we are so mixed up together, and identified in our
> interests, that it must be so. For instance, it's your object to take care of
> number one—meaning yourself."
>
> "Certainly," replied Mr. Bolter. "Yer about right there."
>
> "Well! you can't take care of yourself, number one, without taking
> care of me, number one."
>
> "Number two, you mean," said Mr. Bolter, who was largely endowed
> with the quality of selfishness.
>
> "No, I don't!" retorted Fagin. "I'm of the same importance to you, as
> you are to yourself." (43)[15]

While this passage is undoubtedly ironic in that it incongruously makes
a thoroughly respectable social theory the master theory for a gang of
thieves, it is not at all clear that it can convincingly be read as ironic in
itself. For Fagin's is in fact a *good* lesson that addresses head on a central
ethical difficulty, the conflict between the psychological fact accepted by
the "philosophers"—that people are motivated by the pursuit of pleasure and avoidance of pain—with the ethical altruism that is at the
heart both of Utilitarianism (nobody's pleasure counts for more than
anyone else's) and the Sermon on the Mount (treat everybody as you
would like to be treated yourself). Dickens may be thinking that it is
not a lesson that people like Oliver and Rose—selfless or number-one-
less, we might say, to the core—need to learn, but then his number-one-
less people are not all that believable, nor are they all that numerous.
For *Oliver*'s world, again, is populated largely by people looking out for
number one, and in such a world, as Fagin well recognizes, we must in
fact learn to subordinate our personal number ones to a sort of "general
number one," or, as he says in concluding his lesson, "we . . . all go to
pieces in company."

The narrator of *Oliver* himself seems troubled by some consciousness
of the discrepancy in the novel between its sentimental and skeptical
world views. He records Oliver's growing pleasure in nature after the
anxiety and melancholy surrounding Rose's illness have passed with her
recovery (and, coincidentally, he anticipates John Ruskin's definition of

the pathetic fallacy) by remarking how our own mood affects "even . . .
the appearance of external objects." And this thought leads him to ponder more generally the relation between feelings and reality: "Men who
look on nature, and their fellow-men, and cry that all is dark and
gloomy, are in the right; but the sombre colours are reflections from
their own jaundiced eyes and hearts. The real hues are delicate, and need
a clearer vision" (34). The narrator's language here strongly suggests
that he is directly responding to a passage at the end of the preface of
Thomas Malthus's *Population: The First Essay,* a work of 1798 that had
become a classic text for Utilitarianism and political economy and
among the most important works constituting the intellectual context
of the New Poor Law. Reflecting on his grim thesis that hunger and star-
vation will necessarily check population growth if abstinence won't,
Malthus had written of himself: "The view which he has given of human
life has a melancholy hue, but he feels conscious that he has drawn these
dark tints from a conviction that they are really in the picture, and not
from a jaundiced eye or an inherent spleen of disposition."[16] But the
Dickens narrator's response to this is rather less powerful than we might
expect, and his attributing a somber world view to a diseased condition
does not necessarily brighten his picture. For if the "real hues are delicate, and need a clearer vision," this hardly claims that they are wonderfully bright, nor that they are often graced in fact by that "clearer
vision" of which they are in "need."

It is not just at this rather abstract level of social and psychological
theory that the tension between sentimental and skeptical views is
apparent. The very language of the novel is torn between styles that are
almost uncomfortably hard, even brutal, on the one hand, and sicken-
ingly sweet on the other. Contrast, for example, the novel's opening
paragraph—

> Among other buildings in a certain town, which for many reasons it
> will be prudent to refrain from mentioning, and to which I will assign no
> fictitious name, there is one anciently common to most towns, great or
> small: to wit, a workhouse; and in this workhouse was born: on a day and
> a date which I need not trouble myself to repeat, inasmuch as it can be of
> no possible consequence to the reader, in this stage of the business at all
> events: the item of mortality whose name is prefixed to the head of this
> chapter. (1)

—with this pastoral reflection, which prepares us for Rose's illness—

The memories which peaceful country scenes call up, are not of this world, nor its thoughts and hopes. Their gentle influence may teach us how to weave fresh garlands for the graves of those we loved: may purify our thoughts, and bear down before it old enmity and hatred; but beneath all this, there lingers, in the least reflective mind, a vague and half-formed consciousness of having held such feelings long before, in some remote and distant time; which calls up solemn thoughts of distant times to come, and bends down pride and worldliness beneath it. (32)

It is inviting to attribute the wild difference in styles here to the subject matter: the brutality and awkwardness of the opening satirically reflect the brutality and discomfort of the workhouse; the sweetness of the peaceful country scene is all nectar and honey. But, as in Fagin's lesson about "number one," it is hard actually to locate the satirical point in the opening.

Most apparent in the voice of the first chapter are both distance and discomfort. A few paragraphs in, the narrator speculates about the interval just after Oliver's birth that

if, during this brief period, Oliver had been surrounded by careful grand-mothers, anxious aunts, experienced nurses, and doctors of profound wis-dom, he would most inevitably and indubitably have been killed in no time. There being nobody by, however, but a pauper old woman, who was rendered rather misty by an unwonted allowance of beer; and a parish surgeon who did such matters by contract; Oliver and Nature fought out the point between them. The result was, that, after a few struggles, Oliver breathed, sneezed, and proceeded to advertise to the inmates of the workhouse the fact of a new burden having been imposed upon the parish, by setting up as loud a cry as could reasonably have been expected from a male infant who had not been possessed of that very useful appendage, a voice, for a much longer space of time than three minutes and a quarter.

This is bitter, but is it simply, much less entirely, ironic? For Oliver of course *does* survive his solitary struggle with Nature, and the image of "careful grandmothers, anxious aunts, experienced nurses" and so on does evoke a sense of oppressive, smothering love from which the Brownlow and Maylie circles are not wholly free.[17] The reference to Oliver's voice as "a useful appendage," linked as it is with Oliver's gra-tuitously being identified here as "a male infant," moreover, weirdly introduces an uneasiness about gender that persists in the plot of Nancy (one can't quite call it a subplot, for it eclipses Oliver's) and the misogyny of Fagin and Bill Sikes as well as the beadle Bumble, who, when he is told that he is responsible for his wife's misdeeds, because the law supposes that she acts under his "direction," famously rejoins: "If the law supposes that . . . the law is a ass—a idiot. If that's the eye of the law, the law's a bachelor; and the worst I wish the law is, that his eye may be opened by experience" (51). The narrator in these opening pages, in short, seems not quite in control of his own tone and not quite clear about whether he is satirizing a worldly, antisentimental, and skeptical position or more uncomfortably has been seriously infected by it.

This lack of resolution is apparent still in the novel's end, which is hardly a triumph of sentiment. Nancy's selflessness in rescuing Oliver is rewarded by the most brutal murder in all of Dickens, which, as we saw in the previous chapter, continued to fascinate its author right up until the very end of his life, and which seems moreover actually to have been implicated in his death. Oliver's goodness is itself rewarded, of course, in spite of his illegitimacy: he comes into his father's inheritance, but the terms of his father's will are extremely strange and turn out to be among the chief obstacles put in Oliver's way "to try him," even though the will itself has been destroyed and it requires the intervention of Mr. Brownlow to realize its intentions in fact if not in law. Written when Oliver's mother was pregnant, the will specifies that if the child "were a girl, it was to inherit the money unconditionally; but if a boy, only on the stipulation that in his minority he should never have stained his name with any public act of dishonour, meanness, cowardice, or wrong" (51). If the child *did* thus stain his name, the estate would revert to Oliver's half-brother, Edward Leeford ("Monks"), the vicious child of his father's miserable first marriage. Monks's mother burns the will but is "filled with the impression that a male child had been born, and was alive." Monks thus swears to her,

> if ever it crossed my path, to hunt it down; never to let it rest; to pursue it with the bitterest and most unrelenting animosity; to vent upon it the hatred that I deeply felt, and to spit upon the empty vaunt of that insulting will by dragging it, if I could, to the very gallows-foot. (51)

There are many oddities in this, not the least of which is the continued worrying of the issue of gender: a *girl* would inherit the estate no matter how evil she might turn out to be; a *boy* would lose it all if, while still a child, he did anything in public the least bit shameful, even an act merely mean or cowardly. No moral standard at all applies to girls, it seems, while boys are held to a standard of perfection. The qualification "in his minority" is exceedingly harsh, yet ironically it frees the perfect child to be a most imperfect man without endangering his inheritance. Although Oliver's father has expressed his confidence that his child will share its mother's "gentle nature" and "noble heart" (51), his will fears that a boy will stain his name. But bastards have, in law, no names to stain. Even though the will has been destroyed, and there is no reason to believe that a male child has been born and survived, Monks vows to "hunt it down" and ensure that it fails the will's test. When he and Fagin themselves fail in this (by failing to corrupt Oliver) and Monks's schemes are discovered by Mr. Brownlow, he is literally blackmailed, ironically, into executing the will's provisions (50), though in the end Brownlow, with Oliver's joyful acquiescence, relents and the half-brothers share the estate equally, thus giving Monks further resources with which to demonstrate just how depraved he can be (51).

So the will—itself hardly a coherent document—is utterly destroyed, yet its intention survives if only to be (unsuccessfully) flouted, then is realized and then again and in the end ignored. Oliver survives the excruciatingly difficult test of his moral perfection and presumably retains the arbitrary surname given him by Bumble in the workhouse (2); his fallen mother, "weak and erring," is memorialized with a tablet in the old village church that significantly bears only her Christian name, "Agnes," as though it were she who were illegitimate (53); Rose gives up her adopted name for the identical name in marrying Harry; and the heroic Nancy is of course a bloody and battered corpse, revenged only by the hanging of Fagin and the savage hunting down of her murderous lover, in which the crowd's thirst for blood proves as ugly as his. Indeed. Both Sikes's and Fagin's ends are told largely from their own points of view with inevitably sympathetic, humanizing results.

Dickens's next novels reveal similar attractions to both sentiment and skepticism, but they also demonstrate that Dickens is learning successfully to negotiate his ambivalence—and learning quickly: *Nicholas Nickleby* begins its run in 20 monthly numbers in April 1838, when *Oliver* is only half done, and *Nickleby* itself is little more than half done by the time *Oliver* winds up; *The Old Curiosity Shop* opens for business in a new periodical edited by Dickens called *Master Humphrey's Clock* only six months after *Nickleby* is finished and is itself immediately followed in the same venue by *Barnaby Rudge*.

Nickleby, like *Oliver*, satirizes an institution, and does so even more successfully. The so-called Yorkshire Schools had long been dumping grounds for illegitimate and otherwise unwanted boys, often, like Smike, disabled or ill. But they also occasionally and pathetically attracted parents who were not wealthy enough to send their children to legitimate boarding schools and were gulled by advertisements like the one for Dotheboys Hall (which Dickens modeled closely on actual ones):

> EDUCATION.—At Mr. Wackford Squeers's Academy, Dotheboys Hall, at the delightful village of Dotheboys, near Greta Bridge in Yorkshire, Youth are boarded, clothed, booked, furnished with pocket-money, provided with all necessaries, instructed in all languages living and dead, mathematics, orthography, geometry, astronomy, trigonometry, the use of the globes, algebra, single stick (if required), writing, arithmetic, fortification, and every other branch of classical literature. Terms, twenty guineas per annum. No extras, no vacations, and diet unparalleled. (3)

Many Yorkshire schools were scarcely less dreadful than Oliver's workhouse, but whereas the satire of *Oliver Twist* had little demonstrable effect on poor law reform, Dickens's account of such "schools" as Squeers's so shamed prospective parents that it marked the beginning of their end, and he could truthfully write 10 years later in the preface to the first Cheap Edition that "They are very few now."

The Dotheboys Hall plot of *Nickleby* forms a very small part of the whole, however, even though it is not fully played out until the very end, and as was the case with *Oliver*, it is the *family* plot that dominates. Nicholas finds his way to employment at Dotheboys, then with Vincent Crummles's touring theatrical company, then with the brothers Cheerybles' business, and his sister Kate finds *her* way to employment as a seamstress in Mrs. Mantaini's dressmaking shop and then as companion to the snobbish and hypochondriacal Mrs. Wittiterly all because their father's death after the failure of his worldly speculations has left them and their widowed mother with no resource but their estranged, rich, and miserly uncle Ralph, who takes an instant dislike to Nicholas upon first meeting him and is determined to send him packing before he will undertake to do anything for his sister-in-law and niece. This conflict establishes the basis for the novel's plot, which like *Oliver*'s is essentially that of a romance, though a far more well constructed and conventional one.[18] The contrast in temperament between Ralph and his late brother (also named Nicholas) is striking:

These two brothers had been brought up together in a school at Exeter; and, being accustomed to go home once a week, had often heard, from their mother's lips, long accounts of their father's sufferings in his days of poverty, and of their deceased uncle's importance in his days of affluence; which recitals produced a very different impression on the two; for, while the younger [Nicholas], who was of a timid and retiring disposition, gleaned from thence nothing but forewarnings to shun the great world and attach himself to the quiet routine of a country life, Ralph, the elder, deduced from the often-repeated tale the two great morals, that riches are the only true source of happiness and power, and that it is lawful and just to compass their acquisition by all means short of felony. (1)

With such an inheritance, Nicholas and Kate's challenge is, unlike their timid father, to succeed in "the great world" without adopting the ruthless skepticism of their uncle Ralph.

This challenge is complicated not only by the active antagonism of Ralph, but by their mother, a highly comical character (as we have mentioned, modeled on Dickens's mother) whose nature is compromised by an acceptance of the ways of the world far greater than her late husband's, if far more naïve than her brother-in-law's. Indeed many of her rambling speeches are punctuated by criticisms of her husband's inability to deal with the world, and she is painfully obtuse about the ulterior motives of both Ralph and the circle of young aristocrats to whom he lends money and who outrageously flatter her as they become interested in Kate as potential sexual prey. Mrs. Nickleby, indeed, accepts the world because, while she is perfectly aware of her husband's timidity and ineptness, she is blind to the world's real wickedness and her first instinct is always to believe that worldly success must be a sign of virtue. Thus while Nicholas almost immediately sees through their uncle's schemes, and Kate does so soon after, their mother is conciliatory and apologetic towards him until quite late, and her readiness to take his part painfully prolongs her children's struggle to begin the world and be free of the baleful effects of the previous generation.

Conflicting views about "the great world" are also starkly thematized early in the novel's only two interpolated tales. These are told "against each other" in chapter 6 by two gentlemen in turn—one prematurely gray and in mourning, the other "good-tempered" and "merry-faced"— after Nicholas's trip in a stagecoach to Yorkshire is interrupted by an accident, and his traveling companions and he have to put up at a snug inn for a brief interval while a new coach is made ready. The first purports to tell the story behind York Minster's famous window memorializing five sisters. The youngest of these, a 16-year-old named Alice, plainly recalls Mary Hogarth. One day, as the sisters sit in an idyllic country setting working on their embroidery, they are accosted by a gloomy Benedictine monk, chided for their trivial and vain worldly pursuit, and urged to retreat to a convent. Only Alice defends their "harmless mirth" as creating works that shall one day "awaken good thoughts of by-gone days, and soften our hearts to affection and love." Time passes; the sisters—all but Alice—gradually disperse, take husbands, and lose them to sickness and war. And then Alice dies and the sisters are once again reunited at their old home in mourning for her. The monk returns with his old command to take "the veil," and the sisters are once again almost persuaded. But they look again fondly upon their old embroidery, and Alice's prediction that they would keep pleasant memories alive holds good. Rather than retreat, the sisters commission a glorious stained-glass window for the cathedral, "a faithful copy of their old embroidery work."

> "That's a melancholy tale," said the merry-faced gentleman, emptying his glass.
> "It is a tale of life, and life is made up of such sorrows," returned the other, courteously, but in a grave and sad tone of voice.
> "There are shades in all good pictures, but there are lights too, if we choose to contemplate them," said the gentleman with the merry face. "The youngest sister in your tale was always light-hearted."
> "And died early," said the other, gently.
> "She would have died earlier, perhaps, had she been less happy," said the first speaker, with much feeling. "Do you think the sisters who loved her so well would have grieved the less if her life had been one of gloom and sadness? If anything could soothe the first sharp pain of a heavy loss, it would be—with me—the reflection, that those I mourned, by being innocently happy here, and loving all about them, had prepared themselves for a purer and happier world. The sun does not shine upon this fair earth to meet frowning eyes, depend upon it."

The debate here clearly recalls both the language and substance of the remarks already quoted from *Oliver* about life's "sombre colours," (and behind them Malthus's comments about life's "melancholy hue"). Indeed, the two passages were written almost simultaneously, at the first anniversary of Mary Hogarth's death.[19]

The "merry-faced gentleman's tale" is presented as "a story of another kind." It concerns the Baron of Grogzwig, a hearty lord fond of hunting and "the pleasures of the table, or the pleasures of under the table," who takes it into his head one day to marry. His lady, daughter of the neighboring Baron Von Swillenhausen, proves to be a shrew, who, while providing him with a dozen children, gradually deprives him of all his hobbies and enjoyments. Gradually falling into debt under the pressures of his ballooning family, the baron loses his spirits and decides to kill himself after one last bottle and pipe. He is comforting himself with these when he is interrupted by a horrible apparition, "the Genius of Despair and Suicide," whose job it evidently is to accompany suicides in their final minutes and who tries to hurry the baron along. But the baron does not like to be hurried, and besides he finds it laughable when the apparition tells the baron that his next customer is "a young gentleman afflicted with too much money and leisure." That laugh proves fatal to the genius's mission, for it brings back the baron's spirits:

> "I'll brood over miseries no longer, but put a good face upon the matter, and try the fresh air and the bears again; and if that don't do, I'll talk to the baroness soundly, and cut the Von Swillenhausens dead." With this the baron fell into his chair and laughed so loudly and boisterously, that the room rang with it.

Upon which the apparition utters "a frightful howl" and vanishes.

The mournful man's tale is sentimental and the merry man's tale comic, but otherwise it is hard to see that they are different enough in substance to tell "against each other." They both uphold the values of life and the world against despair and asceticism and are both committed to techniques—therapies, we might say anachronistically—that seek to counter pain and the ultimate evil of death with the memory and hope of pleasure and thus to reconcile us to the world without hardening our hearts and shutting down our feelings—without, in short, letting us become monks or nuns on the one hand, or Ralph Nickleby or his near relations Gabriel Grub and Ebenezer Scrooge on the other.

I ascribe the novel's apparent inability to see that these stories are in some sense the same story to Dickens's continuing conflicts over sentiment and skepticism, though the stories' schematic juxtaposition also tells us that Dickens is in much greater control than he had been in *Oliver,* where we saw his tone vacillating almost wildly, and he seemed at times on the verge of giving himself up to the nightmare vision of reality that informs much of the book. *Nickleby*'s modes and genres are various, but relatively contained. In Alice and the Baron he has coherent answers to despair and doubt, even if he cannot quite decide which one is best or quite see that they both tend the same way.

Likewise, in Nicholas and Kate Dickens finds successful challenges to Ralph's cynicism—ones that are perhaps more parallel than we might expect given the difference of gender. For while Nicholas is full of manly violence and ever ready to thrash a villain like Squeers or Sir Mulberry Hawk (who is bent on ruining his sister), he also has his feminine side; he nurtures Smike with womanly tenderness and gives way to tears on more than one occasion.[20] Kate, for her part, in fact takes care of herself in her brother's absence rather well; she manages to flatten Sir Mulberry while disengaging herself from his unwelcome grip (19), and she has at least limited success in shaming her uncle with his acquiescence in his aristocratic clients' "unmanly course." " 'There is something of that boy's blood in you, I see,' said Ralph . . . as something in the flashing eye reminded him of Nicholas" (28).

As the language here suggests, and as countless critics have noted, *Nickleby* has a peculiarly melodramatic and theatrical air. Theatricality, moreover, is thematized in the central episode of Nicholas's sojourn with Vincent Crummles and his traveling company, in which Nicholas—who is told by Mr. Crummles that he has "genteel comedy in your walk and manner, juvenile tragedy in your eye, and touch-and-go farce in your laugh" (22)—has his first notable success in the world, as actor, adapter, and playwright. He is in this like another famous stage hero who is himself knowledgeable about the stage, mourning a much-loved father, troubled by a foolish mother, and locked in deadly combat with a hated uncle. Indeed, reminders of *Hamlet* are apparent in the very first scene in which we see Ralph, Mrs. Nickleby, and Nicholas and Kate together, when Mrs. Nickleby, in deep mourning, bemoans her loss:

> "Mine was no common loss!" said Mrs. Nickleby, applying her hand-kerchief to her eyes.
> "It was no *un*common loss, ma'am," returned Ralph. . . . "Husbands die every day, ma'am, and wives too."
> "And brothers also, sir," said Nicholas, with a glance of indignation. (3)

Although the play on "common" is somewhat different than Hamlet's "Ay, madam, it is common," it is enough to recall a work that was among Dickens's favorites and that is alluded to again and again, directly and indirectly.[21] *Nickleby* is by no means unique in this among Dickens's works, but the resonances here are peculiarly strong, particu-larly in the central relationship formed by Nicholas, his mother, and his uncle, with Kate and perhaps Smike doubling the Hamlet role (as indeed others do as well: e.g., the mad gentleman in small-clothes [knee-breeches], who woos Mrs. Nickleby by throwing cucumbers and other vegetables over the garden wall at her).

But Nicholas certainly is *not* Hamlet in one important regard: unlike Shakespeare's hero, he has no problems about delay and is never troubled by doubts about his proper course of action or slowed up by philosophizing. Although the punishment of the villain Ralph is certainly protracted, it is not for any holding back on Nicholas's part. It is rather that the full horror of Ralph's most grievous crime, the persecution of Smike in order to wound Nicholas indirectly, isn't really known even to Ralph until the very last number, when "the worst is told," and it is finally discovered that Smike is actually Ralph's own illegitimate child (60). At this point it is Ralph himself who plays Hamlet to his own Claudius and revenges his crime against his own kin in killing himself. If there is an aspect of the novel that serves the function of Hamlet's doubting, rather, it can be identified with the familiar Dickensian technique of doubling ("doubt" and "double" are, remotely at least, cognate)—the doublings already noted of the two interpolated tales, of Nicholas and Kate, of Nicholas and Smike, of Nicholas and Ralph, and so on. For each doubling presents a kind of fork in the road down an alternate reality and invites, to use one of the novel's favorite words, "speculation"—favorite because of its several senses evoking "the world": it refers not only to the kind of *un*worldly philosophical activity engaged in by Hamlet, but also to the worldly financial activities that ruin Nicholas senior (1) and enrich Ralph (2), as well a card game played at multiple points in the novel (9, 14). While Nicholas dashes from one (usually violent) encounter to another, the novel's doublings invite us more thoughtfully to ponder life's might-have-beens.

If the nightmarish quality of *Oliver* is much abated in *Nickleby,* there is still a dark enough view of things to call for a sentimental corrective, supplied in part through the feminine aspects of Nicholas and Kate and especially in their protection of Smike. (That they cannot in the end save him affords opportunities for more pathos in the Mary Hogarth vein, and paves the way also for the next novel and the figure of Little Nell.) A sentimental corrective is perhaps most famously supplied, however, through the exact doubles the Cheeryble twins, who are routinely deplored by critics as not merely improbable but impossible, though Dickens characteristically defends himself in the preface as merely having drawn from life—in this case upon his knowledge of the twin brothers David and William Grant, well-established merchants in Manchester known for their good works (Johnson, 3.3).

Nicholas happens to fall into the Cheerybles' magic circle by purest chance, and while Dickens may have believed them to be faithful copies of living men, he plainly drew as much on the traditions of fairy tale and English pantomime in representing them as on observation.[22] Like Good Fairies, they are the agents who introduce Nicholas and Kate to their respective loves (Madeleine Bray and Frank Cheeryble, the twins' nephew) and, along with Newman Noggs (another figure indebted to the conventions of pantomime), they stage-manage the intricate series of events that lead to Ralph's downfall and the novel's most un-*Hamlet*-like happy ending. Like many of Dickens's benevolent characters, they don't so much embody a *theory* of goodness as Dickens's insistence that there *really are* people in the world who seem too good to be true—"It is remarkable," he writes in the preface, "that what we call the world, which is so very credulous in what professes to be true, is most incredulous in what professes to be imaginary."

If *Nickleby* is Dickens's first sustained attempt to portray a young brother and sister's beginning the world and to worry about the very concept of "the world," it is in his next novel that Dickens first works out something we might call a coherent position on "the world" and where he centrally plays out the implications of *Nickleby*'s interpolated tales. Indeed, *The Old Curiosity Shop* can be regarded as another tale on the theme of "The Five Sisters of York," likewise told by a gray-haired man in mourning (for its narrator, the strange figure of Master Humphrey, reveals himself at the novel's close—most implausibly—to be "the single gentleman," younger brother to Nell's grandfather).[23] It is typically regarded as Dickens's most sentimental novel and is frequently derided on that account; Oscar Wilde famously declared that one must have a heart of stone to read the death of Little Nell without laughing.[24] Certainly it was designed to turn on the tears, and for its contemporary readers it was by and large spectacularly successful in achieving its intended effect, Wilde's remark notwithstanding. Its extraordinary popularity among the Victorians deserves serious attention, therefore. As we shall see, its sentimentality is finely poised against a view of the world that, while it looks conventionally religious, admits of a deeply skeptical interpretation.

The novel is striking today for a note of the perverse that is immediately apparent and never lets up. "Night is generally my time for walking," Master Humphrey announces at its very outset, for the dark affords him "greater opportunity for speculating on the characters and occupations of those who fill the streets" (1). In the midst of such musings he is "arrested by an inquiry" from "a pretty little girl" who has lost her way and begs directions.[25] Humphrey's first thought is of her vulnerability and his own power to do harm: "Suppose I should tell you wrong." This is not so much a question as a statement, for it is actually closed with a period. The thought brings a tear to the child's eye, yet she puts her hand in his "confidingly," and as the pair make their way to her home they exchange mutually curious looks as Humphrey tries unsuccessfully to find out what so young a thing should be doing out alone in the middle of the night.[26] "That, I must not tell," she replies.

Nell's secrecy doubles Master Humphrey's, for he has opened his *Clock* with the words, "The reader must not expect to know where I live." And Humphrey discovers a closer double of himself when he delivers Nell to her home and meets the grandfather with whom she lives alone in a shop,

> one of those receptacles for old and curious things which seem to crouch in odd corners of this town, and to hide their musty treasures from the public eye in jealousy and distrust. There were suits of mail, standing like ghosts in armour, here and there; fantastic carvings brought from monkish cloisters; rusty weapons of various kinds; distorted figures in china, and wood, and iron; and ivory; tapestry and strange furniture that might have been designed in dreams. The haggard aspect of the little old man was wonderfully suited to the place; he might have groped among old churches, and tombs, and deserted houses, and gathered all the spoils with his own hands. There was nothing in the whole collection but was in keeping with himself; nothing that looked older or more worn than he.

After returning to his own equally curious abode, Humphrey cannot help fantasizing about the strange young girl:

> I sat down in my easy-chair, and falling back upon its ample cushions, pictured to myself the child in her bed: alone, unwatched, uncared for, (save by angels), yet sleeping peacefully. So very young, so spiritual, so slight and fairy-like a creature passing the long dull nights in such an uncongenial place—I could not dismiss it from my thoughts.
> . . . I am not sure I should have been so thoroughly possessed by this one subject, but for the heaps of fantastic things I had seen huddled together in the curiosity-dealer's warehouse. . . . I had her image, without any effort of imagination, surrounded and beset by everything that

was foreign to its nature, and farthest removed from the sympathies of her sex and age. If these helps to my fancy had all been wanting, and I had been forced to imagine her in a common chamber, with nothing unusual or uncouth in its appearance, it is very probable that I should have been less impressed with her strange and solitary state. As it was, she seemed to exist in a kind of allegory; and, having these shapes about her, claimed my interest so strongly, that . . . I could not dismiss her from my recollection, do what I would.

"It would be a curious speculation," said I . . . "to imagine her in her future life, holding her solitary way among a crowd of wild, grotesque companions; the only pure, fresh, youthful object in the throng, It would be curious to find—"

I checked myself here, for the theme was carrying me along with it at a great pace, and I already saw before me a region on which I was little disposed to enter.[27]

Two things are remarkable about this passage. The first is how transparent is the eroticism and the fascination in imagining the child's vulnerability amid the grotesque paraphernalia of the shop that provide essential "helps" to the old man's "fancy." The second is that Master Humphrey's "curious speculation," which he dares not play out, is prophetic (if, like him, we conceive Nell to be "solitary" in spite of her being accompanied by her grandfather): the story of her wanderings is indeed about "her holding her solitary way among a crowd of wild, grotesque companions"—as though the "suits of mail" and "fantastic carvings" of the shop were come to life—and that speculation can't be further played out because it can and does lead only to her death, which finds her in virtually the same state that Humphrey now imagines her in: in bed and "surrounded and beset by everything that was foreign to [her] nature," which, as he has told us, is "so spiritual." The similarities are especially forceful if one compares the illustrations for these two scenes. The chief difference is that in the earlier scene Nell is surrounded by a lot of medieval stuff haphazardly disposed around her; in the latter things are a lot tidier, but the medieval trappings are all about her still, and the ancient house in which she dies is itself described as a "ruin" (52, 70). If she exists "in a kind of allegory," it is a strangely static or incomplete one, like Master Humphrey's own "curious speculation." "It would be curious to find—" *what,* exactly?

Nell's fate is to wander across the country in the company of her incompetent and dangerous grandfather (dangerous because his compulsive gambling causes them to flee London, repeatedly threatens them thereafter, and leads him to rob her in the dead of night in a scene that reads as much like a rape as a theft [30]), pursued by other old men who are either frankly villainous, like the sadistic dwarf Quilp, or benevolent but too feeble in their efforts to rescue her, like "the single gentleman" (her grandfather's younger brother, Master Humphrey) and Mr. Garland, who accompanies him and has provided the clue to her whereabouts, thanks to *his* bachelor brother—lots of bachelor brothers in this novel!—dear friend to the old schoolmaster who leads Nell to her final refuge in the village where he has just been appointed. Nell is thus pursued by old men, and in the end she is surrounded by them as well—all oddly unnamed: the schoolmaster, the clergyman, the sexton, the bachelor, and even the grandfather.

One explanation for this static quality in the novel would be to say that really it is not about a young girl who has adventures but comes in the end to die, so much as it is simply about death and how others deal with it. Such a view overlooks Nell's activity; she is indeed far less a nullity and far less passive than Oliver. But from the moment she is first introduced, lost and vulnerable, and imagined in her bed, "having these shapes about her," her fate is sealed. Very soon after she and her grandfather flee London, they stop in a small village with a churchyard, among whose graves Nell feels "a curious kind of pleasure in lingering among these houses of the dead" (17). She stops over "a humble stone which told of a young man who had died at twenty-three years old, fifty-five years ago," when she meets "a feeble woman bent with the weight of years, who tottered to the foot of that same grave and asked her to read the writing on the stone":

> "Were you his mother?" said the child.
> "I was his wife, my dear. . . . You wonder to hear me say that. . . . Older folk than you have wondered at the same thing before now. Yes, I was his wife. Death doesn't change us more than life, my dear." . . .
> Then . . . she told her how she had wept and moaned and prayed to die herself, when this happened; and how when she first came to that place, a young creature strong in love and grief, she had hoped that her heart was breaking as it seemed to be. But that time passed by, and although she continued to be sad when she came there, still she could not bear to come, and so went on till it was pain no longer, but a solemn pleasure and a duty she had learned to like. And now that five-and-fifty years were gone, she spoke of the dead man as if he had been her son and grandson with a kind of pity for his youth, growing out of her own old age, and exalting of his strength and manly beauty as compared with her

own weakness and decay; and yet she spoke about him as her husband
too, and thinking of herself in connexion with him, as she used to be and
not as she was now, talked of their meeting in another world as if he were
dead but yesterday, and she, separated from her former self, were thinking
of the happiness of that comely girl who seemed to have died with him.

This is a remarkable bit of philosophizing about death and selfhood, and
its blurring of the borders between life and death lays the basis for Dickens's later thinking about death, which we shall discuss in chapter 6.
But the writing, we might say, is for Nell not only on the stone, but also
on the wall.

The widow is only one of several mourners whom Nell meets on her
journey, and the most important of these is the kind schoolmaster, who
twice takes Nell and her grandfather in, and whose favorite pupil dies
during their stay—indeed in Nell's very presence (25). It is the schoolmaster who becomes the novel's chief theorist of death and who works
out more systematically than the widow the steps by which death's
pains may be transformed into pleasures. When next by chance they
meet, he is on his way to his new post in the village to which he will take
Nell, and where she will finally die. He asks Nell for a fuller account of
her story and plans, noting that

> "I have a reason (you have not forgotten it) for loving you. I have felt
> since that time as if my love for him who died, had been transferred to
> you who stood beside his bed. If this," he added looking upward, "is the
> beautiful creation that springs from ashes, let its peace prosper with me,
> as I deal tenderly and compassionately by this young child!" (46)

And after they have come to their final resting place, once again surrounded by graves, the schoolmaster develops the lesson further after
Nell confides her sad thought that "those who die about us, are so soon
forgotten." The schoolmaster replies,

> "Nell, Nell, there may be people busy in the world, at this instant, in
> whose good actions and good thoughts these very graves—neglected as
> they look to us—are the chief instruments."
> "Tell me no more," said the child quickly. "Tell me no more. I feel, I
> know it. How could *I* be unmindful of it when I thought of you?"
> "There is nothing," cried her friend, "no, nothing innocent or good,
> that dies, and is forgotten. Let us hold to that faith, or none. An infant, a
> prattling child, dying in its cradle, will live again in the better thoughts
> of those who loved it, and will play its part, through them, in the

redeeming actions of the world, though its body be burnt to ashes or drowned in the deepest sea. There is not an angel added to the Host of Heaven but does its blessed work on earth in those that loved it here. Forgotten! oh, if the good deeds of human creatures could be traced to their source, how beautiful would even death appear; for how much charity, mercy, and purified affection, would be seen to have their growth in dusty graves!"

"Yes," said the child, "it is the truth; I know it is. Who should feel its force so much as I, in whom your little scholar lives again! Dear, dear, good friend, if you knew the comfort you have given me!" (54)

The proper function of death, we might say, then, is to make better people of those it leaves behind and increase life's store of love and good deeds, especially the good deed of providing "comfort."

This is not to deny the religious consolation of heaven, to which the novel makes frequent appeal. But as in *Pickwick,* the other world has a rather worldly flavor, not so much like an inn, perhaps, but rather, being so much peopled by children, a summer camp. In the chapter following the one just quoted, Nell talks with a little boy who has recently lost a brother and expects her soon to follow him:

"They say that Willy is in Heaven now, and that it's always summer there, and yet I'm sure he grieves when I lie down upon his garden bed, and he cannot turn to kiss me. But if you do go, Nell, . . . be fond of him, for my sake. Tell him how I love him still, and how much I loved you; and when I think that you two are together, and are happy, I'll try to bear it, and never give you pain by doing wrong—indeed I never will!" (55)

We look forward to heaven, again, more for the pleasures of companionship than the reward of meeting God, and the thought of meeting up with old friends there makes the living mindful of being good while they are still on earth.

As much as in *Pickwick,* there can be no doubt that the elementary pleasures of comfort and companionship are what good deeds are all about. Moreover, this lesson is brought home not only through Nell herself but also through the novel's major comic characters: Kit Nubbles (the one friend she has who is at all near her own age), Mrs. Jarley, Dick Swiveller and the Marchioness (as well as, negatively, Quilp, whose evil is neatly defined by his sadism). After describing a mournful visit Kit pays to the shop after Nell and her grandfather have quitted it, the narrator comments on him thus:

It must be especially observed in justice to poor Kit that he was by no means of a sentimental turn, and perhaps had never heard that adjective in all his life. He was only a soft-hearted grateful fellow, and had nothing genteel or polite about him; consequently, instead of going home again, in his grief, to kick the children and abuse his mother (for, when your finely strung people are out of sorts, they must have everybody else unhappy likewise), he turned his thoughts to the vulgar expedient of making them more comfortable if he could. (14)

In a similar vein, Mrs. Jarley is likewise said to be

a very kind and considerate person, who had not only a peculiar relish for being comfortable herself, but for making everybody about her comfortable also; which latter taste, it may be remarked, is, even in persons who live in much finer places than caravans, a far more rare and uncommon one than the first, and is not by any means its necessary consequence. (29)

But it may be Dick Swiveller who best expresses the ideal equality of everybody's pleasure when, too ill to take a mug of beer himself, he begs the Marchioness to have one, exclaiming, "It will do me as much good to see you take it as if I might drink it myself" (65).

The *Shop*'s account of pleasure is made more interesting than those in Dickens's previous novels by presenting a richer sense of the dark side of pleasure through Quilp, whose over-the-top sadism provides a persistent and often hilarious as well as scary counter to the novel's pieties about goodness ("I don't eat babies; I don't like 'em" [21]), through Master Humphrey (whose "curious speculation" about Nell we have already examined), and, even more, through Nell's grandfather, whose love for her is grotesque if not downright pathological—as may indeed be hers for him, for the pair neatly exemplify what for the last decade or so has gone by the name of codependency, wherein a (usually addictive, frequently male) person's destructive behavior is abetted by somebody close (frequently female) who consciously or not fears that cure will lead to separation. The grandfather's compulsive gambling—undertaken, he believes, solely to ensure Nell's well-being after he is dead—together with her panic at the thought that they might be parted by well-meaning people were his rage to gamble to be known ("Separation from her grandfather was the greatest evil she could dread" [24]) certainly presents a classic configuration.

But it would be provincial to write off their relationship as merely sick, especially since there is very little that is unconscious about the novel's idealization of Nell's love for her grandfather. It is not, that is to say, that the novel is itself blind to his failings; how could it be when the novel is all we have to go on in seeing them for ourselves? Rather, the novel praises Nell's devotion *in spite of* the unworthiness of its object. From the very beginning, the self-centeredness and ineffectiveness of her grandfather's care of her are apparent, even, to some extent, to himself. "It is true," he says to Master Humphrey, "that in many respects I am the child, and she the grown person." And Humphrey notes also "something feeble and wandering in his manner," though "convinced that he could not be . . . in a state of dotage or imbecility" (1). The implication from chapter 1 on is that he is on the verge of madness, and this is of course borne out not only when his addiction to gambling leads him to rob Nell herself, but also in the end, when he is pathetically unable to recognize even that she is dead. If *Nickleby* was haunted by the ghost of *Hamlet,* it is, as many of its first readers noticed, *King Lear* that provides the backdrop to the *Shop.* But the question of curing the grandfather's madness or curing Nell of her attachment to him are no more real questions for the novel than curing Lear or his daughter would be for Shakespeare's tragedy, even though we all recognize the unreasonableness of Cordelia against the rationality, say, of Regan and Goneril. What to us appears to be a pathological carelessness about self is exactly what Dickens celebrates, again, as selflessness.

We might expect to find an explanation for such carelessness about self in religious or spiritual terms. After all—and to return to the terms with which this chapter began—care of the self, which nowadays we take effectively to be a duty, belongs to the realm of the mechanical, the calculating logic of self-interest and profit-and-loss decried by Carlyle and what I have called the party of the spirit. But is it a particularly religious or spiritual selflessness that Dickens promotes in *The Old Curiosity Shop?* Here again the conflict between sentiment and skepticism remains apparent. For, on the one hand, the novel's pronouncedly religious atmosphere bears, as we have seen, a decidedly secular reading (as in its lessons about death and even heaven), while on the other it does not, we might say, sentimentalize selflessness *essentially* so much as by way of a self-conscious act of will and, as it were, under special circumstances, the most important of which, perhaps, would be that approved selflessness is mutual. It is certainly good to be selfless amid similarly good people who are selfless themselves, and it may be good to be selfless vis-à-vis those we love—though Nell's case certainly puts that criterion to the test.

The ultimate negation of self is of course death itself—which limit Nell's case not only tests but reaches. The novel no more essentially sentimentalizes death, however, than selflessness. Immediately before she meets the schoolmaster for the second time, Nell is reduced to begging:

> Towards the afternoon, her grandfather complained bitterly of hunger. She approached one of the wretched hovels by the way-side, and knocked with her hand upon the door.
> "What would you have here?" said a gaunt man, opening it.
> "Charity. A morsel of bread."
> "Do you see that?" returned the man hoarsely, pointing to a kind of bundle on the ground. "That's a dead child. I and five hundred other men were thrown out of work, three months ago. That is my third dead child, and last. Do you think I have charity to bestow, or a morsel of bread to spare?" (45)

There are beautiful deaths, like Nell's, and then there are simply ghastly ones like that of this anonymous and sexless "dead child," who ends up "a kind of bundle on the ground." Which death is ours, this episode seems to suggest, may be a matter of pure chance.

This is an even starker vision of death than that of Scrooge's in the *Carol*, presented to him by the Ghost of Christmas Yet To Come; for Scrooge has at least himself to blame for his projected death, and he has, moreover, the power to alter it. Indeed, it is as stark as any death in Dickens's work.[28] Viewed against so desolate a backdrop, Nell's death needs to be recognized not as the natural way to go, but rather pointedly as a work of very human art—not in the obvious sense of being Dickens's creation, but rather as created by Nell herself and those around her. Its artificiality, contrivance, and affectation thus are not so much critical lapses as precisely its point.

I have been arguing that it is in the *Shop* that Dickens first works out a coherent position on "the world," that we find this position most succinctly articulated in the schoolmaster's lessons about dealing with death, and that it remains committed to the goods of the earlier novels—pleasure generally and the domestic pleasures of companionship and comfort most particularly. While his writing has been on an increasingly sentimental trajectory, its sentimentalism remains in these earliest works juxtaposed with and informed by a remarkably secular vision that we can see in its down-to-earth conception of the good, its reluctance to endorse any explicit religious doctrine, and its frequently bleak portrayals of what life and especially death can be like at their worst—as well as its frequent eruptions of material that is simply ghoulish. This conflict of sentiment and skepticism, as I have styled it in this chapter, remains vivid and unresolved throughout the rest of Dickens's career, though it is appropriate to close our account of it here with *The Old Curiosity Shop* because, perhaps with the exception of *A Christmas Carol* and the Christmas Books generally, it will never be clearer or cleaner than here. Indeed, rather against the grain of Dickens criticism that tends to see his evolution as moving from lighter to darker veins, I believe that the skeptical legacy of the enlightenment and the (generally unconscious) attraction to the party of the mechanicals is actually stronger in his earlier career, and we shall follow up the interests of this chapter by seeing in chapter 6 how the later Dickens is generally kinder to what we might call the mystical side of religion on the one hand, and less apt on the other, if not to be ghoulish, at least to be brutally so, than had been the still quite young man who authored *Pickwick, Oliver, Nickleby,* and the *Shop.*

Chapter Five

Domesticity and Dirt

Just as the tension between sentiment and skepticism is lifelong for Dickens, so too is that between what I shall here term domesticity and dirt: the urge to be snug and safe, to control and protect, on the one hand, and the restless and sometimes even reckless urge to sow disorder and danger on the other. Nor indeed are they unconnected. As we have seen, the realm about which Dickens tends to be sentimental and in which he locates the good *is* the domestic. But the tension we examined in the previous chapter is chiefly about ways of *viewing* the world and their ethical implications. What will concern us here, in addition to the theme of domesticity, are ways of *being in* the world—aspects of character that seem even more fundamental and almost instinctual.

While in the last chapter we concentrated on roughly the beginning third of Dickens's career, here it is for the most part the middle third that will command our attention. And there are of course good biographical reasons why the domestic comes into special prominence in this period, for it is the period in which the home of the young married couple becomes the home of a very sizable family. Dickens's first three children were actually born before *The Old Curiosity Shop* was complete (1841); but a further seven arrived during the period that concludes with the publication of *Bleak House* (1853). So it is in this period that youth gives way to middle age, romance gives way to more mundane concerns, and managing and even policing the family eclipse or at least control grander designs. It is a time, in short, for growing up and for seeing to the growing up of others and for wishing one didn't have to.

Barnaby Rudge and *Martin Chuzzlewit,* the two novels that immediately follow the *Shop,* both demonstrate an ambivalence about home and growing up that is much more obvious than in anything Dickens had written previously—or subsequently, perhaps. Each takes its name from a young man whose growing up is problematic. Each also, however, significantly elaborates our view of "the world" and interests itself, for the first time in Dickens's work, in detailed questions about society and the nation. Domestic order is seen as necessarily and mutually connected with the social order.[1]

Barnaby is a historical novel, dealing with the anti-Catholic riots in London led by the half-mad young Protestant fanatic Lord George Gordon for just over a week in June 1780, when several hundred people were killed and tremendous damage was done to property, chiefly through the burning of homes owned by Roman Catholics or their sympathizers by a mob of tens of thousands. Gordon's madness is doubled in the character who gives the work its title and who joins the mob: Barnaby is repeatedly described as an "idiot" (e.g., 3), but he is also given the conventional stage mannerisms and appearance of a madman or fool. Neither Gordon nor Barnaby are characters who could ever grow up—the narrator says of Barnaby that "his childhood was complete and lasting" (25)[2]—and their mingled immaturity and madness embody an inner "disorder of . . . mind" (3) reflected in the outer civil disorder of the riots, which prefigure the terror of the French Revolution (the subject of course of Dickens's other historical novel, *A Tale of Two Cities*).

Martin Chuzzlewit's theme is what Dickens calls "the commonest of all the vices" in the preface to the first edition (1844), what he spells out as "Selfishness" in the preface to the Cheap Edition (1850); it is a theme he has made familiar already from the earliest novels, but in taking its eponymous young hero to America, where he learns for the first time to care for somebody else—Mark Tapley, who is forever seeking out the most distressing circumstances so as to bring some "credit" to himself by remaining "jolly" (e.g., 5) and who has nursed the younger Martin through a serious fever—*Chuzzlewit* brings national identity (and nations' selfishness) into consideration as well. English selfishness is embodied comically by the hypocrite Pecksniff and the nurse Sairey Gamp and more darkly by young Martin (though he redeems himself after his trials in America), his cousin Jonas Chuzzlewit, and Jonas's associate in crime, Montague Tigg (a.k.a. Tigg Montague). American selfishness is embodied by virtually everybody Martin and Mark meet in their travels (most notably, perhaps, in the swindlers Zaphaniah Scadder and General Choke, who sell Martin and Mark a parcel of land for development in the town of Eden, which turns out to be a malaria-infested swamp on the banks of the Mississippi). The American variety of egoism, where it does not involve outright fraud, consists in a bullying chauvinism and self-aggrandizement: it seems that almost everyone Martin meets is heralded as "one of the most remarkable men in our country" (16, 21, 22, 33). Martin's experiences in America of course very directly parallel Dickens's own when he made his first triumphant

tour of the United States and Canada in 1842, and which he elaborated
also in *American Notes*.

Dickens's ambivalence about homes and growing up shows itself in
these novels not so much through plot or theme, for there is no question
that these come down in the end squarely in favor of domestic and social
order. It is rather the sheer vitality of the imagination and language that
suggests a kind of will to chaos. Although terrible, the descriptions of
the Gordon riots are at the same time exhilarating, and Dickens was
clearly swept up by their excitement: he writes to Forster about his
account of the rioters' breaking into London's greatest prison and free-
ing its prisoners—characteristically identifying with their violence—"I
have just burnt into Newgate, and am going in the next number to tear
the prisoners out by the hair of their heads" (Forster, 2.9). Nor does the
far milder *Chuzzlewit* escape the impulse to violence, above and beyond
its one attempted and one successful murder. In a passage made classic
by Dorothy Van Ghent, who first singled it out 50 years ago,[3] the narrator describes what ought to be a relatively peaceful scene, the view from
the rooftop of Todgers's, the lodging house where Pecksniff and his
daughters stay while visiting London:

> the revolving chimney-pots on one great stack of buildings seemed to be
> turning gravely to each other every now and then, and whispering the
> result of their separate observation of what was going on below. Others,
> of a crook-backed shape, appeared to be maliciously holding themselves
> askew, that they might shut the prospect out and baffle Todgers's. The
> man who was mending a pen at an upper window over the way, became
> of paramount importance in the scene, and made a blank in it, ridicu-
> lously disproportionate in its extent, when he retired. The gambols of a
> piece of cloth upon the dyer's pole had far more interest for the moment
> than all the changing motion of the crowd. Yet even while the looker-on
> felt angry with himself for this, and wondered how it was, the tumult
> swelled into a roar; the host of objects seemed to thicken and expand a
> hundredfold; and after gazing round him quite scared, he turned into
> Todgers's again, much more rapidly than he came out; and ten to one he
> told M. Todgers afterwards that if he hadn't done so, he would certainly
> have come into the street by the shortest cut: that is to say, head-fore-
> most. (9)

Not just for the narrator and his peculiarly animistic imagination, that
is, but for *any* "looker-on," the turbulent cityscape becomes violent,
potentially threatening even the madness of self-destruction. The
cityscape, we might say, is *itself* potentially the mob of *Barnaby Rudge*.

It is also notably through the vitality of the rogues and villains that the will to irresponsibility and chaos breaks through, for their language often simply cuts loose from the conventional even as it takes off from it. When Mrs. Gamp declares that "Rich folks may ride on camels, but it an't so easy for 'em to see out of a needle's eye" (25), she commands the language, as Steven Marcus notes, with "the god-like dominion of the comic poet," and affirms a radical "freedom from conditions" and "mastery over circumstances."[4] Pecksniff's language and imagination are similarly irrepressible. Recalling a student whom he had dismissed (after the student had discovered his real character), Pecksniff declares:

> I remember thinking once myself, in the days of my childhood, that pickled onions grew on trees, and that every elephant was born with an impregnable castle on his back. I have not found the fact to be so; far from it; and yet those visions have comforted me under circumstances of trial. Even when I have had the anguish of discovering that I have nourished in my breast an ostrich, and not a human pupil—even in that hour of agony, they have soothed me. (6)

It may seem unfair to pair Mrs. Gamp with Mr. Pecksniff and thus include her among the novel's rogues, for in the end she turns out to be on the side of good and is instrumental in bringing the murderer Jonas Chuzzlewit to justice. But she is certainly devoted to her own ease and is at least technically dishonest both about her attachment to drink and in her frequent allusions to her imaginary conversations with her mythical friend, Mrs. Harris, which have the remarkable feature of "invariably winding up with a compliment to the excellence of her [Mrs. Gamp's] nature" (25). Indeed, a genius for making things up is as necessary a skill for a hypocrite as for a novelist and connects therefore not just Pecksniff with Gamp but all his great pretenders with Dickens himself.[5] Fiction may be defined as harmless pretense—that is, not really intended to deceive—and while Pecksniff certainly does aim to deceive, surely part of our pleasure in him is that so much of his deception is in fact transparent. We love to see him make himself up, so to speak, and cut loose.

If their language betrays sympathy with rebellion, the plots and explicit elaboration of theme in *Martin Chuzzlewit* and *Barnaby Rudge,* as I have said, come down unambivalently on the side of domestic and social order, and in both novels the drama centers on sons (or grandsons in the case of the two Martin Chuzzlewits). Dickens employs his characteristic technique of doubling, moreover, so that, as in *Nickleby,* there are in each novel more than one pair of fathers and sons (or father-and-son-like pairs)—no less than five such, indeed, in *Barnaby.* These pairs most often find themselves in serious—even deadly—conflict of a fairly classic kind, such as between Anthony Chuzzlewit and his son Jonas, who attempts to kill his father out of impatience to inherit his estate or, in *Barnaby,* Sir John Chester and his son Edward, whom Sir John disowns when Edward refuses to give up his pursuit of the niece of his father's oldest enemy, or Sir John and his illegitimate son Hugh, who is a prominent rioter and on whose behalf Sir John refuses to intercede when he is sentenced to be hanged. But while father-son conflicts never entirely lose their relish for Dickens, they reach their clear zenith here. It is as though something about the son's rebellion against paternal authority gets sufficiently worked out after these two novels for Dickens to turn to a rather deeper probing of the family in which, as we shall presently see, he now becomes interested in a version of the domestic in which women and the feminine come forward to play a far more substantial and troubling role.

Excepting *David Copperfield* and *Great Expectations,* in the novels after the mid-forties the relations between fathers (or guardians or uncles) and daughters (or wards or nieces) largely eclipse those of fathers and sons. Thus Florence Dombey survives her brother Paul in *Dombey and Son* (1848), and the remainder of the novel is about her father's coming to acknowledge her; Esther Summerson is the clear protagonist of *Bleak House* (1853), and her plot's final movement turns on the question of whether she will marry her guardian; Louisa Gradgrind's relationship with her father overshadows that of her brother Tom in *Hard Times* (1854); the motherless Amy Dorrit devotes herself to her father in the novel named after her, *Little Dorrit* (1857); Lucie Manette's relationship with her father is central to *A Tale of Two Cities* (1859); and Lizzie Hexam, Bella Wilfer, Pleasant Riderhood, and Jenny Wren all have complicated and intricately observed relationships with their fathers in *Our Mutual Friend* (1865).[6] To be sure, this had been the case in *The Old Curiosity Shop* as well, but Nell, like Oliver, is something of a cipher, and of course she doesn't make it past childhood. The train of Dickensian daughters that follow her, by contrast, includes several of Dickens's most complex and evolving characters. It is in these next novels, too, that Dickens begins to present other women who are not just complex but also powerful and downright dangerous—Edith Granger *(Dombey),* Rosa Dartle *(Copperfield),* Lady Dedlock and Mademoiselle Hortense

(*Bleak House*), Miss Wade (*Little Dorrit*), and Miss Havisham (*Great Expectations*).

Michael Slater is, I believe, the first critic to call attention to this deepened attention to women (243). Why it should occur at this point is not at all obvious, however, for it accompanies no obvious turn of events in Dickens's life.[7] On the contrary, Alexander Welsh sees in the relatively uneventful period between early 1842, when Dickens traveled to the United States, and late 1846, when he began *Dombey and Son*, a creative "moratorium," marked by restless travel (to Italy, Switzerland, and France, as well as America) and introspection (it is in this interval that Dickens writes the fragment of an autobiography he shared only with Forster and, later, Catherine). Welsh borrows the term *moratorium* from the psychoanalyst Erik H. Erikson, who uses it to describe a period of marking time or prolonged adolescence often found in people destined for historical achievement (10). Of course, in the case of a writer as energetic as Dickens, the term *moratorium* is relative, for during this interval he publishes not only *Martin Chuzzlewit* and *American Notes* but also *Pictures from Italy* and the first four Christmas Books (the *Carol, The Chimes, The Cricket on the Hearth,* and *The Battle of Life*), and he founds a newspaper (The *Daily News*). Nevertheless, the frenetic pace established by the writing of the first five novels clearly has much abated.

The turn towards the feminine—by which I shall mean most broadly Dickens's increasing interest in women, his interest in locating feminine qualities in males, especially admirable ones, and his increasing skepticism about characteristics coming to be identified in his culture as masculine—coincides with the introspection that accompanies the "moratorium." I believe it is connected, too, with an accompanying "growing up" that is perhaps more apparent in the fiction than in the life. Certainly it is during this period that most critics see Dickens as coming into his artistic maturity and beginning to produce works of conspicuous coherence. *Dombey and Son* (1846–48) is the first novel for which complete number plans survive,[8] and it is moreover a text that is everywhere thematically anxious about wholeness and falling apart—as though Dickens's artistic worries about coherence had infected his characters.[9] We have seen that anxiety already in Fagin's concern about his gang's "going to pieces in company" (*Oliver,* 43). In *Dombey* it is not just a worry about the community going to pieces, however, but more fundamentally about individual identities and even bodies (Dombey's name is itself an anagram of "embody"). The elderly Mrs. Skewton is a sort of living mummy who is so much made up of makeup, false hair, and false

teeth that she disintegrates into ashes every night (27); after she is felled
by a stroke, her attendants take "her to pieces in very shame, and put
the little of her that was real on a bed" (37). Other characters' bodies are
literally fragmented, like Captain Cuttle, who has lost an arm, and, cli-
mactically, the villain, Carker, who is run over by a train, "beaten down,
caught up, and whirled away upon a jagged mill, that spun him round
and round, and struck him limb from limb, and licked his stream of life
up with its fiery heat, and cast his mutilated fragments in the air" (55).
Carker's death reminds us that even in the most domestic of Dickensian
settings grotesque and appalling violence is never far away.

Growing up is even more explicitly a theme and no less problematic
in *Dombey* than in the two preceding novels, and its plot makes this
strikingly plain at the same time that it marks the turn to the feminine.
For the novel begins, as its title suggests, as yet another tale of fathers
and sons. Paul Dombey is a prosperous and proud merchant whose wife
dies in giving birth to his second child and first son, also named Paul.
Dombey senior invests all his hopes and expectations in little Paul as
future heir to the firm. As Dickens had written to Forster outlining his
plan: "I design to show Mr. D. with that one idea of the Son taking
firmer and firmer possession of him, and swelling and bloating his pride
to a prodigious extent" (Forster, 6.2, letter of 25–26 July 1846). Little
Paul does not actively resist his father's plans for him—indeed he
accepts and even embraces his special status—but he is a strange child,
with an almost eerie aura:

> He was childish and sportive enough at times, and not of a sullen dispo-
> sition; but he had a strange, old-fashioned, thoughtful way, at other
> times, of sitting brooding in his miniature arm-chair, when he looked
> (and talked) like one of those terrible little Beings in the Fairy tales, who,
> at a hundred and fifty or two hundred years of age, fantastically repre-
> sent the children for whom they have been substituted. (8)

His being "old-fashioned" thus suggests not only that there is something antique in his manner but also that he has literally been fashioned
old. While perfectly dutiful towards Dombey senior, the affections of
this odd, motherless child nevertheless incline powerfully towards his
older sister, Florence, who, being a girl, is regarded by her father as of no
account whatsoever. Just a quarter of the way through the novel's serial-
ization, little Paul—not exactly unexpectedly—dies. Thus, as Miss Tox
strikingly puts it, "Dombey and Son" turns out to be "a Daughter after
all" (16).

Unaccountably, Dickens canceled Miss Tox's remark in all editions after 1858, even though Miss Tox alludes to it at the novel's end (59) and Dickens had already thought it up when he wrote the letter to Forster just quoted, for he features it there as the climax of the number; he also thought to include it in the number plans (Stone, 67). Kathleen Tillotson plausibly suggests that the cancellation may have been due to a desire not to mar the pathos of the chapter's end, which concludes with little Paul's death scene and the narrator's final gloss on the "old-fashioned": "The fashion that came in with our first garments. . . . The old, old fashion—Death!" and "that older fashion yet, of Immortality!"[10] Yet precisely that change of emotional gears was obviously important to Dickens; indeed, he emphasized it with double spacing and by printing a line between the narrator's invocation of death and Miss Tox's remark. Its eventual omission thus remains curious.

Miss Tox's thought is strikingly put, moreover. She speaks not as though little Paul had died, but as though either the son or the firm had undergone a sex change. Indeed, in translating "Dombey and Son" into a "Daughter," she also (by taking the ambiguous phrase to identify not the business, but its two principals, as the narrator too often does) fuses Dombey and his son into a single, female entity. Or we might say she offers not just a translation, but a formula: one Dombey and Son *equals* one Daughter. We could hardly ask for a clearer signal of the turn to the feminine than this.[11]

Pride goeth before a fall; the remaining three-fourths of *Dombey* is of course the story of how the hitherto negligible Florence comes to be actively and jealously hated by her father for the love little Paul had borne her, even as her love for him strengthens, and how events bring Dombey and his firm to ruin, when in an abyss of despair he finally does the right thing and asks Florence for forgiveness. Dombey's troubles with women are complicated by his decision to remarry. He chooses a woman as proud as himself, the beautiful and aloof Edith Granger (Mrs. Skewton's daughter), a widow who has also lost a small son. Her motives in marrying are mixed. In accepting Dombey she at once accedes to her mother's intense pressures to sell herself in marriage and ends them; she and her mother become financially secure; and she acquires what she self-destructively believes to be a fitting partner (for she hates herself for having sold herself)—a man as hard-hearted as herself and one whose hardness of heart is likewise an unnatural and defensive pose, albeit one that has become second nature. But in the fact that both partners share a common loss, there is an implicit if small hope for the marriage's success. It is Florence who upsets the marriage—ironically, for, recognizing her father's aversion for her, she wants nothing but his happiness and hopes the marriage will both please him and allow her to learn from Edith how to please him. Edith indeed softens to her, but this only further hardens Mr. Dombey towards Florence—for Edith has not softened to her husband—and he is tormented by the young woman his daughter has become and towards whom everybody important to him inclines, while he remains isolated and "unapproachable" (53).[12]

The crisis in both his marriage and his relationship with Florence is reached when Dombey commands Edith to suppress her shows of affection for Florence. This he effects through James Carker, manager of the firm, and Edith finds intolerable the humiliation of such an indirect communication via a subordinate, as well as the nature of the command. She asks for a separation, and when Dombey refuses she flees with the disloyal Carker to the Continent, though in spite of all appearances and Carker's own expectations, she proudly refuses to become his lover and quickly abandons him once they arrive in France. When Florence hurries to comfort her father (and before anyone knows that Edith has not in fact eloped), he strikes out at Florence: "he lifted up his cruel arm, and struck her, crosswise, with that heaviness, that she tottered on the marble floor; and as he dealt the blow, he told her what Edith was, and bade her follow her, since they had always been in league" (47). Florence flees, not to return until a year later and more, after her father's firm has fallen, he is ruined, and she has married Walter Gay, her childhood protector and sweetheart, and given birth to a son.

Florence's sudden return is prompted, she says, by the experience of becoming a parent herself and the recognition that comes with it of what she had done to her father in leaving him—in spite of his abuse. It is well timed, for it occurs when Dombey has hit bottom—he has just begun to imagine taking his own life and is ready at last to recognize that it is not Florence who needs forgiveness: "As she clung closer to him, in another burst of tears, he kissed her on her lips, and, lifting up his eyes, said, 'Oh my God, forgive me, for I need it very much!' " (59). Here we are once more not far from *Lear,* nor *The Old Curiosity Shop*—except that unlike Nell's grandfather, Dombey does recognize his sin, and unlike both *Lear* and the *Shop,* this work has a happy ending.[13] After a terrible illness and delirium, Dombey survives to play, not only with his grandson, little Paul, but his granddaughter:

> no one, except Florence, knows the measure of the white-haired gentleman's affection for the girl. That story never goes about. The child her-

self almost wonders at a certain secrecy he keeps in it. He hoards her in his heart. . . . He is fondest of her and most loving to her, when there is no creature by. The child says then, sometimes:

"Dear grandpapa, why do you cry when you kiss me?"

He only answers "Little Florence! Little Florence!" and smooths away the curls that shade her earnest eyes. (60)

That happy ending is for modern readers likely, however, to be tempered by the hoarding and secrecy so reminiscent of Nell's grandfather as well as the replications in the children's names, which, if nothing more sinister, at least hint that the past is never really past.

We are likewise liable to squirm at both Florence's returning to beg her father's forgiveness after being beaten by him and her attempt to extract from Edith a request for his forgiveness when the two women are brought together for one final meeting before Edith departs for exile in the south of Italy with her cousin Feenix. It is an awkward scene, because, as an ostensibly fallen woman, Edith is no fit company for a respectable married woman like Florence, and the encounter has to be delicately managed by Cousin Feenix with the permission of Walter. Florence is perfectly proper—"I have not shrunk back from you, mama, because I fear you, or because I dread to be disgraced by you. I only wish to do my duty to papa. I am very dear to him, and he is very dear to me"—and her propriety leads Edith bitterly to declare her innocence at least of adultery. Florence elicits from Edith what is at best a partial appeal to Dombey for forgiveness only after much almost legalistic wrangling.[14] When Dombey comes to recognize his own fault in what Edith calls "the dark part of our married life," then, she says, "I will be repentant too. . . . I will try, then, to forgive him his share of blame. Let him try to forgive me mine!" (61).

But the disappointment we may feel on the one hand in Florence's unquestioning obedience to her father and in everybody's unquestioning acceptance of Edith's exile (although one can imagine far worse fates than spending the rest of one's days in southern Italy with Edith and Cousin Feenix) are on the other hand tempered by the novel's insistent questioning of the masculine and feminine more generally. For while patriarchy is never seriously questioned, gender certainly is—and particularly what we might call the division of behavior associated with gender. Captain Cuttle may be a crusty old salt, but the care he lavishes upon Florence in her flight from her father is exquisitely tender. He is so moved by her plight "that he fairly overflowed with compassion and gentleness," and he kisses her hand "with the chivalry of any old knight-errant," but then walks "on tip-toe out of the room" (48)—hardly a knightly move. He proves to be a cook of "extraordinary skill" (49). Walter, who is no less chivalric than the captain, is also no less delicate. He is described as Dombey's complete opposite: "The boy, with his open face, and flowing hair, and sparkling eyes, panting with pleasure and excitement, was wonderfully opposed to Mr. Dombey" (6). Finding Florence under the captain's protection, he insists that she have a proper chaperon, and when Florence upbraids him with the constrained manner he bears towards her, he remains so sensitive to her superior social situation that it is left to her to make the proposal.

The two marriages outside of Florence and Walter's that are held up as exemplary, the Toodleses' and the Tootses', provide similar examples. In both cases there is a striking handing over of authority from husband to wife. Mr. Toodles defers to his wife's business sense in contracting with Dombey for her services as a wet nurse, and Toots's marriage to Susan "the Nipper" similarly inverts the commercial masculine pride of Dombeyism in several ways. Toots always defers to Susan's judgment, and his greatest delight in his marriage is the succession of girls that Susan bears him: "The oftener we can repeat that most extraordinary woman," he exclaims, ". . . the better!" (62).

There is no formula whereby we simply can predict the novel's attitude towards the wide variety of characterological and biological mixes of gendered attributes that the novel offers—its manly men, womanly women, unmanly men, unwomanly women, manly women, womanly men, and so on. *Dombey* actually refers to "manliness" only on three occasions, each of them ironic (23, 29, 38). What the novel clearly dislikes is not manliness as such, however, but less gendered characteristics like toughness—of the kind manifested by Dombey or his apoplectic friend Major Bagstock, for example: "Joey B. . . . [is] hard-hearted, Sir, is Joe—he's tough, Sir, tough" (7). The emotional firmness punningly associated with the Dombey "firm" looks masculine enough in Mr. Dombey, but it is found in women as well, like his sister Mrs. Chick, who exhorts his dying first wife in the first chapter to "make an effort."[15] Unlike her brother, she never comes to think differently and in the end attributes the failure of the firm to *his* failure to make an effort (58). Insofar as firmness is characteristic of Edith, moreover (and it is characteristic of her vis-à-vis virtually everyone except Florence and Cousin Feenix), it also damns her.

What the novel really likes, conversely, is "heart," and it has again no formula explaining to which sexes those qualities do or ought to belong, for "Heart" is, like toughness, relatively ungendered and is as much associated with men as women—for example, as much with the magnificent if half-imbecile Toots or Captain Cuttle and the circle at the ironically named Wooden Midshipman as with Florence (whom the Captain dubs "Heart's Delight" [23]).[16] Indeed, it is the Wooden Midshipman—Walter's uncle's (Solomon Gills's) nautical instrument shop, named after the carved and painted figure of a midshipman peering through a sextant that stands above its signboard (4)—that is the novel's primary example of a well-functioning household, notwithstanding the irony of its being a place of business nor its all-male composition (at least until Florence takes refuge there). The irony of the shop's name of course is that it is Mr. Dombey and his circle who are wooden—he is actually described as "laying himself on a sofa like a man of wood, without a hinge or joint in him" (26), and Major Bagstock is said to be "wooden-featured" (7). Uncle Sol, Captain Cuttle, and young Walter Gay are on the contrary all openness and animation, and all of them sooner or later dissolve in tears (9, 32).[17] Even the Wooden Midshipman itself is not above such dissolution, for the chapter in which Walter is (falsely) reported to have drowned in a shipwreck is titled "The Wooden Midshipman Goes to Pieces" (32), connecting "heart" also with the theme of wholeness.

This evident intention to uncouple "toughness" and "heart" from their identification with men and women respectively helps save the novel from falling into insipid stereotype; it does not, however, actually eclipse considerations of gender, and we can still recognize behind its intention what I am calling loosely a positive turn to the feminine—not, that is, a turn to an essential or "real" feminine, but a turn to what Dickens's culture (and to some extent ours) identifies as such. Most broadly, the novel idealizes the domestic over the "world" (meaning, as in *Nickleby,* the worlds of business and society) and idealizes the feminine over the masculine; it urges everybody to be more open, fluid, and honest and less rigid, proud, and contained. In a sharp irony, this is exactly what Edith's mother has urged: " 'What I want,' drawled Mrs. Skewton, pinching her shrivelled throat, 'is heart. . . . What I want is frankness, confidence, less conventionality, and freer play of soul. We are so dreadfully artificial' " (21). The problem with Mrs. Skewton's pronouncement is not that it is untrue; it is simply that she doesn't herself mean or believe it.

Along with the turn to the feminine arrives a concomitant idealization of and working out of a coherent position on childhood that marks an advance beyond Dickens's earlier ambivalences without altogether resolving his conflicts about growing up.[18] If Dickens's earlier children and young people had been ciphers (Oliver, Nell) or rather conventional stage figures (Nicholas, Kate) or incapable of growing up (Smike, Barnaby) or just very, very resistant to growing up (Martin), there is a breakthrough of sorts on this score in *Dombey*. A comparison of Paul and Florence with Nicholas and Kate is instructive. Although, as we saw in the last chapter, Nicholas and Kate each on occasion betray both feminine and masculine aspects (Nicholas weeps, Kate decks Sir Mulberry), each is, conventionally and superficially at least, respectively manly and womanly in the main (Nicholas does most of the fighting, Kate does most of the weeping), and they obviously double one another, functioning as a conventionally gendered pair running along parallel tracks. Considered in terms of Dickens's evolving thinking about gender and growing up, we can see that they signal a roughly stable parity after the near hysteria about gender in *Oliver Twist*. But neither can be said to grow up, exactly, for neither is at all different at the end of the novel than at the beginning.

The situation of Paul and Florence is of course very different, most obviously so in that only one of them survives, the sister[19]—as is marked again in Miss Tox's marvelous formula about Dombey and Son's turning out to be a Daughter after all. And a further difference is apparent in the clear implication that Paul's failure to thrive is connected with his father's stifling of his childhood, thanks to Dombey senior's inability to see in him anything but his "son and heir" (5).[20] When Dombey remarks to Mrs. Pipchin, to whom Paul has been sent to board, "My son is getting on. . . . Really, he is getting on," the narrator notes that "There was something melancholy in the triumphant air with which Mr. Dombey said this. It showed how long Paul's childish life had been to him, and how his hopes were set upon a later stage of his existence" (11). Growing into manhood is not possible for little Paul because he has never been allowed a childhood, nor, to the extent that his father represents the values of "the world," is it desirable. If there is a healthy path to adulthood, it lies with traits identified as feminine, and once this is recognized, a much fuller account of what it means to be grown up becomes possible.

There is in addition a connection between the turn to the feminine and an attention to interior life that is quite new in Dickens, who has often and quite inaccurately been characterized as limited to portraying the externals of character and one-dimensional characters at that.[21]

Anyone who doubts that Dickens can portray a complicated interior life should reread the first dozen or so paragraphs of *Dombey* chapter 43, "The Watches of the Night," which painstakingly and painfully recounts Florence's silent witnessing of the falling apart of her father's marriage and the tortured division of her loyalties between him and Edith. In *Dombey,* we may say, Dickens has found a psychology in two senses, therefore—both as a coalescing theory of what it takes and means to grow up and as a technique for narrating the workings of mind. And the discovery of that psychology also marks his coming to maturity as a novelist.

David Copperfield occupies a unique place in Dickens's work in the extra-ordinary closeness of at least some of the events recounted to those in Dickens's own life. As we saw in chapter 2, whole sections in the early parts have been lifted with only minor revision from the autobiographical fragment. It was Dickens's favorite novel and has always been a great favorite with Dickensians, but it has proved a difficult novel for most recent critics to deal with.[22] Just because David is so evidently *like* Dickens both in the details of his childhood and in his adult careers as shorthand writer and successful novelist, and yet is in so many ways idealized and personally *unlike* Dickens, he has proved a more difficult, even uncomfortable, character to talk about than other first-person narrators like Esther Summerson or Pip. The turn to psychology and to the problem of growing up remains apparent, for *Copperfield* is a classic bildungsroman—perhaps *the* classic example of such in British fiction. And the turn to the feminine is apparent too, though less clearly so for the obvious reason that its protagonist is a boy.

But David's sex is in question from the very beginning—from before the beginning, in fact, for his elderly aunt, Betsey Trotwood, who arrives to assist in his birth, takes it as self-evident that he will in fact be a girl, whom she has efficiently already named Betsey Trotwood Copperfield. Aunt Betsey's presentiment is connected with her own history, for she was unhappily married to a man who is supposed to have beaten her and from whom she separated long ago, after buying him off—a highly unusual occurrence under mid-nineteenth-century English law, because whatever property a woman brought to a marriage would normally have become the husband's. In order for Miss Betsey to have any money with which to buy her husband off, she must have had going into the marriage a settlement: property held unalterably in her name and therefore protected from the provisions of the Common Law. Divorce would have been enormously expensive and not granted under like circumstances except upon proof of "intolerable" cruelty.[23] Aunt Betsey has reassumed her maiden name and gone off to live as a single woman (but in company with another of Dickens's holy fools, the remarkably named Mr. Dick). Her project is to protect her presumed niece "from reposing any foolish confidences where they are not deserved" and thus from her own fate and "her own old wrongs." But when Copperfield and Daughter turns out to be a Son after all, she vanishes, "like a discontented fairy" (1), only to reenter the novel when young David flees from London and the miserable life of drudgery at the warehouse (identical in all essentials with Warren's Blacking) of his stepfather, Mr. Murdstone, the wine merchant—from which point on she assumes the role of fairy godmother.

Even before his flight to Aunt Betsey, gender becomes an issue again when Mr. Murdstone sends David off to boarding school and he comes under the notice of James Steerforth, the school's most popular boy, who alternately exploits and protects him. David learns that the headmaster's daughter is supposed to be "in love with Steerforth; and I am sure," he writes, "as I sat in the dark, thinking of his nice voice, and his fine face, and his easy manner, and his curling hair, I thought it very likely." The feelings are mutual, as the dialogue that closes David's first day in Steerforth's company reveals:

> "Good night, young Copperfield," said Steerforth. "I'll take care of you."
> "You're very kind," I gratefully returned. "I am very much obliged to you."
> "You haven't got a sister, have you?" said Steerforth, yawning.
> "No," I answered.
> "That's a pity," said Steerforth. "If you had had one, I should think she would have been a pretty, timid, little, bright-eyed sort of girl. I should have liked to know her. Good night, young Copperfield."
> "Good night, sir," I replied.

The adult David here immediately interjects an ominous note of things to come:

> I thought of him very much after I went to bed, and raised myself, I recollect, to look at him where he lay in the moonlight, with his handsome face turned up, and his head reclining easily on his arm. He was a person of great power in my eyes; that was, of course, the reason of my

mind running on him. No veiled future dimly glanced upon him in the moonbeams. There was no shadowy picture of his footsteps, in the garden that I dreamed of walking in all night. (6)

That image of Steerforth lying "with his handsome face turned up, and his head reclining easily on his arm" returns of course in the novel's next-to-last number, after Steerforth has seduced and abandoned David's childhood playmate Little Emily and then is drowned in a shipwreck just off the Yarmouth shore before David's eyes and his body is washed up on the beach, where, David writes, "I saw him lying with his head upon his arm, as I had often seen him lie at school" (55). But long before this David and Steerforth meet again as young men in London, and Steerforth, prompted by David's innocence, gives him a nickname: "my dear Daisy—will you mind my calling you Daisy? . . . You romantic Daisy!" (20).

In *Oliver Twist* we saw Dickens splitting himself into the innocent and passive Oliver on the one hand and the knowing and active Artful Dodger on the other. In *Copperfield* there is a comparable splitting that sees a more pronounced femininization of the idealized self, while the petty street crimes of the Artful Dodger grow up, so to speak, and become Steerforth's adult crime of seduction—or, to take the example of another of David's doubles, Uriah Heep's lusting after David's ultimate love, Agnes Wickfield.

David's own love relationships are comparatively tame, if not quite asexual. He is thoroughly infatuated with the spoiled Dora Spenlow (modeled, as we have seen, on Maria Beadnell), but even when married (for Dickens allows himself in fiction the victory that life denied him) they make but a childish pair. When David does his best to be firm in the matter of housekeeping, to which Dora is singularly ill-suited (the young couple is mercilessly taken advantage of, even robbed, by their servants), she begs him to think of her as but a "child-wife" (44), to which request he wisely acquiesces, if not without lingering difficulty. For he cannot resist some efforts to "form" Dora's mind, and only with repeated failure does it occur to him that "perhaps Dora's mind was already formed" (48). It may be because Dora is innately incapable of growing up, or because "Doady"—thus has David been nicknamed by Dora, ostensibly as a "corruption of David" (41), though rhyming with "Toady" it sounds like something rather nasty—is slow in giving up his attempts to form her, or both, but in any case Dora wastes away and finally dies, clearing the decks for a marriage between David and Agnes.

Everyone except David sees this coming, including Dora, who, we are
led to infer, tells Agnes she hopes that she will fill the void left by her
death (53). David has known Agnes since childhood and always and
insistently thinks of her as a sister (18, 24, 25, 35, 39, 42, 60, 62). She
may be "good," "beautiful," "earnest," and "disinterested," as Betsey
says of her (60), but while she is grown up and capable in every department in which Dora was not, she has very little of flesh and blood about
her. Following Aunt Betsey's usage (for Betsey is never *entirely* reconciled to the fact that David has turned out to be a boy), she always
addresses David as "Trotwood"; Betsey, to her credit, generally reduces
this to "Trot."

David comes to see in his first love "The first mistaken impulse of an
undisciplined heart." That phrase is uttered by Annie Strong as she
recounts the story of how in marrying the much older Dr. Strong she
has been saved from a marriage to Jack Maldon, a childhood sweetheart
who comes to no good and with whom she now realizes she has had
nothing in common. She further opines that "There can be no disparity
in marriage, like unsuitability of mind and purpose" (45). Her words
immediately strike David powerfully, though he is slow in appreciating
their bearing on his own circumstances:

> Those words of Mrs. Strong's were constantly recurring to me, at this
> time; were almost always present to my mind. I awoke with them, often,
> in the night; I remember to have even read them, in dreams, inscribed
> upon the walls of houses. For I knew, now, that my own heart was undis-
> ciplined when it first loved Dora; and that if it had been disciplined, it
> never could have felt, when we were married, what it had felt in its secret
> experience.
> "There can be no disparity in marriage, like unsuitability of mind and
> purpose." Those words I remembered too. I had endeavoured to adapt
> Dora to myself, and found it impracticable. It remained for me to adapt
> myself to Dora; to share with her what I could, and be happy; to bear on
> my own shoulders what I must, and be still happy. This was the disci-
> pline to which I tried to bring my heart, when I began to think. It made
> my second year much happier than my first; and, what was better still,
> made Dora's life all sunshine. (48)

It is tempting to see in David's almost priggish attitude towards Dora
warnings of ill things to come in Dickens's own marriage and a resur-
gence of Dombeyism. Critics have by and large not taken David's side
and have found Dora a lot more fun than Agnes. But it is important to
recognize an attempt here on David's part to find some grown-up mid-

dle ground between the extremes of "heart" and "toughness." If that
project does not fare terribly well in *Copperfield*, it is far more successfully
realized in Dickens's next novel, the one that in the twentieth century
has come to be recognized as his most influential and highly regarded,
even as its very modernity marked for his contemporaries a sometimes
baffling turn.[24]

The goods of the domestic sphere in *Dombey* and *Copperfield* are ones that
have been familiar to us since *Pickwick:* companionship, mutuality, and
comfort. To these we now may also add the good of cleanliness, which
the Victorians were fond of noting is next to godliness,[25] and such
closely related ideas as neatness, orderliness, coziness, snugness—all of
which were fundamental to Dickens's notion of a happy home. Good
housekeeping is for him an external discipline parallel to the internal
discipline of the heart. The Wooden Midshipman's charm is partly that
it is so nautical in its ambiance that it is itself very like a ship in its
arrangements: "the shop itself, partaking of the general infection,
seemed almost to become a snug, sea-going, ship-shape concern, wanting only good sea-room, in the event of an unexpected launch, to work
its way securely to any desert island in the world" (4). The cleanliness of
the shop is useful and protective. The disorder of David and Dora's
home is uncomfortable, but not dangerous. In *Bleak House,* dirt and disorder are positively deadly, and they threaten not merely homes, but the
very country—indeed, the very world.

Bleak House is by no means the first of Dickens's works to worry
about dirt and disorder. *Oliver Twist* shows off some very nasty neighbor-
hoods, and *The Old Curiosity Shop,* we have said, essentially moves Nell
from a messy bedroom to a tidy one. The swamp called "Eden" in *Chuzzlewit* is pestilential, and even Mr. Pickwick has an encounter with dirt
when he is imprisoned. But the dirt of *Bleak House* is pervasive and,
indeed, fundamental. London is everywhere foully polluted (at mid-
century Londoners still poured raw sewage into the Thames and got
their drinking water from it), and its terrible sanitation threatens not
just the poor and not just city dwellers: its heroine almost dies in the
country of smallpox transmitted from a "pestiferous and obscene" (11)
London burial ground in the courtyard formed by the backs of dwellings
and so crammed with bodies that the very bones threaten to spill into
the kitchen windows of the adjacent houses (16). Cleaning things up is a
central, and for the first time in Dickens's career, perhaps never-ending,
even hopeless task.

The novel begins with a frequently analyzed tour de force: the omniscient third-person narrator's description of a London fog that seems to reach out and envelop all England and that explicitly embodies the moral fog that hangs over the court of Chancery, the highest court in the land, the court established once upon a time to provide equity when the common courts of law fail to provide it, but whose self-interested inefficiency has over centuries grown into a monstrous evil. But before there is the fog, there is mud:

> London. Michaelmas term lately over, and the Lord Chancellor sitting in Lincoln's Inn Hall. Implacable November weather. As much mud in the streets as if the waters had but newly retired from the face of the earth, and it would not be wonderful to meet a Megalosaurus, forty feet long or so, waddling like an elephantine lizard up Holborn Hill. Smoke lowering down from chimney-pots, making a soft black drizzle, with flakes of soot in it as big as full-grown snowflakes— gone into mourning, one might imagine, for the death of the sun. Dogs, undistinguishable in mire. Horses, scarcely better; splashed to their very blinkers. Foot passengers, jostling one another's umbrellas in a general infection of ill temper, and losing their foot-hold at street-corners, where tens of thousands of other foot passengers have been slipping and sliding since the day broke (if this day ever broke), adding new deposits to the crust upon crust of mud, sticking at those points tenaciously to the pavement, and accumulating at compound interest. (1)

Or, more precisely, there is chaos. The anthropologist Mary Douglas has defined dirt as "essentially disorder," or matter out of its proper place, thus associating dirt with a much wider field than impurity and danger.[26] But in the world of *Bleak House* chapter 1, it is not too much to say that everything is out of order, or that there is order in nothing. Conversely, when chaos rules, nothing can very well be said to be out of order either. For chaos is primordial.

The mud in which everything is "undistinguishable" thus suggests several things: the universe in its original state before even the elements have been sorted out (smoke falls, snow is black, soot is drizzle), before even the beginning of time ("if this day ever broke"), the world immediately after the biblical flood ("as if the waters had but newly retired from the face of the earth"), and possibly the primitive goo out of which life may have evolved ("it would not be wonderful to meet a Megalosaurus"), as well as inorganic geological processes ("adding new deposits to the crust upon crust of mud").[27] The reference to "the death of the sun" suggests yet another possibility—that far from being embroiled in a primordial soup, it is the end of the world (and time) that we are witnessing.

Cleanliness in such a context isn't just *next* to godliness; it *is* godliness, for creation is the fundamental act of organizing matter and giving it its proper place. To Dickens's contemporaries the mud of *Bleak House*'s opening would of course also have suggested something much closer to home—the mess left behind by all those horses and dogs (the cleaning away of which gives Jo the crossing sweeper his occupation and makes him useful, especially to Victorian women in their long dresses).

Compounding its disorder, *Bleak House* begins with a dizzying array of frames of reference. Its first sentence could be a dateline, and its second likewise locates its time and place with almost journalistic precision. But the opening's incomplete sentences and lack of finite verbs also prepare us for its unsettling cosmic resonances. We know exactly where we are, yet may be excused for being confused on that score too. We seem at once to be in a very specific time and place and in some timeless or mythical realm as well. Is this a mere Lord Chancellor or a Lord of a more powerful kind, perhaps not a benevolent one? Brilliant as the opening is, it pointedly leaves us in the dark. It does not help that we are introduced in this same first chapter to a lawsuit with the unhelpful and ominous name of JARNDYCE AND JARNDYCE, which, we are told, "has, in course of time, become so complicated that no man alive knows what it means":

> Scores of persons have deliriously found themselves made parties in Jarndyce and Jarndyce without knowing how or why; whole families have inherited legendary hatreds with the suit. The little plaintiff or defendant who was promised a new rocking-horse when Jarndyce and Jarndyce should be settled has grown up, possessed himself of a real horse, and trotted away into the other world.

Although marvelously fanciful, that last sentence, encapsulating an entire life, also spells out a grim truth. It is characteristic of Dickens, who, we have noted, worked briefly in a firm of solicitors when scarcely out of his boyhood, that he gets his facts right, even when they seem most exaggerated. People really could be made interested parties to Chancery suits involuntarily (becoming potential heirs if the suit involved an estate)—and by the same token could not get out of them until the suit was resolved. Jarndyce and Jarndyce, like other suits described in the novel, and as Dickens notes in his preface, is modeled on several actual and equally complicated cases, some of which lasted upwards of a hundred years and were likewise exhausted by court costs before coming to an actual settlement. One of these did not end until almost 10 years after Dickens's own death and 25 years after the writing of *Bleak House*.[28] No wonder then that Chancery should assume an awful, even religious, aura.

> How many people out of the suit Jarndyce and Jarndyce has stretched forth its unwholesome hand to spoil and corrupt would be a very wide question. . . . Shirking and sharking in all their many varieties have been sown broadcast by the ill-fated cause; and even those who have contemplated its history from the outermost circle of such evil have been insensibly tempted into a loose way of letting bad things alone to take their own bad course, and a loose belief that if the world go wrong it was in some off-hand manner never meant to go right.

While particular suits can ruin particular people, the more general evil of Chancery (here plainly invoking Dante's circular conception of Hell in the *Inferno*) is a way of thinking about the world that "insensibly" infects virtually everybody (for Chancery's power was so proverbial that the phrase "In Chancery"—the title of chapter 1—denoted an inextricable hold in wrestling). Sharking is bad enough, but it is the shirking that really frightens Dickens, for the most noxious temptation is to believe "that if the world go wrong it was in some off-hand manner never meant to go right"—which is, logically, to believe that it was meant to go wrong or, in other words, as much as to say that wrong *is* right. Thus the cosmic chaos of the mud and fog reflects an equally fundamental moral chaos—a denial of ethical guideposts and an attendant escape from any idea of responsibility.

But it is quite wonderful too how Dickens's third-person narrator manages to entertain and somehow even to make us feel safe in the midst of so despairing a vision. No doubt this is because everything seems to be out of control *except* for that narrative voice, which is masterful and witty, entirely at ease, and therefore infinitely reassuring. (That masterfulness and even a hint of omniscience too will be passed on to Inspector Bucket, the detective who makes a magical appearance a third of the way through, almost as though the omniscient narrator had dropped into the novel as a character.)

Reassuring too, perhaps, is a pattern of repetition and circularity established at the very outset. It is apparent in countless little details, like the very name of the suit, or that image of circles of evil just quoted. It is apparent too in the way the narrative keeps coming back upon itself through the repetition of images or simply returning to the same places. J. Hillis Miller in a classic reading has discussed this circularity,[29] but he is anticipated by G. K. Chesterton, who further connects circularity with growing up and the domestic:

> The thing is no longer a string of incidents; it is a cycle of incidents. It returns upon itself; it has recurrent melody and poetic justice; it has artistic constancy and artistic revenge. . . . The story circles round two or three symbolic places. . . . People go from one place to another place; but not from one place to another place on the road to everywhere else [as had been typical of earlier works]. . . . The whole story strays from Bleak House and plunges into the foul fogs of Chancery and the autumn mists of Chesney Wold; but the whole story comes back to Bleak House. The domestic title is appropriate; it is a permanent address. (Chesterton 1911, 150–51)

But repetition can also be ominous, especially when it seems beyond our control. And in this novel we have good reason to question whether repetition is a narrator's voluntary technique or the unwilled echo of something more sinister.

Even in the "permanent address" of the novel's title there is a note of something the very opposite of domestic: it is a *bleak* house. D. A. Miller notes that "bleak" is cognate with both "black" and "bleach" (as it is too, we might note, with "blank" and "blind"), and he closes his important essay on the novel by quoting the remark (made by Mr. Jarndyce [6]) that "Bleak House has an exposed sound."[30] What even the prescient Chesterton apparently did not perceive is that the novel's domesticity is at its very center undermined. Nor perhaps did Dickens himself (and in spite of his own characters' better understanding), for the few comments he makes about the novel in his letters that actually refer to the writing (as opposed to the novel's sales figures, about which he is always attentive and specific) are surprisingly cheerful given its darkness. He writes to his friend Mrs. Richard Watson (whose home provides a model for the great Dedlock estate at Chesney Wold), about "the point I have been patiently working up to" in the 10th or 11th number, that "I hope it will suggest to you a pretty and affecting thing" (22

November 1852), though it is hard to conceive of anything there as "pretty," since it entails the heroine, Esther Summerson's, almost dying of smallpox and making the agonizing discovery of her mother's identity (agonizing because her mother, Lady Dedlock, can never publicly acknowledge her nor indeed even privately beyond a single furtive encounter). Likewise he writes to Mrs. Watson the following year that "I like the conclusion very much and think it *very pretty indeed*" (27 August 1853, Dickens's emphasis), and while it may count on balance as a happy ending (Esther's marriage follows soon after the death of Richard Carstone), "pretty" is again among the very last words that modern readers are likely to pin on it. For the novel ends as it begins, with an incomplete sentence—indeed, with a dash, and the enigmatic phrase "—even supposing—" (67).

Esther appears suddenly as a first-person narrator in chapter 3, and after the gloom of Chancery and London generally, not to mention the rainy dreariness of both Chesney Wold and the Dedlock house in town, to all of which we are introduced in the first two chapters, and the gloom of Esther's own early childhood as she has described it, it is no wonder that our arrival at Bleak House itself a few chapters later should feel positively cheery. But all the little oddities of the house that in one light appear charming and quaint admit a threatening reading as well, especially as revealed in the tour that John Jarndyce gives Esther and his orphan cousins, Ada Clare and Richard Carstone, when he first greets them and takes them under his protection in the chapter called "Quite at Home" (6). It is worth quoting in full:

> It was one of those delightfully irregular houses where you go up and down steps out of one room into another, and where you come upon more rooms when you think you have seen all there are, and where there is a bountiful provision of little halls and passages, and where you find still older cottage-rooms in unexpected places with lattice windows and green growth pressing through them. Mine, which we entered first, was of this kind, with an up-and-down roof that had more corners in it than I ever counted afterwards and a chimney (there was a wood fire on the hearth) paved all around with pure white tiles, in every one of which a bright miniature of the fire was blazing. Out of this room, you went down two steps into a charming little sitting-room looking down upon a flower-garden, which room was henceforth to belong to Ada and me. Out of this you went up three steps into Ada's bedroom, which had a fine broad window commanding a beautiful view (we saw a great expanse of darkness lying underneath the stars), to which there was a hollow

window-seat, in which, with a spring-lock, three dear Adas might have been lost at once. Out of this room you passed into a little gallery, with which the other best rooms (only two) communicated, and so, by a little staircase of shallow steps with a number of corner stairs in it, considering its length, down into the hall. But if instead of going out at Ada's door you came back into my room, and went out at the door by which you had entered it, and turned up a few crooked steps that branched off in an unexpected manner from the stairs, you lost yourself in passages, with mangles in them, and three-cornered tables, and a native Hindu chair, which was also a sofa, a box, and a bedstead, and looked in every form something between a bamboo skeleton and a great bird-cage, and had been brought from India nobody knew by whom or when. From these you came on Richard's room, which was part library, part sitting room, part bedroom, and seemed indeed a comfortable compound of many rooms. Out of that you went straight, with a little interval of passage, to the plain room where Mr. Jarndyce slept, all the year round, with his window open, his bedstead without any furniture standing in the middle of the floor for more air, and his cold bath gaping for him in a smaller room adjoining. Out of that you came into another passage, where there were back-stairs and where you could hear the horses being rubbed down outside the stable and being told to "Hold up" and "Get over," as they slipped about very much on the uneven stones. Or you might, if you came out at another door (every room had at least two doors), go straight down to the hall again by half-a-dozen steps and a low archway, wondering how you got back there or had ever got out of it.

It is not wonderful that Chancery or the slum neighborhood of Tom-all-Alone's, with its horrendous and filthy burial ground, nor even Chesney Wold with its "Ghost's Walk" and attendant legend should be frightening locales, for all of these are haunted by past (as well as present) wrongs. Indeed, since Bleak House has its own unpleasant history—having once been owned by the Tom Jarndyce who let it fall into a ruin (8), gave his name to Tom-all-Alone's, and "blew his brains out one day" (1) in despair over the lack of progress of the suit—it is not from that perspective wonderful that it should be frightening too. But what *is* wonderful here is that, transformed as it has been by Mr. Jarndyce's domestic attentions, and as successful as those changes are clearly understood to have been ("How changed it must be!" Esther enthuses on hearing the house's history [8]), there is still an almost nightmarish undertone, perhaps all the more nightmarish for being invisible to Bleak House's inhabitants themselves. A room that has more corners in it than can be counted afterward is positively surreal. A

window-seat with a "spring-lock" in which three dear people might be
"lost at once" is an amenity we might do without. Green growth is
pleasant in its place, but not "pressing" through one's windows. Mangles—clothes wringers—are useful household appliances, but also suggest mutilation and torture. A chair that is "also a sofa, a box, and a
bedstead" may be not only useful but ingenious, but a bedstead that is
also a box suggests to me a coffin, and its looking "in every form something between a bamboo skeleton and a great bird-cage" likewise
evokes death and imprisonment as well as the frightening image of a
bird as big as a person. That it has "been brought from India nobody
knew by whom or when" explicitly refers to the alien and indirectly
refers back to Jarndyce and Jarndyce's being so ancient "that no man
alive knows what it means"—just as the horses outside that "slipped
about very much" also return us to the novel's very beginning. But it is
perhaps the architecture of Bleak House that is most unsettling. It is
not just in those uncountable corners that the house is "irregular." It
would be a challenge to construct a model of it just as it is a challenge
too merely to walk around in without getting lost or going round in
circles and unaccountably returning to the same place and "wondering
how you got back there or had ever got out of it."

More remains to be said about repetition in *Bleak House,* but we ought
first to focus on Esther Summerson and her narrative, for it is Esther who
ostensibly opposes Chancery's evil. If the evil of Chancery is that it sows
moral chaos and a general tendency to leave bad things alone and shirk
responsibilities—if Chancery is, like the universe (in Mr. Jarndyce's
view), "rather an indifferent parent" (6), then Esther, illegitimate and
orphaned though she may be, epitomizes good parenting—and good
housekeeping. The Lord Chancellor is presumed to be the nation's moral
center. He presides over the House of Lords, is the highest judge in the
land, is in theory the last refuge for people seeking justice (the Chancellor
bears the title "Keeper of the King's Conscience"), has special responsibility for the custody of the insane, and serves as legal guardian to countless
wards (like Richard and Ada, orphaned minors who happen to be parties
to Chancery suits). But, against Chancery's singular failure to take care of
anyone except its own lawyers, it is Esther who provides such a center
and helps illustrate Dickens's belief that institutions are simply incapable
of human functions like parenting. More particularly, she embodies the
maxim that "charity begins at home," which explains also why there are
in the novel so many outstandingly ineffective career philanthropists, like
Mrs. Jellyby, whose "Telescopic Philanthropy" sends emigrants to Borrio-

boola-Gha on the banks of the Niger to cultivate coffee and the natives but who cannot see the misery of England's poor nor manage her own family (4), or Mrs. Pardiggle, who delivers evangelical tracts to the illiterate poor and tortures her own children by forcing them to devote their pocket money to such charities as the "Infant Bonds of Joy," whose members must pledge "never, through life, to use tobacco in any form" (8).

Before Esther encounters either the law or organized philanthropy, however, her world is defined by the harsh religion of her godmother (and aunt in fact), Miss Barbary, who brings her up "in rigid secrecy" after she discovers signs of life in Esther when she had been "laid aside as dead" immediately after her birth (36). Miss Barbary almost succeeds on one memorable birthday in making Esther believe it would have been better had she never been born. "Submission, self-denial, diligent work, are the preparations for a life begun with such a shadow on it" (3), she tells little Esther, evoking the shame of her illegitimate birth.[31] But devastated as Esther is by these injunctions, she does not adopt them uncritically:

> I went up to my room, and crept to bed, and laid my doll's cheek against mine wet with tears, and holding that solitary friend upon my bosom, cried myself to sleep. . . . [H]ow often I repeated to the doll the story of my birthday and confided to her that I would try as hard as ever I could to repair the fault I had been born with (of which I confusedly felt guilty and yet innocent) and would strive as I grew up to be industrious, contented, and kind-hearted and to do some good to some one, and win some love to myself if I could.[32]

Miss Barbary's commands assume the burden of original sin and subsequent personal sin besides (of the kind that is passed from parents to children); they enjoin Esther to be obedient and deny the claims of self entirely. But Esther modulates them significantly. Obedience is not among her stated goals, and selflessness here is aimed at happiness, her own as well as that of others. She even permits herself the final goal of winning some love to herself, and this becomes of course the defining project of her life—she recalls her birthday resolution at crucial moments, as when she first encounters her mother, Lady Dedlock, long before she realizes their relationship (18) and in her smallpox crisis (35)—though she is dutiful enough and conflicted enough to be embarrassed about wanting to be loved when she goes so far as to allow the wish into consciousness. "It seems so curious to me to be obliged to write all this about myself!" she writes apologetically (3), "As if this narrative were the narrative of *my* life! But my little body will soon fall into the background now."

There have been readers enough who have wished Esther's little body *would* fall into the background. But of course it does not:

> I don't know how it is I seem to be always writing about myself. I mean all the time to write about other people, and I try to think about myself as little as possible, and I am sure, when I find myself coming into the story again, I am really vexed and say, "Dear, dear, you tiresome little creature, I wish you wouldn't!" but it is all of no use. I hope any one who may read what I write will understand that if these pages contain a great deal about me, I can only suppose it must be because I have really something to do with them and can't be kept out. (9)

This may seem disingenuous to modern readers, though critical opinion has shifted in the last 40 years or so and seems more forgiving of Esther's coyness—more willing to see in it real division, real discomfort, real disability, and real struggle than an arch and backhanded call for attention.[33] Dickens has chosen for himself a very awkward rhetorical task, not only in impersonating a woman, but in having to write via Esther's almost pathological self-abnegation while demonstrating just how very good she is at winning "some love" for herself—for once beyond her hellish childhood with Miss Barbary she manages to make virtually *everybody* love and admire her. And this of course becomes for some readers another irritation; if we grant Esther on the one hand the crippling effects of her upbringing and having fully earned thereby the right to be thoroughly neurotic, we would still perhaps on the other rather not see her so *entirely* successful in overcoming those obstacles.[34]

Indeed, Esther is almost uniquely successful, for her story is in the end presented as, with one interesting exception, the only conventionally happy one: she gets her man and raises her family. Ada and Richard fall in love and marry and have a child, but Richard cannot escape Chancery's contagion, and it kills him. Lady Dedlock flees in shame when her story becomes known to the Dedlock family lawyer, Mr. Tulkinghorn, and he threatens to reveal it to her husband, Sir Leicester; she dies of exposure before Esther and Mr. Bucket can find her. John Jarndyce would be happy to have married Esther, but loses out to Allan Woodcourt. Caddy Jellyby escapes her own domestic nightmare and marries the dancing master, Prince Turveydrop (himself exploited by a selfish parent), but their child, in a very sad irony for a musical family, turns out to be deaf and dumb. All in all, there are precious few intact and happy families in *Bleak House*.

The interesting exception is the Bagnets. Matthew Bagnet is a former soldier who plays the bassoon, owns a musical instrument shop, is
married to an enormously resourceful wife who has accompanied him
across the globe in his army days, and has three happy children, each
named "from the places of their birth in barracks": Quebec, Woolwich,
and Malta (27). What makes them interesting is the transparent fiction
husband and wife entertain that Matthew is in charge. "Discipline must
be maintained," he proclaims, over and over, but he never delivers an
opinion himself, always resorting instead to the formula: "Old girl, . . .
tell him my opinion" (34). The discipline that must be maintained is
therefore a fiction too, though it is one that neither husband nor wife
acknowledge in front of one another, even as Matthew is happy to
acknowledge it to his friend the ex-trooper George:

> "She is a treasure!" exclaims Mr. George.
> "She's more. But I never own to it before her. Discipline must be
> maintained. It was the old girl that brought out my musical abilities. I
> should have been in the artillery now but for the old girl. Six years I ham-
> mered at the fiddle. Ten at the flute. The old girl said it wouldn't do;
> intention good, but want of flexibility; try the bassoon. The old girl bor-
> rowed a bassoon from the bandmaster of the Rifle Regiment. I practised
> in the trenches. Got on, got another, get a living by it!" (27)

Indeed, one reading of Mr. Bagnet's motto, therefore, is that it is the fiction itself that must be maintained, even while it remains transparent.

This peculiar protocol was no doubt charming to most of Dickens's
contemporaries, whereas it offends most of ours. But it is important to
recognize how far it in fact undermines the stereotype, nay, the actuality,
of male authority, while paying it lip service—especially, again, given the
remarkable rarity of intact or happy families in the novel. Mrs. Bagnet
once found her way home to Europe from "another quarter of the
world—with nothing but a grey cloak and an umbrella" (27), and late in
the novel she again embarks alone on an only slightly less adventurous
journey from London to Chesney Wold and back to reunite her husband's
old friend trooper George and his mother, Mrs. Rouncewell, housekeeper
of the Dedlocks' country estate: "[Y]ou take care of the children, old
man, and give me the umbrella! I'm away to Lincolnshire" (52).

Esther herself of course much more closely conforms to good Victorian codes of feminine conduct—at least superficially. She certainly
behaves deferentially to men (and her elders) generally. Perhaps the
most striking example occurs just before her marriage, when she
believes she is about to wed her guardian, John Jarndyce, but is sud-

denly and literally handed over by him to Allan Woodcourt, the young surgeon whose love she has resigned herself to losing after her face has been badly scarred by smallpox. This pious fraud can be explained, if not justified, by the fact that Esther has in the meantime accepted Mr. Jarndyce's proposal, for Victorians don't go back on promises to marry easily. (Indeed, it was being found guilty of breach of promise that wound Mr. Pickwick up in jail.) Nevertheless, we might imagine other ways of managing such a switch—ones that would allow Esther at least some agency. As it is, she registers no objection and passively and quite delightedly allows herself to be handed from one man to the other.

This may recall Florence Dombey's extreme obedience to Mr. Dombey, but there are of course important differences. Nobody except Miss Barbary has abused Esther, so her dutifulness is towards a man who has been nothing but kind and has rescued her from the shadow of her birth; she really is and always has been in love with Allan; her marriage to John Jarndyce, we are led to believe, would on both sides have been companionable, not romantic—nor sexual; indeed, though Jarndyce's proposal makes her feel thankful, it also makes her cry "very much" (44). So Esther's passivity and dutifulness simply put her in reach of that love she has for so long hoped to gain for herself, and her agency is therefore quite real, if indirect. The pious fraud—an increasingly popular device with Dickens as his career evolves—thus becomes a vehicle that lets duty and pleasure perfectly coincide.

Esther's deference is on important occasions merely apparent, however. It gives way to resistance and even rebellion when need be. She resists Mrs. Pardiggle's call to join her in what Esther terms her "rapacious benevolence":

> At first I tried to excuse myself for the present on the general ground of having occupations to attend to which I must not neglect. But as this was an ineffectual protest, I then said, more particularly, that I was not sure of my qualifications. That I was inexperienced in the art of adapting my mind to minds very differently situated, and addressing them from suitable points of view. That I had not that delicate knowledge of the heart which must be essential to such a work. That I had much to learn, myself, before I could teach others, and that I could not confide in my good intentions alone. For these reasons I thought it best to be as useful as I could, and to render what kind services I could to those immediately about me, and to try to let that circle of duty gradually and naturally expand itself. All this I said with anything but confidence, because Mrs. Pardiggle was much older than I, and had great experience, and was so very military in her manners. (8)

Behind Esther's apparent diffidence there is a powerfully articulated ethic that we shall return to presently (and that, via the image of a "circle of duty," advances the novel's own interest in circularity, another topic to which we have dutifully promised to return).[35] For the moment we may note the persistence of her "protest" even in the face of manners so very "military" and also the rhetoric of Esther's description of this encounter, which is pointedly ironic. For Esther's real reasons for declining Mrs. Pardiggle's invitation have of course nothing to do with any lack of benevolent qualifications of her own; the lack she points to in herself, rather, is precisely Mrs. Pardiggle's deficiency. Esther is being downright sarcastic with Mrs. Pardiggle, who is simply too stupid to get the point.

Esther more directly charges a much more formidable—and in no way stupid—opponent, the parasitical Mr. Skimpole, with irresponsibility when he encourages Richard's entanglement in the hopeless lawsuit, though she again claims to speak "timidly enough, he being so much older and more clever than I." Skimpole takes the point and returns it upon her, ostensibly as a compliment, though it is barbed: "When I see you, my dear Miss Summerson, intent upon the perfect working of the whole little orderly system of which you are the centre, I feel inclined to say to myself—in fact I do say to myself very often—*that's* responsibility!" (37). Readers who have resisted falling in love with Esther may applaud this, and it is perhaps telling that Dickens allows Skimpole, who is a thoroughly bad man in the tradition of Steerforth and his like—aesthetes who are charming and talented but utterly selfish and careless of any harm they might do others—to hit the nail so nearly on the head.

For Skimpole has seen Esther's doctrine of her little "circle of duty" at work and does not at all like what he sees there. "System" is rather a bad word in this novel. Esther herself has found Mrs. Pardiggle rather "too businesslike and systematic" (8), and Mr. Jarndyce refers to Chancery as a "monstrous system," setting another ruined suitor, Mr. Gridley, off on an extended rant about "the system," which is by everyone in the legal establishment offered as the source of all his woes and which conveniently therefore absolves its members from any individual responsibility (15). That Esther may be seen therefore not so much as Chancery's *good* opposite, but rather and more directly as its *double,* an evil twin, is in fact an implication of D. A. Miller's influential reading in *The Novel and the Police.* He argues, along generally Foucauldian lines, that while moral policing is a function made desirable and necessary by Chancery's rather orderly power to do evil on the one hand and the actual moral disorder it sows on the other, and that while policing is represented as in the service of the domestic goods that Chancery so conspicuously endangers and fails to realize, policing in fact gives "rise to the very regimentation it was supposed to curtail" (104). "Mr. Bagnet's famous catchword" that "Discipline must be maintained" therefore "formulates what is no less the objective than the condition of the family in Dickens's representation of it" (105).

Thus there is an ambiguity about Esther and the ideal of the domestic no less than about Chancery, and each is pulled between extremes of orderliness or "system" versus incomprehension, pollution, and chaos. But beyond ambiguity, even, is a persistent feeling of uncanniness that the novel generates, a feeling of weirdness that approaches horror and that is particularly unsettling because it is characterized by an uncertainty that may lead us to fear that we are in the grip of the supernatural. We have seen something of this in Esther's first description of Bleak House, which is *at once* charming and sinister. We see it too in the novel's interest in and deployment of circularity, for as Freud notes in his essay on the uncanny, repetition when it is insistent is uncanny in itself.[36]

Uncanny too, Freud notes, is that particular form of unwilled repetition known as *déjà vu*, which Dickens had described, oddly not once but twice, in *David Copperfield*.[37] But what was an extraordinary and therefore abnormal (if significant) experience for David becomes pervasive and therefore almost normal in the world of *Bleak House*, where we continually have the unsettled experience of returning upon our own tracks without entirely realizing it (as, for example, when the narrative, having left us at the end of chapter 1 with the Chancellor on the brink of speaking as he says with "both the young people . . . and satisfy[ing] myself on the subject of their residing with their cousin," returns literally to the other side of the door via the circuitous route of the world of fashion and the Dedlocks in chapter 2, and then the story of Esther's whole early life in chapter 3, which culminates with Esther's participation in that promised interview between the Chancellor and Richard and Ada). It is an experience significantly shared by many characters *within* the novel, moreover, most often through the half-recognition in Esther's or Lady Dedlock's of a familiar face. Mr. Guppy, having recently met Esther, has such an experience of *déjà vu* when he sees Lady Dedlock's portrait at Chesney Wold (7). Mr. George meets Esther and believes he has met her before (probably unconsciously recognizing not her mother's face but that of his old companion her father) (24). And Jo, already unsettled by the delirium of smallpox, when he meets Esther is terrified by her uncanny likeness to both Lady Dedlock and the passionate Mlle. Hortense (who strikingly resembles both Esther and Lady Dedlock and will go on to murder Mr. Tulkinghorn and cast suspicion on Lady Dedlock): "If she ain't the t'other one, she ain't the forrenner. Is there *three* of 'em then?" (31).[38]

Freud's essay has a much richer resonance with *Bleak House* than can be explored here, but we may note that "uncanny" is the English for Freud's *unheimlich*—a literal rendering of which is "unhomely." That is a nice coincidence, given the novel's unhomely title, and suggests that Dickens isn't just incidentally making use of the uncanny as a powerful aesthetic technique, but that there is a significant thematic consonance between the uncanny and the domestic as well.

One biographical fact is relevant here. At the end of March 1851, Dickens's father died after undergoing—without anesthesia—what Dickens described in a letter to Catherine as "the most terrible operation known in surgery" (25 March). Apparently he had for some time suffered from a stricture of the urethra but did not seek help until it was too late. His urethra had ruptured, urine infiltrated his scrotum, and gangrene set in (Pilgrim letters, 6:333 n 4.). "He bore it with astonishing fortitude," Dickens continues, "and I saw him directly afterwards—his room a slaughterhouse of blood." But John Dickens survived the operation only to fall into delirium and succumb a few days later. Naturally his father's death, which would under less ghastly circumstances have been distressing enough, given his very strong and conflicting feelings about his father, was deeply upsetting. For a week or two Dickens could not sleep, though he kept up a frenetic professional pace and made good use of his sleeplessness by touring London slums in the middle of the night with the policeman who became the model for Inspector Bucket. Out of this experience came several articles, including "On Duty with Inspector Field" and "Lying Awake" for *Household Words* (collected in *Reprinted Pieces*) and, rather later, "Night Walks" for *All the Year Round* (describing his "amateur experience of houselessness" and reprinted in *The Uncommercial Traveller*). I am convinced that out of it too came much *Bleak House* material. For one thing, *Bleak House* effectively condemns the previous generation's moral lapses and irresponsibilities in a manner quite new to Dickens: Esther's father, Captain Hawdon, is of John Dickens's generation—the generation of the Romantics—as are some other alternately oppressive and negligent fathers: Mr. Turveydrop and Harold Skimpole. For another, the novel worries that the sins of the fathers may be visited on their children ("according," Miss Barbary would add, "to what is written" [3]) and at the same time fears the disappearance of moral authority altogether.

Indeed, the most significant legacy of Dickens's reaction to his father's death may have been the novel's distinctive atmosphere—its sense of the inescapable burden of the past (the ultimate circularity), its feeling that the world is in the midst of some cosmic calamity, and its troubled vacillation between on the one hand the despairing beliefs that things can never be understood and were never meant to go right and on the other an almost paranoid belief that everything is connected in a vast cosmic conspiracy that capriciously and blindly grinds its victims down. The third-person omniscient narrator famously asks:

> What connexion can there be between the place in Lincolnshire, the house in town, the Mercury in powder, and the whereabout of Jo the outlaw with the broom, who had that distant ray of light upon him when he swept the churchyard-step? What connexion can there have been between many people in the innumerable histories of this world who from opposite sides of great gulfs have, nevertheless, been very curiously brought together! (16)

The answer of course is that everybody turns out to be connected to everybody else, though hardly in straightforward ways. (Even after Esther's parentage is sorted out, lots of questions remain about Miss Barbary's relations with her sister, Lady Dedlock, and we never find out exactly how she is in turn related to John Jarndyce, nor how he is related to Richard and Ada—we never get beyond the statement made by Jarndyce's lawyer to the Chancellor in chapter 1: "I am not at the moment prepared to inform the court in what exact remove he is a cousin, but he *is* a cousin" [1]). The law-stationer Mr. Snagsby is but one of many characters who are caught up in mysteries that are to them utterly confounding. He "cannot make out what it is that he has had to do with. Something is wrong somewhere, but what something, what may come of it, to whom, when, and from which unthought of and unheard of quarter is the puzzle of his life" (25). His shrewish wife takes the opposite tack. Puzzled by the apparent familiarity between her husband and Jo, the crossing-sweeper, Mrs. Snagsby "sees it all. . . . It is as clear as crystal that Mr. Snagsby is that boy's father" (25), though her surmise is laughably off the mark. The Snagsbys' little domestic comedy plays out in small the same epistemological dilemma faced by more important characters and, indeed, the novel's readers—the dilemma between having to believe that under the spell of Chancery nothing makes sense and that everything makes all too terrible sense.

Even Esther, who always knows how to *behave* well, does not escape the epistemological muddle. "I have a great deal of difficulty in beginning to write my portion of these pages, for I know I am not clever" (3), her narrative begins, and while she is far more clever than she knows, she is genuinely confused about many aspects of her identity and self. When she first comes to London and is ushered into Chancery, she is infected by Chancery's hypnotically circular spell:

> Everything was so strange—the stranger from its being night in the daytime, the candles burning with a white flame, and looking raw and cold—that I read the words in the newspaper without knowing what they meant and found myself reading the same words repeatedly. . . . Then I went on, thinking, thinking, thinking; and the fire went on, burning, burning, burning . . . —for two hours. (3)

At the end of that same eventful day, when she not only encounters Chancery but meets Ada and Richard, and then stays with them at the Jellybys', she tries to fall asleep with the unhappy Caddy Jellyby lying with her head on Esther's lap:

> At first I was painfully awake and vainly tried to lose myself, with my eyes closed, among the scenes of the day. At length, by slow degrees, they became indistinct and mingled. I began to lose the identity of the sleeper resting on me. Now it was Ada, now one of my old Reading friends from whom I could not believe I had so recently parted. Now it was the little mad woman [Miss Flite] worn out with curtsying and smiling, now some one in authority at Bleak House. Lastly, it was no one, and I was no one. (4)

Such moments, when Esther's identity and even sense of external reality become radically uncertain, recur—most significantly just before she falls ill with smallpox and then in the delirium of its fever (31, 35).

Esther's little but potentially expanding "circle of duty" can be understood as a defense against such radical uncertainty. In a world in which all the big questions are unsettled (who am I? who's in charge here? what's it all about?), the safest course is to attend to the little things immediately around one that just obviously need doing and then move on to the next and the next. This is the logic of Esther's housekeeping. It happens also to be the logic of Dickens's "master," Carlyle, discussed at length in the previous chapter, and the doctrine of work he elaborates in *Sartor Resartus,* in which he describes his own crisis of identity and religious doubts, also following hard upon the death of his father: "To me the Universe was . . . one . . . immeasurable Steam-engine, rolling on it its dead indifference, to grind me limb from limb." Doubt he resolves by turning away from speculation towards action: " '*Do the Duty which lies nearest thee,*' which thou knowest to be a Duty! Thy second Duty will already have become clearer."[39]

Esther's narrative of course makes up only half the novel, which is strikingly divided between its omniscient third-person narrative and hers. No two narrators could be more apparently different. The one is clearly figured as masculine, masterful, and confident, its conventional omniscience at once accented by its writing always in the present tense and playfully called into question, for while it knows everything in the present and can travel instantaneously across the country, pass through walls, and read people's minds, it at least pretends not to know the future. It is the voice of the consummate showman or exhibitor, always inviting us to "Look here!" (11)—and also look at him. The other is figured feminine: diffident and uncertain, self-belittling, but without confidence even in that, "for I may be very vain, without suspecting it—though indeed I don't," as Esther perplexedly and perplexingly writes (3).

The narrators do, for all their differences, share important interests, of course. The third-person narrator often takes us into people's heads and poignantly invites us to imagine what it must be like to be Jo, who is illiterate and so ignorant that he has more in common with the animals whose wastes he sweeps away than the people whose delicacy he offends (16). This sympathetic move (to which we shall return in chapter 7) bespeaks precisely "the art of adapting . . . [one's] mind to minds very differently situated" that Esther has told Mrs. Pardiggle is so necessary for real charity (8), and it suggests an account of *Bleak House* as a whole as an instrument enabling the imaginative sympathy that leads to real charity. (Charity begins at home—not only at Bleak House the house, but more generally at *Bleak House* the novel.) Yet never before has Dickens the novelist been so manifestly and formally at odds with himself, nor will he be again. On the one hand, his "masculine" narrator has never been in finer voice. But the turn towards the feminine that we first noted in Florence Dombey is even more pronounced here. The masculine narrator may have the first word, but Esther has the last, even if she ends, as the novel had begun, with an incomplete sentence.

Chapter Six
Love and Death

If *Bleak House* marks Dickens's becoming, as Chesterton had written, fully grown up as a novelist, and if Dickens is in that novel himself interested in what it means to be grown up and has come to embrace with less conflict than ever before the discipline and even policing of self and family entailed in being grown up, then in his next novel he shows a striking reaction (and a return to some of the concerns of *Dombey*). For *Hard Times* explicitly takes up the cause of the child and imagination and even has a good word to say about untidiness. Esther knew from the defining day of that memorable birthday that she wanted to win some love for herself, and she never needed to ask herself what love is—nor indeed how to get it; she only wanted the chance to do so. *Hard Times* wonders and worries about what love is, however, and its tolerance for untidiness is connected with that worry. Wondering and worrying about love will prove a constant theme in Dickens's later career. So too will coming to terms with and indeed eventually embracing untidiness, even when untidiness takes its most extreme form in the disorder and dissolution that is death. There had been many deaths in *Bleak House*—more indeed than in any other of the novels—and while there was at least a poetic justice in a few of them (like Krook's via Spontaneous Combustion), none of them was remotely redemptive. But in the last third of Dickens's career, which is interrupted of course by his own sudden death, there is a significant move towards a more religious or spiritual reading of death than in anything he had previously produced—even than in his most overtly sentimental treatment of death, in *The Old Curiosity Shop*.

Unexpectedly for a novel tolerant of untidiness, *Hard Times* is spare and schematic. It tends for this reason to be one of the least favorite novels among Dickensians and is conversely sometimes championed by critics who don't generally warm to Dickens. It is polemical and often taken to be a tract against Utilitarianism—although that judgment calls for serious qualification, because while Dickens does indeed have some people identifiable as Utilitarians in his sights, as we saw in chapter 4 his own ethics line up rather neatly with the Utilitarians in that he identifies the good with pleasure and evil with pain.[1] It is "Inscribed" to Carlyle, who, as we have seen, certainly figured himself as an enemy of Utilitarianism, and the novel's polemic allies itself pointedly not so much with Carlyle's doctrine of work (as had *Bleak House*) as with his railing against the Mechanical. But the novel's thrust is not in theory anti-Utilitarian. On the contrary, its criticisms are everywhere made from a Utilitarian standpoint, for, consistent with all Dickens's writings, the novel imagines no good other than pleasure and no evil other than pain. What it does object to are habits of mind and theories of psychology, education, and political economy that were indeed identified with the circle that formed around Bentham and therefore became identified with Utilitarianism. That circle included many men who, like Thomas Gradgrind (or, at the opposite end of the spectrum, like Thomas Carlyle, for that matter), did indeed have little interest in pleasure.

As Dickens wrote to his friend the publisher (and Utilitarian) Charles Knight, "My satire is against those who see figures and averages and nothing else . . . the addled heads who would take the average of cold in the Crimea during twelve months, as a reason for clothing a soldier in nankeen on a night when he would be frozen to death in fur" (30 December 1854).[2] His target therefore is "rationalism" of a peculiarly reductive and indeed *irrational* kind. The novel begins with another famous tour de force: a monologue delivered by the hardware-merchant-turned–politician and educator Mr. Gradgrind to a class of children in the school he owns, presided over by its teacher Mr. M'Choakumchild. Gradgrind speaks to praise "Facts" and put down "Fancy" and "Wonder"—everything, indeed, that suggests imagination and does not come down to a matter of calculation, "a mere question of figures" (1.2), and he is in this a good Victorian exponent of positivistic science and member of what we called in chapter 4 the party of the mechanicals. This is the principle that governs his home and his school as well as the factory owned by his friend Bounderby, who is also the town's banker:

> The M'Choakumchild school was all fact . . . and the relations between master and man were all fact, and everything was fact between the lying-in hospital and the cemetery, and what you couldn't state in figures, or show to be purchaseable in the cheapest market and saleable in the dearest, was not, and never should be, world without end, Amen. (1.5)

The domination of Fact over the children in M'Choakumchild's school and the Gradgrind home, as well as over the factory's "hands," can in the Dickens world come to no good:

Is it possible, I wonder, that there was any analogy between the case of the Coketown population and the case of the little Gradgrinds? Surely, none of us in our sober senses and acquainted with figures, are to be told at this time of day, that one of the foremost elements in the existence of the Coketown working-people had been for scores of years, deliberately set at nought? That there was any Fancy in them demanding to be brought into healthy existence instead of struggling on in convulsions? That exactly in the ratio as they worked long and monotonously, the craving grew within them for some physical relief—some relaxation, encouraging good humour and good spirits, and giving them a vent—some recognized holiday, though it were but for an honest dance to a stirring band of music—some occasional light pie in which even M'Choakumchild had no finger—which craving must and would be satisfied aright, or must and would inevitably go wrong, until the laws of the Creation were repealed? (1.5)

The narrator here pointedly rebels against the "key-note" of Coketown (as Gradgrind's town is named), which is "never wonder!" (1.8). And yet he does so in a curious and ironic way, for he follows a logic that is itself calculating, even arithmetical—a matter of number ("set at nought") and "ratio"—and that appeals to those "of us in our sober senses and acquainted with figures." As so often happens with Dickens's irony, the apparent object of satire is actually partially endorsed, for the calculation here is a perfectly good one, and the narrator's predictions of course come true.

So it is not really "facts" and "calculation" that are the enemy, but bad facts and poor calculation. It is a fact that people crave and need fancy, and Mr. Gradgrind's failure to see this raises the possibility therefore not that he is wrong to think mechanically about the mind but that he is an imperfect mechanic.

And yet there is another complication that may after all return Dickens as a member in good standing of the Carlylean party of the anti-mechanicals, and this has to do with the nature of Wonder or Fancy. While it may be a fact that these are basic human needs that we ignore at our peril, it is not so easy to satisfy them. Although the craving for Fancy can be figured as a need for "physical relief," Fancy and Wonder are also matters of spirit and by that very fact resist definition. They are not simple commodities purchasable at the local store.

But they *are* purchasable at that rather special and transitory store, the Circus. When we first meet Gradgrind's two elder children, Tom and Louisa, they have been caught by their shocked father peeping through a fence and trying to get a view of the goings-on at "Sleary's

Horse-Riding" (1.3). Owing to their supposed corruption under this wicked influence, Gradgrind and Bounderby repair to Sleary's to dismiss from school Sissy Jupe, daughter of one of Sleary's performers, who has gained temporary admission while the circus is in town. It turns out that Signor Jupe, whose talents are failing, has run away, perhaps in the belief that his presence will do his daughter more harm than good. As it turns out, Gradgrind will take Sissy in, and her inability to get over her fanciful, imaginative way of thinking will make her both a terrible student in the Gradgrind school and a thoroughly healthy influence in his home, though she will be unable to save either Louisa from a horrible and loveless marriage to Bounderby and an almost-elopement with a scoundrel in the Carker tradition or her brother Tom from committing a serious theft from Bounderby's bank.

It will take Gradgrind until the very end of the novel, when Sleary helps the disgraced Tom flee the police and escape abroad, to learn the lessons of the circus and appreciate the claims of imagination. But for the reader the lesson is plain when the circus people are first described:

> There were two or three handsome young women among them, with their two or three husbands, and their two or three mothers, and their eight or nine little children, who did the fairy business when required. The father of one of the families was in the habit of balancing the father of another of the families on the top of a great pole; the father of a third family often made a pyramid of both those fathers, with Master Kidderminster for the apex, and himself for the base; all the fathers could dance upon rolling casks, stand upon bottles, catch knives and balls, twirl hand-basins, ride upon anything, jump over everything, and stick at nothing. All the mothers could (and did) dance, upon the slack wire, and performed rapid acts on bare-backed steeds; none of them were at all particular in respect of showing their legs; and one of them, alone in a Greek chariot, drove six in hand into every town they came to. They all assumed to be mighty rakish and knowing, they were not tidy in their private dresses, they were not at all orderly in their domestic arrangements, and the combined literature of the whole company would have produced but a poor letter on any subject. Yet there was a remarkable gentleness and childishness about these people, a special inaptitude for any kind of sharp practice, and an untiring readiness to help and pity one another, deserving, often of as much respect, and always of as much generous construction, as the every-day virtues of any class of people in the world.
>
> Last of all appeared Mr. Sleary: a stout man . . . , with one fixed eye and one loose eye, a voice (if it can be called so) like the efforts of a bro-

ken old pair of bellows, a flabby surface, and a muddled head which was
never sober and never drunk. (1.6)

Coming right after the obsession with order and policing in *Bleak House,*
this is a remarkable passage. There is a blurring of gender that ought by
now to be familiar enough, but there is further a blurring of families.
The circus people are at once untamed and sexual, civilized and innocent. Most remarkable is that their untidiness and domestic disorderliness not only are tolerated but seem necessary to their "gentleness and
childishness . . . , [their] special inaptitude for any kind of sharp practice, and . . . untiring readiness to help and pity one another." Even
Sleary's bodily disorders and half-drunkenness appear to be somehow
necessary to his role as spokesman for Fancy, for, as he unpretentiously
lisps the circus philosophy, "People must be amuthed, . . . they can't be
alwayth a working, nor yet they can't be alwayth a learning."

It is perhaps not clear if Sleary's muddled head (echoed in the refrain
of the factory hand Stephen Blackpool, who repeatedly exclaims, " 'Tis
a' a muddle!" [1.11]), his drunkenness, and his lisp tell us simply that
imagination and art in a world ruled by Gradgrinds are so marginalized
that they can speak only in what appear to be distorted and half articu-
late ways, or if beyond this there is something essentially inarticulate
and messy about them. There is at least the suggestion that the latter is
the case in Sleary's final statement of the "Sleary philosophy" in the
novel's penultimate chapter, "Philosophical" (3.8). Here Sleary tells
Gradgrind the marvelous story of the return of Merrylegs, Sissy's
father's old dog, who had run away with him when he fled the circus:

> "Thquire, you don't need to be told that dogth is wonderful ani-
> malth."
> "Their instinct," said Mr. Gradgrind, "is surprising."
> "Whatever you call it—and I'm blest if I know what to call it,"—
> said Sleary, "it ith athonithing. The way in with a dog'll find you—the
> dithtanthe he'll come!"
> "His scent," said Mr. Gradgrind, "being so fine."
> "I'm blest if I know what to call it," repeated Sleary, shaking his head,
> "but I have had dogth find me, Thquire, in a way that made me think
> whether that dog hadn't gone to another dog, and thed, 'You don't happen
> to know a perthon of the name of Thleary, do you? Perthon of the name of
> Thleary, in the Horthe-Riding way—thout man—game eye?' " (3.8)

While Mr. Gradgrind has by this point almost learned his lesson, he still
tries to reduce a living mystery (what Carlyle calls "Natural Supernatu-

ralism") to something that looks like fact and explanation—mere "instinct." Sleary's (Carlylean) point is that some truths just can't be spoken or named. To give a name to the ways of the dogs is to pretend to a knowledge we cannot have, and it is precisely this ineffability that may be registered in Sleary's lisp.

And yet the ineffable needs to be uttered too in some form if it is to have any power to resist the explicit calculations and reductions of "fact." Sleary takes Merrylegs' return as a certain sign that Jupe is dead and buried, and since there is no way of deciding "whether her father bathely detherted her; or whether he broke his own heart alone, rather than pull her down along with him," the men agree (in another pious fraud) that nothing is to be gained in telling Sissy of this, for as Gradgrind says, she has dearly held onto the bottle of liniment that her father had sent her for just before his flight, "and she will believe in his affection to the last moment of her life." Sleary concludes:

> "It theemth to prethent two thingth to a perthon, don't it, Thquire?" said Mr. Sleary, musing as he looked down into the depths of his brandy and water: "one, that there ith a love in the world, not all Thelf-intereth after all, but thomething very different; t'other, that it hath a way of ith own of calculating or not calculating, whith thomehow or another ith at leatht ath hard to give a name to, ath the wayth of the dogth ith!"

So the sacred unspeakable in the end gets its name—"a love in the world"—even if it "hath"—the lisp here neatly coincides with the biblical—its own manner of "calculating or not calculating" that remains mysterious and inexplicable.

Sleary's account of love can easily be charged with sentimentality—as well as vagueness. While the use of the word "philosophical" here is to some extent ironic, Dickens pretty clearly means also to offer Sleary as a serious antagonist to the "philosophers"—political economists, really, like Thomas Malthus or David Ricardo—against whom he has been writing since the days of *Oliver Twist* and those very "philosophical" men responsible for the theory behind the workhouse as well as Fagin's more sophisticated musings about "number one." In the account's explicit effort to resist definition, it of course joins that respectable party of the spirit we identified in chapter 4, and in its troubling the question of definition it certainly rises well above simple sentiment. Sissy's loves (we are told in the final chapter about "happy Sissy's happy children" [3.9]) are on the other hand perfectly unselfconscious and untroubled. But in Louisa's story we have a much darker account that raises worries not just about love's usual vicissitudes, but about its very nature. Louisa has her forerunners in Edith Dombey and even angrier women, like Rosa Dartle in *Copperfield* or Mlle. Horstense in *Bleak House*. But Dickens here gives a disturbed sexuality a new prominence and indeed centrality.

Louisa's capacity for love is plainly distorted by her stifling upbringing, which has grotesque consequences as well for her brother. As the narrator ironically marvels, "It was altogether unaccountable that a young gentleman whose imagination had been strangled in his cradle, should be still inconvenienced by its ghost in the form of grovelling sensualities; but such a monster, beyond all doubt, was Tom" (2.3). Tom's disturbance exaggerates masculine traits. He is sensual, yet entirely and coldly devoted to "number one" (1.9 and 14). Louisa's disturbances exaggerate feminine traits. She is selflessly devoted to her worthless brother and lets herself be pushed into an arranged marriage with the repulsive and middle-aged Bounderby by Tom (who expects a position in Bounderby's bank as his reward) and their father, even though she makes plain to both that she has no love for Bounderby—is indeed repelled by him. Her reaction to a prenuptial kiss that Bounderby begs of her says it all:

> [Bounderby] went his way, but she stood on the same spot, rubbing the cheek he had kissed, with her handkerchief, until it was burning red. She was still doing this, five minutes afterwards.
>
> "What are you about, Loo?" her brother sulkily remonstrated. "You'll rub a hole in your face."
>
> "You may cut the piece out with your penknife if you like, Tom. I wouldn't cry!" (1.4)

This looks downright masochistic, except that it yields Louisa no pleasure.

Like Edith Dombey, Louisa brings herself to the brink of an elopement, and the implication is that where Edith's motives were chiefly to revenge herself upon Mr. Dombey for his humiliation of her, Louisa's sexuality has actually been aroused by the worldly and cynical Mr. Harthouse, who insinuates himself upon her initially by claiming an interest in saving her brother from the ruin that plainly awaits him (for he gambles and loses). Although at the last minute she fails to keep her appointment with Harthouse and returns desperately to her father, thus barely avoiding even the appearance of becoming a fallen woman (Edith, it will be recalled, avoided technical adultery, but not the appearance of it, having left the country with Carker), there is no question of her continuing to live with Bounderby, who declares a separation when his ultimatum that Louisa return to his bed only two days following her aborted elopement goes unanswered (3.4). The narrator in the final chapter foretells Bounderby's death (of "a fit" in the street) five years hence and also, almost cruelly, raises the hope of a new start for Louisa only to dash it:

> Herself again a wife—a mother—lovingly watchful of her children, ever careful that they should have a childhood of the mind no less than a childhood of the body, as knowing it to be even a more beautiful thing, and a possession, any hoarded scrap of which, is a blessing and happiness to the wisest? Did Louisa see this? Such a thing was never to be. (3.9)

Louisa will have the recompense of "happy Sissy's happy children loving her; all children loving her" and herself "grown learned in childish lore," but whether her failure to remarry is to be understood as a mere matter of ill luck (Coketown hardly providing a rich crop of eligible men), the inability to overcome her crippling upbringing, or a Victorian punishment for having *almost* fallen, is not apparent.

Bleak House and *Hard Times* are angry books both. Each identifies a social system and habits of mind that threaten to overrun institutional life and produce moral chaos on the one hand and the death of wonder on the other. That each can imagine no institutional solution to the problem it portrays, but pins its hopes rather on individual heroics and varying combinations of discipline and love (or disciplines of the heart, to recall the language of *David Copperfield*), hardly lessens its bitterness. *Little Dorrit* likewise identifies a social evil, likewise can imagine no institutional solution, and likewise looks to individual hearts for remedies, but now locates bitterness and anger as the very core of the problem.

As critics since Edmund Wilson's classic essay in *The Wound and the Bow* have unfailingly noted, *Little Dorrit* figures society as one vast prison.[3] Like Chancery or Gradgrindery, the Marshalsea debtors' prison (in which, as we have seen, John Dickens was jailed for several months while young Charles toiled at Warren's Blacking) is at once the target of topical satire and represents a larger evil, though one considerably more complex than anything Dickens has previously identified. And the prison is not the novel's only satirical subject, for *Dorrit* is famous as well for the Circumlocution Office, which to its contemporaries was a transparent representation of the civil service generally and more particularly the Treasury—which played a role in an enormous range of public business. The Marshalsea and the laws governing debtors have in common with the civil service some features of Chancery, especially long-standing inefficiency ("Whatever was required to be done, the Circumlocution Office was beforehand with all the public departments in the art of perceiving—how not to do it" [1.10]), a devotion to antiquated and illogical procedures, and an institutional habit of evading responsibility that encourages individual evasions—Dickens's first idea for a title was to call it "Nobody's Fault" (Forster, 7.1). The novel's portrait of the swindler Mr. Merdle also draws on a great speculative bubble that had burst the year before and satirizes greed and the perennial hope of getting something for nothing as well as the blind faith in mere appearance and pretense that such hope engenders. Through it all run the twin themes of trusting to Providence and blaming Providence instead of tending to the Carlylean virtues of keeping quiet and getting down to work.

Providence also figures importantly in the story of Arthur Clennam, who becomes in the end the lover and husband of little Amy Dorrit, the "Child of the Marshalsea" (as she is called from having been born and grown up within its walls). Or rather it figures importantly in the life of his mother, Mrs. Clennam, a character in the Miss Barbary line who believes that she and Providence are on especially good terms. Her religion is Calvinist, Old Testament, unrelentingly grim. Confined to a wheelchair, she lives Scrooge-like in an old house in the heart of London's business district and governs the family firm and prays that her enemies "might be utterly exterminated" (1.3). As in *Bleak House,* Providence has its often purely secular way of connecting the most unlikely persons and places, however, helped especially by the crowding of urban life: "And thus ever, by day and night, under the sun and under the stars, climbing the dusty hills and toiling along the weary plains, journeying by land and journeying by sea, coming and going so strangely, to meet and to act and react on one another, move all we restless travellers through the pilgrimage of life" (1.2).[4] But whereas in *Bleak House* connections had always something uncanny about them, which is to say that there always remained something confused and unresolved about them, in *Little Dorrit* Providence tends to act in rather more definite ways.

Amy Dorrit may appear to be a straightforward incarnation of Esther Summerson, and indeed she *is* another apparently selfless woman who manages for everyone about her but eventually wins some love for herself. But significantly it is Arthur Clennam who has the psychologically crippling stern religious upbringing that must be overcome before he can manage a love life for himself, while Amy has been since her eighth year motherless, and far from being stern, her father—William, called since the time he became its tenant of longest standing "the Father of the Marshalsea"—is an almost helpless old man, "effeminate" and "irresolute" (1.6). Little Dorrit therefore is as much in the Little Nell (and Cordelia) line as any other—except that happily she does not die.

Unlike her older brother and sister, Amy has lived her entire life in the Marshalsea, which historically resembled a very shabby college or inn more than a jail. Like the Oxford or Cambridge colleges, it had a high surrounding wall and gated entry with a lodge that housed a turnkey instead of a porter, and its inmates half seriously referred to themselves as Collegians. Prisoners might occupy larger or smaller sets of rooms depending on their ability to pay (and many prisoners had some ability to pay; the point of incarceration was after all to *make them* pay; John Dickens's family continued to employ a workhouse girl as servant while they were in the Marshalsea). But unlike her siblings and father, Amy avoids the "prison taint" (1.1) that pervades not just the Marshalsea but the novel. Ironically, she is almost the only figure in the novel who in some sense never really is imprisoned.

What being in prison signifies is extremely complex. It may be an external or internal state, and the jailer is as often oneself as some other person or public entity. Mrs. Clennam regards herself as a prisoner and commands her son to "look at me, in prison, and in bonds here" (1.5). Her paralysis, however, is clearly self-imposed and indeed hysterical; at the end of the novel she discovers that she can in fact walk when she wants to. Foreshadowing his criminal fraudulence, Mr. Merdle continually clasps "his wrists as if he were taking himself into custody" (1.33), and in the end he cheats the gallows by performing the ultimate act of self-arrest: he cuts his own throat. Mrs. Merdle laments the unnatural state of "Society [which] suppresses us and dominates us" (1.20), though in claiming to be "a child of nature" she is no more genuine than Mrs. Skewton had been—she plays by Society's "arbitrary" rules most willingly.

It is notable that the Marshalsea and the very tangled laws involving insolvency actually come in for very little straightforward satirical treatment—unlike the Circumlocution Office—and its inmates are treated sometimes satirically, sometimes merely contemptuously, but often pityingly. The doctor who delivers Little Dorrit consoles her father thus:

"We are quiet here; we don't get badgered here; there's no knocker here, sir, to be hammered at by creditors and bring a man's heart into his mouth. Nobody comes here to ask if a man's at home, and to say he'll stand on the door mat till he is. Nobody writes threatening letters about money, in this place. It's freedom, sir, it's freedom! I have had to-day's practice at home and abroad, on a march, and aboard ship, and I'll tell you this: I don't know that I have ever pursued it under such quiet circumstances, as here this day. Elsewhere people are restless, worried, hurried about, anxious respecting one thing, anxious respecting another. Nothing of the kind here, sir. We have done all that—we know the worst of it; we have got to the bottom, we can't fall, and what have we found? Peace. That's the word for it. Peace." (1.6)

Part of the complexity of being imprisoned is that while we are surely meant to deplore the doctor's resignation as a failure of will, nevertheless he has a point, for the novel at the same time likewise deplores the fact that people in "Society" really *are* "restless, worried, hurried about, anxious respecting one thing, anxious respecting another." The satire constituted by the Merdle plot makes just this point, and when Arthur Clennam allows himself to be caught up in "this fatal mania" (2.26) and to invest everything he and his partner, Daniel Doyce, own in the Merdle enterprise, we understand that he has thereby joined the ranks of the restless and forgone "freedom" and "peace." This longing for peace is underscored by the novel's very end, which describes Amy and Arthur after she has rescued him from his debts and immediately after their wedding, walking out from the little church next to the prison, "looking at the fresh perspective of the street in the autumn morning sun's bright rays": "They went quietly down into the roaring streets, inseparable and blessed; and as they passed along in sunshine and shade, the noisy and the eager, and the arrogant and the froward and the vain, fretted, and chafed, and made their usual uproar" (2.34). The freedom and peace praised by the doctor thus are by no means unworthy ends, and even his claim that they can be found within the prison's walls, while on the face of it absurd, turns out to have some merit.

The truth of this claim is apparent in the figure of Little Dorrit herself, who embodies a certain moral freedom and serenity in spite of having been born in jail and in spite of being taken for granted by her whole family as in effect their servant ("It was the family custom to lay it down as family law, that she was a plain domestic little creature, without the great and sage experience of the rest. This family fiction was the family assertion of itself against her services. Not to make too much of them." [1.20]). And the claim's truth is apparent too in a theme introduced even before we enter the Marshalsea. For the novel begins in a prison in Marseilles (where we meet its central villain, Monsieur Rigaud) and moves on to a group of English travelers in the same city who are being held in quarantine. Upon their release, one of them, Mr. Meagles, remarks, "One always begins to forgive a place as soon as it's left behind; I dare say a prisoner begins to relent towards his prison, after he is let out." Forgiving one's prison even before one is let out proves no less important to the novel than forgiving it later.

In what may well be the twentieth century's best single essay on Dickens, Lionel Trilling observes of *Little Dorrit* that "it is part of the complexity of this novel which deals so bitterly with society that those of its characters who share its social bitterness are by that very fact condemned."[5] The bitterness may in other words be "justified," but giving in to bitterness has effects as damaging as the social injustice that gives rise to it.

The clearest example of the destructiveness of bitterness is provided by Arthur's mother, who, we learn at the novel's end, is not his mother in fact. She has devoted her life to punishing her husband for having illegitimately fathered Arthur upon a young singer shortly after the Clennams' arranged marriage took place (a fact that strengthens her likeness to Miss Barbary).[6] She believes herself providentially "appointed" (2.30) not only to punish him but to persecute the poor girl he loves, to torment herself with the memory of her being wronged, and to bring up Arthur ignorant of his birth and in the same state of "wholesome repression" that had characterized her own education.

Another striking example is evident in the enigmatic figure of Miss Wade. She is among that group of quarantined travelers, and it is she who, upon hearing that causal remark about forgiving one's prison, vehemently protests: "If I had been shut up in any place to pine and suffer, I should always hate that, and wish to burn it down, or raze it to the ground. I know no more" (1.2). She appears intermittently in the novel, chiefly as urging the Meagles' resentful servant, Tattycoram (in many ways an opposite double for Little Dorrit), to rebel against what she feels is their condescending usage, and later she appears as her protector and companion when the girl does run away. While Miss Wade's conduct and character are deplored, she is uniquely given the chance to tell her own story in a chapter wholly given over to her autobiography (and titled—undoubtedly *not* by her—"The History of a Self-Tormentor").[7] As Trilling notes, she reveals herself in her autobiography to be "the exact inversion of Esther Summerson" (59); whereas Esther is diffident about her brain power, eager to make the best of everything, and eager to please, Miss Wade is proud, angry, and determined not to be pushed around; she begins her narrative with the announcement: "I have the misfortune of not being a fool" (2.21). Tattycoram eventually returns to the Meagles' household, having encountered only wretchedness in her life with Miss Wade, but when Mr. Meagles tries to persuade her to come back, he confronts the older woman with a curious charge: "I don't know what you are, but you don't hide, can't hide, what a dark spirit you have within you. If it should happen that you are a woman, who, from whatever cause, has a perverted delight in making a sister-woman as wretched as she is (I am old enough to have heard of such), I warn her against you, and I warn you against yourself" (1.27). This passage has routinely come to be interpreted as Dickens's eminently Victorian way of signaling readers in the know that Miss Wade is a lesbian. But while there are details of her life that could support that view (including her passionate childhood attachment to another girl; "I so loved that unworthy girl," she writes, "that my life was made stormy by my fondness for her" [2.21]), she also tells of her falling in love and becoming engaged to one man and letting herself be seduced by another (Henry Gowan, the cynical painter—and partial reincarnation of Harold Skimpole—who later marries the Meagles' daughter Pet).[8] In any case, what Meagles and Dickens ask us to notice is the "perverted delight" not of loving but of inflicting suffering. What Miss Wade records as the repeated "wicked injury" of her life is that people are endlessly telling her that she has "an unhappy temper"—an ambiguous phrase that can refer to somebody who is characteristically unhappy, or to somebody who has an unfortunate personality, or to somebody with a tendency to lose her temper—as well as to somebody, like Miss Wade, who is all of these.[9] Like Mrs. Clennam, she punishes herself while making everyone about her miserable, and she has a special mission, it seems, to punish the father even more than the child. It is no doubt significant in this connection that Dickens gives her the name of the surgeon who had performed on his own father in his last illness that "most terrible operation known in surgery" (Pilgrim letters, 6:333 n. 3).

Miss Wade, like others of the socially embittered in the novel, claims to see through society's false surface, which from her perspective consists of a charitable exterior that conceals an intention to keep her down (we are led to believe that she is, like Esther, illegitimate). Mrs. Clennam likewise believes she sees clearly through her husband's respectable exterior and can accurately reckon up his moral worth. But the truth of such perceptions in *Little Dorrit* is as dubious as the bitterness to which they give rise, and pretense in the world of the novel is not merely endemic but inescapable. The starkly drawn (if not always successfully maintained) distinction between Fact and Fancy in *Hard Times* becomes here what Janice Carlisle calls "an inquiry into the moral status of fictions"—one, indeed, that yields no easy answers.[10] For the first time in Dickens's career, he begins to worry in his work about that faculty of imagination whose wholesome effects he has always taken for granted.[11]

Pretense seems to be nourished by the prison taint. Among the Dorrits it takes the form of pretending to an uncompromised gentility, and this in turn leads them to pretend that Amy is neither in effect their servant nor that she leaves the prison every day to go out to work. Likewise, she conceals from her employer, Mrs. Clennam, where she lives. While Amy herself has no social pretensions, of course, she conspires in the "family fiction" and "had always upon her the care of preserving the genteel fiction that they were all idle beggars together" (1.7). It is an interesting fiction because, like so many of Dickens's ironies, it is literally true—except for Amy and her sister Fanny (who, following the example of Dickens's own sister Fanny, boards outside the prison), they pretty much *are* idle beggars. The irony depends upon the fact that the conventional phrase "idle beggar" is one that the idle rich easily apply to themselves in jest.

Amy even generates several fictions of her own. When her brother Tip becomes himself a prisoner, Little Dorrit embarks upon "the pious fraud" of concealing the fact from her father (1.7), in which deception Tip fully participates, feigning not to know why it is important (1.8), though it is at least implied that the prison taint may more fundamentally alter perceptions:

> One solid stationary point in the looseness of this gentleman's character, was, that he respected and admired his sister Amy. The feeling had never induced him to spare her a moment's uneasiness, or to put himself to any restraint or inconvenience on her account; but, with that Marshalsea taint upon his love, he loved her. The same rank Marshalsea flavour was to be recognized in his distinctly perceiving that she sacrificed her life to her father, and in his having no idea that she had done anything for himself. (1.20)

When Amy visits Arthur late one evening—the first night she has ever been away from the Marshalsea—she pretends to her father that she is at a party, and when Clennam is struck by this, she answers his questioning glance by saying, "I hope there is no harm in it. I could never have been of any use, if I had not pretended a little" (1.14).

Amy's greatest fiction involves Arthur. She learns in the end that Mrs. Clennam is not his mother in fact but promises Mrs. Clennam that she will not disclose the secret for as long as the old woman lives. But beyond this, she evidently decides to keep the secret forever, for immediately before their marriage she asks that Arthur indulge her in an "odd fancy," which is to burn a piece of paper. It is the one document that reveals the story of his parentage (2.34). This final pious fraud of Amy's recalls Sleary's and Mr. Gradgrind's agreeing not to tell Sissy about her father's death, and we may guess that the reasoning is the same—that this too is an instance in which the truth can do no good, or, as Sleary puts it, "There'th nothing comfortable to tell; why unthettle her mind, and make her unhappy?" (3.8).

The logic here is Utilitarian and secular; the only good is comfort or pleasure, and even the truth may be sacrificed to that end when the telling of it would have no other consequence than causing pain. But there is a more literal or orthodox piety connected with Amy's fraud as well. In making her plea for secrecy, Mrs. Clennam continues her bitter self-justification, to which Amy responds with a little sermon:

> "O, Mrs. Clennam, Mrs. Clennam," said Little Dorrit, "angry feelings and unforgiving deeds are no comfort and no guide to you and me. My life has been passed in this poor prison, and my teaching has been very defective; but, let me implore you to remember later and better days. Be guided only by the healer of the sick, the raiser of the dead, the friend of all who were afflicted and forlorn, the patient Master who shed tears of compassion for our infirmities." (2.31)

Comfort is still the cardinal good, but there is also a new and unambiguously religious note being struck here, one that speaks of that most spectacular of miracles, the raising of the dead. It looks forward to Dickens's next novel, *A Tale of Two Cities,* whose end ("It is a far, far better thing that I do, than I have ever done") is almost as famous as its beginning ("It was the best of times; it was the worst of times") and that not only itself looks forward, in Sydney Carton's words, to "a far, far better rest . . . than I have ever known," but also directly quotes John 11:25–26: "I am the Resurrection and the Life, saith the Lord" (3.15, and see also an earlier instance in 3.9). The first book of the novel, moreover, comprising the first six chapters, is titled "Recalled to Life."

A Tale of Two Cities significantly connects its interest in resurrection with love. Taking advantage of the accident of their close physical resemblance, Carton sacrifices himself, switching places in jail with his successful rival for the hand of Lucie Manette, Charles Darnay, who has been condemned to the guillotine during the Reign of Terror, ironically because of a letter written long ago by Lucie's father, cursing the noble family with which Darnay happens to be connected. Both Darnay's initials and Carton's first name echo Dickens's own, and in his preface he provides some hints of an autobiographical interest, telling us that the plot occurred to him while he was acting in his friend Wilkie Collins's *The Frozen Deep* (where, it will be recalled, he met Nelly Ternan) and that "a strong desire was upon me then, to embody it in my own person." He continues: "Throughout its execution, it has had the complete possession of me; I have so far verified what is done and suffered in these pages, as that I have certainly done and suffered it all myself." It is difficult to know just what to make of this intense claim. What would it mean "to embody it" in his own person? Merely to act it out (as he has just acted out in Collins's play the role of another hero who lets himself sacrificially die so that his rival can marry the woman they both love)? Or actually to live it and, as it were, die it?

Dying for love or almost dying for love or being resurrected for love—along with killing for love—will be great themes of the last novels, though these streams of thought are interrupted, apparently, by one of Dickens's greatest if least characteristic books, *Great Expectations*. For while that novel's major lovers, or would-be lovers, Pip (the narrator) and the eccentric elderly recluse, Miss Havisham, *are* in varying senses dying for love, there is hardly any resurrection in store for them, and this most ironically titled novel is instead all about disappointment. Just because it has so little of transcendence about it, it feels in many ways like Dickens's most grown-up and most realistic novel—"realistic" in the connected senses of being without illusions and being narrated in the postromantic mode "realism."

This is not to say that Dickens deprives himself or us of his characteristic pleasures. Pumblechook and Wopsle; Wemmick and his aged parent; the Havisham relations who gather to fawn and drool over the riches they hope to inherit; Mr. Trabb the tailor's "audacious" boy, who refuses to show Pip any deference when he comes upon his expectations (19); Pip's dark double, Orlick, who kills Pip's sister, Mrs. Joe, and almost succeeds in killing Pip—all these do the familiar comedic and villainous Dickensian business. But the underlying tone of the novel is so consistently elegiac and haunted, its "hero" is so manifestly unheroic, self-deluded, and burdened with stifling guilt and shame, and its original ending—clearly the more fitting ending, though Dickens allowed himself at the last minute to be talked into replacing it with an ambiguous and arguably happy one[12]—is so unrelievedly sad, that *Great Expectations* belongs as much in the company of Gustave Flaubert's *Madame Bovary* or *Sentimental Education* as even in the company of his more "realistic" English contemporaries Thackeray, Trollope, or George Eliot.

Great Expectations is often read as a satire on snobbery (somewhat in the vein of Thackeray, many of whose early works take snobbery as a besetting social problem).[13] Pip actually never uses that word, but he does charge himself in his social ambitiousness with unfaithfulness to his brother-in-law, Joe Gargery, the blacksmith (who is as much a father to him as anything else), and there is no question that in his eagerness to become a "gentleman" Pip cheerfully turns his back on Joe and the whole ethos of work and the working class associated with the forge—including Biddy: the girl who chiefly teaches him to read, to whom he confides his passion for Miss Havisham's disdainful ward, Estella, and whom he imagines at novel's end that he really ought to marry, but who turns out instead to have just married Joe. Q. D. Leavis has effectively put down this conventional reading, however, by pointing to the obvious fact that Pip could never have been content in the world of the forge, nor indeed should he have been.[14] His wish to be a gentleman may be a tangle of motives, many of which are twisted in themselves, but it also propels him away from a very provincial setting into the greater world beyond. Joe is certainly lovable and faithful, but we take the measure of his mind when he comes up to London to visit the newly wealthy Pip, who asks him if he has taken in any sights: " 'Why, yes, Sir,' said Joe, 'me and Wopsle went off straight to look at the Blacking Ware'us. But we didn't find that it come up to its likeness in the red bills at the shop doors: which I meantersay,' added Joe, in an explanatory manner, 'as it is there drawd too architectooralooral' " (27). Although the full shame carried in the reference to the blacking warehouse would in 1859 have been apparent actually only to four people, all of Dickens's readers should have readily understood Joe's limits from his bumpkin's belief that a blacking factory he has seen represented in advertising bills was a distinguished cultural landmark of the great metropolis.

Pip's desire for a bigger and finer life and his passion for Estella are inextricably tied to the impression made upon him by Miss Havisham, the weird old woman who has brought her life to a sudden stop after being abandoned by her lover on what was supposed to have been her wedding day, and who lives 25 years later amid the ruins of that day in her ironically named mansion, Satis House,[15] still wearing her bridal gown, her very wedding cake an untouched, moldering, and vermin-infested pile upon her long table, and herself reminding Pip of nothing so much as a "ghastly waxwork" he had once seen at a fair and that seemed now uncannily to have come to life (8). Stranger still is the "sick fancy"[16] that has led her to employ this young boy: "I am tired. . . . I want diversion, and I have done with men and women. Play." But for all the implied perversity and decay of Miss Havisham's life and fancies—its sexual frustration and morbid delight in same, as well as the sugges-tion of voyeurism, aimed at a child, no less—there is something deeply fascinating and compelling about them. As Pip haltingly pleads when his performance anxiety prevents him even from pretending to play (for it is ironically his work to pretend to spontaneity): "it's so new here, and so strange, and so fine—and melancholy—." And the perversity proves catching, for the evident masochistic delight Miss Havisham takes in her broken heart immediately provides Pip with a model for his own passion for the young and beautiful Estella, whom Miss Havisham is bringing up—it is the one forward-looking project in her otherwise sus-pended life—to break men's hearts.[17]

It is Estella who first tells Pip he is "coarse" and "common" (8), and the self-conscious shame that this excites engenders also Pip's wish to be a "gentleman." Pip well understands the irrationality of this. "I used to think," he writes later, "with a weariness on my spirits, that I should have been happier and better if I had never seen Miss Havisham's face, and had risen to manhood content to be partners with Joe in the honest old forge" (34). And he will realize too that his passion for Estella has only brought him misery: "I never had one hour's happiness in her soci-ety, and yet my mind all round the four-and-twenty hours was harping on the happiness of having her with me unto death" (38). After hearing his first "lunatic confession" of wanting to be a gentleman on Estella's account, Biddy lays out clearly the madness of his attraction and the vanity of desiring a girl who has cruelly taunted him:

"Do you want to be a gentleman, to spite her or to gain her over?" Biddy quietly asked me, after a pause.

"I don't know," I moodily answered.

"Because, if it is to spite her," Biddy pursued, "I should think—but you know best—that might be better and more independently done by caring nothing for her words. And if it is to gain her over, I should think—but you know best—she was not worth gaining over."

Exactly what I myself had thought, many times. Exactly what was perfectly manifest to me at the moment. (17)

But self-awareness can do little good when self-awareness is itself so much the basis of Pip's problem.

What it *means* to be a gentleman is itself a thorny question—one we shall take up again in the next and final chapter. The central difficulty about gentility is that while it is in theory and origin a matter of "breeding" (the word derives from the Latin for "clan" or "tribe" but can ambiguously refer to upbringing in addition to birth), it is also a matter of what Pip calls "the stupendous power of money" (19), as well perhaps as a matter of a nature deeper even than birth or family—a matter of one's moral being. Pip's friend Herbert Pocket's father subscribes to the theory "that no man who was not a true gentleman at heart, ever was, since the world began, a true gentleman in manner. He says, no varnish can hide the grain of the wood; and that the more varnish you put on, the more the grain will express itself" (22). But appealing as such a classless moralization of gentility may be (this is the move of course that yields our most common sense of the word "gentle"; a parallel move occurs in the history of the word "kind"), the idea of gentility in practice does not escape considerations of family name, manners, and wealth.

Pip's plot of course turns on his delusion that Mr. Jaggers, the mysterious lawyer who suddenly appears one day to announce that Pip has "great expectations," is really Miss Havisham's emissary, that she means to raise Pip to Estella's level, and that they will eventually marry.[18] He has circumstantial reasons for this misreading (Jaggers is Miss Havisham's lawyer in fact, and Miss Havisham does nothing to disabuse Pip of his mistake when he circumspectly expresses his gratitude in saying good-bye to her), though it is in retrospect no less lunatic for him to believe in her benevolence than to love Estella in the first place. Yet so powerful is the fantasy of having a fairy godmother that almost all readers are greedily taken in as well.

No less powerful is the repugnance to the idea that Pip's real benefactor is Abel Magwitch, the terrifying convict who jumps out from behind a tombstone in the novel's first chapter and threatens Pip with a hideous death if he does not bring him food and a file in secret. Pip's attraction to the fineness (however bizarre and decayed it may be) of Satis House no doubt draws on the guilt and shame of his connection with the convict and his having stolen from his sister food and drink and from Joe's forge a file.[19] In the middle of the novel, when Pip is living the life of the young gentleman in London, he is troubled by Mr. Jaggers's being primarily a criminal lawyer and a defender indeed of criminals of the lowest kind, and he finds himself one day

> thinking how strange it was that I should be encompassed by all this taint of prison and crime; that, in my childhood out on our lonely marshes on a winter evening I should have first encountered it. . . . While my mind was thus engaged, I thought of . . . Estella, proud and refined, . . . and I thought with absolute abhorrence of the contrast between the jail and her. (32)

So it is doubly appalling (if less surprising, for this passage clearly anticipates the plot's critical turn and prepares us for a characteristically Dickensian shiver of *déjà vu* a few chapters later) when Magwitch appears one night and reveals himself as Pip's secret benefactor.

And added to the noxious "taint of prison and crime" (we should note the explicit echo of *Little Dorrit* here) is a further horror, that Pip is actually Magwitch's creation: "The imaginary student pursued by the misshapen creature he had impiously made," Pip writes, "was not more wretched than I, pursued by the creature who had made me, and recoiling from him with a stronger repulsion, the more he admired me and the fonder he was of me" (40). Pip thus invites us to imagine him as Frankenstein's monster—and in so doing also offers a perceptive early reading of Mary Shelley's novel, in spite of his apparent misreading. In *Frankenstein* it is the creator who recoils in horror from his creature, who at first only seeks acceptance. But Pip rightly understands that the monster's pain and moral awareness are greater than his creator's and that the monster therefore is in some ways less monstrous than his creator. There is an intimation here too of the accepted modern reading of Victor Frankenstein and his creation as doubles locked in a mutual pursuit of mingled attraction and repulsion.

But Miss Havisham's importance is hardly eclipsed by Magwitch's revelation, for her story closely parallels his and indeed is intertwined with his. She too has created a monster and to very similar purpose. Magwitch wants general revenge on a world that regards him as vulgar and particular revenge against his partner in crime, Compeyson, who has succeeded more or less in passing himself off as a gentleman. It turns out that Compeyson is also the man who abandoned Miss Havisham on what was supposed to have been their wedding day, so that her vengeful desire to raise Estella to be loved and break the hearts of men is another version of Magwitch's project. (It turns out too, of course, that Estella is actually Magwitch's daughter, further connecting this unlikely couple.) Even as he upholds the desirability of being a gentleman, Magwitch subverts the notion that there is something intrinsically fine about a gentleman, making it a mere matter of money: "If I ain't a gentleman, nor yet ain't got no learning, I'm the owner of such" (39). Miss Havisham likewise upholds an ideal of love while subverting it. On the one hand she is, however grotesque, a model of faithfulness; on the other she turns love inside out: she says to Pip, urging him on in his passion for Estella, "I'll tell you . . . what real love is. It is blind devotion, unquestioning self-humiliation, utter submission, . . . giving up your whole heart and soul to the smiter—as I did!" (29). And she is even more successfully vengeful than the convict, for in Estella she produces the perfectly dispassionate and invulnerable heartbreaker and in Pip the perfect masochist.

Only Miss Havisham comes to recognize the monstrousness of her creation. Rather like Joe, Magwitch has insuperable limits, and while Pip learns to love and even revere him—for his fidelity (again like Joe's) is absolute—Pip also maintains a measure of superiority as well as distance by making Magwitch the object of yet another Dickensian pious fraud (in revealing to him on his deathbed that his daughter lives and that Pip loves her, but leaving him with the false inference that Estella returns Pip's love). Miss Havisham, by contrast, finally sees in Pip the reflection of her own misery. After confessing to her that "I am as unhappy as you can ever have meant me to be," Pip pours out his heart before the two women in an "ecstasy of unhappiness" as he makes his final and most powerful declaration of love to Estella, who has just revealed that she is to be married to Bentley Drummle:

> You are part of my existence, part of myself. You have been in every line I have ever read, since I first came here, the rough common boy whose poor heart you wounded even then. You have been in every prospect I have ever seen since—on the river, on the sails of the ships, on the marshes, in the clouds, in the light, in the darkness, in the wind, in the woods, in the sea, in the streets. You have been the embodiment of every graceful fancy that my mind has ever become acquainted with. The stones of which the strongest London buildings are made, are not more

real, or more impossible to be displaced by your hands, than your presence and influence have been to me, there and everywhere, and will be.
Estella, to the last hour of my life, you cannot choose but remain part of
my character, part of the little good in me, part of the evil. But, in this
separation I associate you only with the good, and I will faithfully hold
you to that always, for you must have done me far more good than harm,
let me feel now what sharp distress I may. O God bless you, God forgive
you! (44)

While Estella greets this speech with "incredulous wonder," Miss Havisham "seemed all resolved into a ghastly stare of pity and remorse." The
next time Pip visits her, after Estella has been married, Miss Havisham
abases herself, begs his forgiveness, and cries out "twenty, fifty times
over, What had she done!" (49).

Pip willingly forgives Miss Havisham as, "compassionating her," he
likewise sees in her the mirror of *his* own misery, and he absolves her of
responsibility for his (though not Estella's) unhappiness by claiming—
quite wrongly, to my mind—that he "should have loved . . . [Estella]
under any circumstances."[20]

The question of who really *is* Pip's creator is thus very complex. The
analogy with Frankenstein is complicated by the doubling of Miss Havisham and Magwitch, and even Magwitch's role as creator is qualified by
the fact that before there was Pip the gentleman there was Pip "the
small bundle of shivers . . . beginning to cry" as he tries to apprehend
"the identity of things" and to infer the character and even likeness of
his dead parents from the inscriptions on their tombstones on that one
"memorable raw afternoon towards evening" with which the novel
begins (1). Indeed, the very first fact we learn about Pip is that—like
Peepy in *Bleak House* (4)—he is self-named.[21] Magwitch, indeed,
endorses this act of self-creation by making it a condition of Pip's expectations that Pip "always bear the name of Pip" (18); so Philip Pirrip
becomes Pip Pirrip (and possibly Pip Gargery), but finally (and legally)
Mr. Philip Pip.

Pip's plot begins actually to move when he not only provides Magwitch with food and drink but takes pity on him as well, for "fearful" as
the convict is, he is also "lamed by stones, and cut by flints, and stung
by nettles, and torn by briars" (1). "Pitying his desolation, and watching
him as he gradually settled down upon the pie," Pip writes, "I made
bold to say, 'I am glad you enjoy it' " (3). This happens on Christmas
day, no less, but the Christ evoked is not the miracle-working resurrectionist of *A Tale of Two Cities;*[22] it is instead Christ the human sufferer

and comforter (and Pip's pitying Magwitch here also of course looks forward to his pitying Miss Havisham much later on). As Joe says to Magwitch just after his arrest, "We don't know what you have done, but we
wouldn't have you starved to death for it, poor miserable fellow-crea-
tur.—Would us, Pip?" (5).

Thus the origin of Pip's fortunes is an act of charity. But while charity
(like happiness) remains here as everywhere in Dickens a matter of the
familiar domestic comforts and pleasures, even these turn out to be
exceedingly rare commodities in this, one of Dickens's least comfortable
works. Wemmick's home may qualify as truly cozy: having all the trappings of a fort—complete with miniature cannon, drawbridge, and
moat—it is a comic and quaint realization of the maxim (enshrined in
English common law) that a man's home is his castle. Its owner is likewise the perfect realization of the separation of private and public
spheres, for not only his sentiments but his very body alters as he moves
between his Walworth home and Jaggers's office. If Wemmick's Castle
epitomizes comfort, it also proclaims comfort's fundamental alienation
from the world of the novel, however. Joe's forge may likewise be an
embodiment of domestic pleasure, at least in the end, after Joe's sister
has died and Joe has married Biddy. But of course this is a hearth from
which Pip is excluded, except occasionally to look in avuncularly upon
his own double in the form of Joe and Biddy's little boy, also named Pip.

The (revised) ending of *Great Expectations* evokes the end of *Paradise Lost,*
for Pip takes Estella's hand in his and, like Adam and Eve, they walk out
of the ruined garden (59). However one chooses to read Pip's telling us
that he "saw no shadow of another parting from her," therefore (that is,
whether he sees no shadow because they simply never part again,[23] or he
sees no shadow because, true to character, he just doesn't see into the
future very well, or he sees no shadow because, immediately upon leaving the garden, they *do* part for real and good, and so there is no shadow
to be seen beyond that), in any case the ending clearly registers a fall.
Treated "most cruelly" by her husband, Bentley Drummle, separated
and then widowed, Estella tells Pip (in all versions, though in slightly
different words) that "suffering has been stronger than all other teaching, and has taught me to understand what your heart used to be," and
it is the fact and teaching and self-consciousness of suffering that are
undeniably the novel's legacies.

But how different is Dickens's next (and last completed novel), *Our
Mutual Friend,* in spite of its being more thoroughly steeped in death

than any other of his works; indeed, it begins with Gaffer Hexam, a
"waterside character" (1.12), and his daughter Lizzie in a rowboat on the
Thames one evening, dragging the river for dead bodies and whatever
wealth they may have on them. (The unfinished *The Mystery of Edwin
Drood* might have vied for this morbid honor, but Dickens's own sudden
death when it was exactly half finished forever leaves us guessing on this
score as on so many others[24]). Indeed, *Our Mutual Friend* closes on the
note of death as well, for in his "Postscript in Lieu of Preface," Dickens
concludes by briefly recounting that a portion of the novel's manuscript
was with him in his carriage during the spectacular and terrifying railway
accident at Staplehurst (discussed in chapter 3 in connection with Dickens's having had also with him in the carriage Nelly Ternan), and he adds
an odd thought: "I remember with devout thankfulness that I can never
be much nearer parting company with my readers for ever, than I was
then, until there shall be written against my life, the two words with
which I have this day closed this book:—The End."[25]

Lots of people die in earlier novels, of course. *Bleak House* not only
kills off the brickmaker's baby, Captain Hawdon, Mr. Gridley, Mr.
Krook, Mr. Tulkinghorn, Jo, Lady Dedlock, and Richard Carstone, but
gives to each a proper death scene; it also narrates the deaths of Tom
Jarndyce and the Lady of Sir Morbury Dedlock and leaves us anticipat-
ing Mlle. Hortense's hanging. All but Sir Morbury's Lady (who becomes
the Ghost of the Ghost's Walk) stay dead, moreover. Fewer people die in
Our Mutual Friend, but nothing that dies here seems able to rest in
peace; resurrection and reanimation are virtually the norm, as is appropriate to a work so particularly interested in death by drowning, for
water is mythically as well as literally as much associated with birth (and
second births or rebirths) as with death. The very first body that Gaffer
Hexam pulls out of the river, he tells his daughter, is her "living" and
her "meat and drink," and it seems indeed a lively meal, for in being
towed behind his boat, it "lunged itself at him sometimes in an awful
manner when the boat was checked, and sometimes seemed to try to
wrench itself away, though for the most part it followed submissively. A
neophyte might have fancied that the ripples passing over it were dreadfully like faint changes of expression on a sightless face" (1). The body
also occasions a little philosophical exchange with Gaffer's rival, Rogue
Riderhood (who before drowning for good and all will nearly drown
himself later on and be the subject of a remarkable scene of resuscita-
tion), on the question whether a dead man can have money: "What
world does a dead man belong to? T'other world. What world does

money belong to? This world. How can money be a corpse's? Can a corpse own it, want it, spend it, claim it, miss it?" (1.1). But t'other world and this have a way of confusing one another in this novel, above and beyond the obvious fact that a corpse can, through the wonderful instrument of a *will*, indeed have money and spend it.[26]

Our Mutual Friend is in fact about a will, one written, moreover, by a man who is afraid of coming back to life, for he "directs himself to be buried with certain eccentric ceremonies and precautions against his coming to life" (1.2). No fool he. His son John Harmon is by its terms to inherit his father's fortune, consisting of several mounds of rubbish and "upwards of one hundred thousand pounds" in cash (1.8), accumulated by old Harmon in his business as a dust (i.e., trash) contractor, for fortunes may be made among the things that people throw away. But his father has attached a perverse stipulation: that John—who has left the country and started his own small business in distant parts after a serious quarrel with his father—marry Bella Wilfer, a young woman whom his father had seen but once one Sunday morning in the street, when she was only four or five, throwing a tantrum and pummeling her own father because he wouldn't go the exact way she wanted. John's aversion to marrying merely for money sets his plot in motion. He intends to reenter the country and scout his prospective bride in disguise before deciding how to proceed, but thanks to an incredibly complex and improbable series of events involving a man he has met during his crossing—and who happens to resemble him (shades of Sidney Carton and Charles Darnay)—no sooner does he arrive than he is drugged, robbed, and almost murdered by drowning in the Thames. But he survives, while the double who has assumed his clothing drowns, and his double's body is naturally presumed to be his, thus allowing Harmon to assume a whole new identity (as John Rokesmith) and prove the worth of not only Bella but the Boffins, the faithful Harmon servants who have inherited the Harmon estate after John is declared dead. Not even the wills stay dead, however, for new ones keep turning up in the dust mounds, and their burials and discoveries propel several of the novel's many plots.

Indeed, *Our Mutual Friend* has more plots than any of Dickens's works and is unique in having two main love plots that are themselves barely connected, for in addition to the John and Bella plot there is the plot of Lizzie Hexam and her lover, the indolent gentleman and barrister Eugene Wrayburn (whose circle embraces a large number of important characters and their subplots—the Veneerings, Podsnaps, Lammles, Mr.

Twemlow, and Lady Tippins). Almost the only noncoincidental connection between these main plots is Eugene's friend Mortimer Lightwood—another indolent lawyer whose only client is the Boffins and through whom Eugene happens to encounter Lizzie early on in the aftermath of John Harmon's supposed drowning, for it is her father who discovers the body and seeks Mortimer out (because he has found on the body a note with Mortimer's name upon it); Eugene idly accompanies his friend on this waterside excursion and thus meets Lizzie, whom he at first seeks merely to educate after her father drowns, but then pursues and protects after she is pursued in turn by Bradley Headstone, a teacher with whom her selfish brother Charlie (shades of Louisa and Tom Gradgrind) is in training as a pupil-teacher and who, like Eugene, becomes enthralled by her. Bradley's hatred of his rival leads to his nearly drowning Eugene after mauling him at the river's edge, but Lizzie rescues Eugene, and Bradley is himself shortly thereafter locked in a struggle (with Lizzie's father's old partner, Rogue Riderhood, who has through his knowledge of Bradley's attack on Eugene been blackmailing him) in which both men drown.

The clearly symbolic dust mounds that dominate the cityscape of *Our Mutual Friend,* like the mud and fog of *Bleak House* or the prisons of *Little Dorrit,* have generally been taken as indicative of the novel's dark modernity. If Dickens's satires on the law and bureaucracy look forward to Kafka,[27] *Our Mutual Friend* surely looks forward to T. S. Eliot and "The Wasteland."[28] But without in any way denying the novel's continuing modernity, we need also to note how different the ethos of Dickens's novel is from that of Eliot's poem. Just as nothing dead in this novel seems to be able to stay dead, so nothing thrown away stays thrown away. The whole point about the dust mounds, in fact, is that they are not a desert but a treasure.[29] We nowadays are proud of ourselves for recycling a fraction of what we dispose of; the Victorians had no such word as *recycling,* perhaps because they recycled *everything* as a mere matter of course.

In his great work *London Labour and the London Poor,* Henry Mayhew includes a chapter, "Of the Street-Finders or Collectors," in which he details a fantastic array of nightmen, scavengers, bone-grubbers, rag-gatherers, sweeps, cigar-end finders, wood-gatherers, dredgers, sewer-hunters, and mud-larks.[30] A typical subgroup of such collectors are the "pure-finders," who collected dogs' dung, chiefly for use in the tanning and dressing of leather (as for example—and notably—in the binding of books). Dogs' dung was sufficiently valuable, indeed, that enterprising collectors actually found ways to adulterate it (with ground-up mortar). Mayhew estimates between two and three hundred Londoners solely engaged in this one occupation (2:142).

Among the more unusual of *Our Mutual Friend*'s not-to-be-wasted commodities is the amputated leg of Silas Wegg, street seller of ballads, fruits, and candies (and himself a figure who might have walked out of Mayhew's volumes). This has been purchased by Mr. Venus, a taxidermist and "Articulator of human bones," which, because of a peculiar twist in the bone, has proved difficult to work into the miscellaneously assembled skeletons that are Venus's stock in trade, and as a result becomes the subject of a remarkable negotiation between its original and current owners:

> "Where am I?" asks Mr. Wegg.
>
> "You're somewhere in the back shop across the yard, sir; and speaking quite candidly, I wish I'd never bought you of the Hospital Porter."
>
> "Now, look here, what did you give for me?"
>
> "Well," replies Venus, blowing his tea: his head and face peering out of the darkness, over the smoke of it, as if he were modernizing the old original rise in his family: "you were one of a warious lot, and I don't know."
>
> Silas puts his point in the improved form of "What will you take for me?"
>
> "Well," replies Venus, still blowing his tea, "I'm not prepared, at a moment's notice, to tell you, Mr. Wegg."
>
> "Come! According to your own account I'm not worth much," Wegg reasons persuasively.
>
> "Not for miscellaneous working in, I grant you, Mr. Wegg; but you might turn out valuable yet, as a—" here Mr. Venus takes a gulp of tea, so hot that it makes him choke, and sets his weak eyes watering; "as a Monstrosity, if you'll excuse me."
>
> Repressing an indignant look, indicative of anything but a disposition to excuse him, Silas pursues his point. . . . "I have a prospect of getting on in life and elevating myself by my own independent exertions," says Wegg, feelingly, "and I shouldn't like—I tell you openly I should not like—under such circumstances, to be what I may call dispersed, a part of me here, and a part of me there, but should wish to collect myself like a genteel person."
>
> "It's a prospect at present, is it, Mr. Wegg? Then you haven't got the money for a deal about you? Then I'll tell you what I'll do with you; I'll hold you over. I am a man of my word, and you needn't be afraid of my disposing of you. I'll hold you over. That's a promise." (1.7)

Wegg may have nothing remotely transcendent about him beyond his leg's continuing life as a valuable commodity,[31] but, true to his name, Mr. Venus is an idealist and lover, the object of whose affections is Pleasant, daughter of Rogue Riderhood. Pleasant, however, objects to the business, and initially rejects Venus's proposal:

> "She knows the profits of it, but she don't appreciate the art of it, and she objects to it. 'I do not wish,' she writes in her own handwriting, 'to regard myself, nor yet to be regarded, in that bony light.' " (1.7)

The power of his art is quite real, however (and he wins Pleasant in the end), and when he declares of one of his stuffed specimens—a stuffed canary—"There's animation! On a twig, making up his mind to hop!" (1.7), we doubt neither his skill nor the transforming imagination that underlies it.

Imagination, indeed, is as central a theme here as in any of the later works and as much tied up with romance, romantic love, make-believe, and fictions as it was in *Hard Times* or *Little Dorrit*. And while it is here not nearly so dangerous or beyond control as in *Great Expectations,* it remains problematic. Among the novel's prime imaginers is Jenny Wren, a crippled doll's dressmaker of no more than 12 or 13 who befriends and protects Lizzie (who is herself no mean imaginer), and who is, like Pip, self-named (her real name is Fanny Cleaver). She pretends that her drunken father is her child, and that the dolls whose clothes she makes and mends are real, and that she will marry one day as a sort of bothersome social duty, and that she will be hard upon her husband, for "no intentions were stronger in her breast than the various trials and torments that were, in the fulness of time, to be inflicted upon 'him' "—whoever he might turn out to be (2.2).[32] Most strangely, she pretends that the little garden her friend Riah has built on his housetop is heaven, and she calls down to him as he mounts the stairs "out of a Glory of her long bright radiant hair, . . . like a vision: 'Come up and be dead! Come up and be dead!' " (2.5).

The most extended imagining in the novel, however, involves its most controversial turn of plot and Dickens's final "pious fraud" (4.13). This is Mr. Boffin's elaborate masquerade, part of a conspiracy entered into with his wife and young John Harmon after Mrs. Boffin recognizes that John Rokesmith, the young man her husband has hired as his private secretary, actually is Harmon. Boffin's pretense is that in his newfound wealth he has become a miser. The point of the deception is to prove that the petulant and spoiled, but also charming (more *for* her temper than in spite of it) Bella, who has come to live with the Boffins to benefit from the wealth they have inherited in her place, is not the mercenary creature she presents herself (even to herself) as being, that she is rather "the true golden gold at heart" (4.13). (Among her very first declarations in the novel had been that "I love money, and want money—want it dreadfully" [1.4].) It is Boffin's pretended miserliness and concomitant wretched treatment of Harmon that finally elicits Bella's love for Harmon and proves that her love for him is far stronger than her love of money. What has made the fraud especially troubling for readers is that it is so extended (it covers almost half the novel, beginning in number 12) and is enacted as much on them as on Bella, for until Boffin reveals his deception, readers really have no reason to suspect that his deteriorating character is anything but genuine, so plausible is his performance. Edwin Eigner likens the fraud to the ornate deceptions and artifices of the late Shakespeare romances, and there is indeed a striking mingling at once of magic and fallenness about Boffin's masquerade.[33] This is in my view no error on Dickens's part but a self-conscious, postromantic gesture that accepts and even revels in the artifice of its own magic.[34]

The feeling is really quite different from anything we have seen in early Dickens—even though several critics, beginning with Chesterton, find here "a happy return to the earlier manner of Dickens at the end of Dickens's life" (Chesterton 1911, 207). The happiness is indeed here: Lizzie and the badly battered Eugene marry, as do Bella and John; Jenny, we are led to believe, has found her "him" in the form of Sloppy, and Mr. Venus wins his Pleasant when he promises to confine himself "to the articulation of men, children, and the lower animals . . . [to] relieve the lady's mind of her feeling respecting being—as a lady— regarded in a bony light" (4.14). The novel ends, indeed, on the word "gaily." But its happiness is nonetheless muted by its consciousness of a fall, and it cannot entirely shake off its dust nor step outside the circle of its bony light.

But muted, too, if not quite absent, are the conflicts between sentiment and skepticism and domesticity and dirt that we saw dominating the first two-thirds of Dickens's career. Dickens at the end of his life, that is, is notably neither so given to the extremes of sentimentality and harsh doubt that we find, for example, in *Oliver* or *The Old Curiosity Shop,* nor so worried about controlling or even just tidying up the realm of the domestic as he has been in *Dombey* or *Bleak House.* The brutal joking of

Bob Sawyer about dissection and appetite or the ghoulishness of the interpolated tales in *Pickwick* outdo anything in *Our Mutual Friend.* The man in the *Shop* who can point to "a kind of bundle on the ground" and bluntly declare: "That's a dead child. . . . That is my third dead child, and last" simply has no place in the late Dickens, where a body is always more than meat. If, following Mary Douglas's relativizing definition, dirt is matter out of place, by the time of *Our Mutual Friend* Dickens has come to realize that everything indeed does have its place—and therefore its value. Putting things in their proper places of course is what discipline and cleaning are all about, but by the end of his life Dickens's idea of what constitutes the "proper" has itself relaxed, and he is far more willing to allow that perhaps he does not himself know where all the proper places are and that things will in any case and on their own find them.

Chapter Seven

Conclusion: Dickens and the Middle Class

After seeing Eugene and Lizzie happily married and Eugene's firmly deciding not to "sneak away with her, as if I were ashamed of her" to "one of the colonies" (4.16), *Our Mutual Friend* ends with a brief chapter that reassembles the circle in which we first met Mortimer and Eugene. Mortimer goes to a Veneering dinner party to listen to "The Voice of Society" (as the chapter is titled) and its opinion of the marriage. Predictably, that opinion is not favorable. "Society" here, as in *Little Dorrit*, is powerful but quintessentially inauthentic—indeed the aptly named Veneerings themselves are not merely *nouveau riche* but actual frauds, who, we are told, will "make a resounding smash next week" (4.17). "Society" is offended that a gentleman has married a waterman's daughter who has worked in a paper mill and who, most damagingly, has no money. Yet there is at the dinner table one dissenting voice, that of the ordinarily mild-mannered Twemlow, who would, by virtue of his kinship with a Lord, be old money—if he had any to speak of. On the question of the marriage, he expresses the view, "rather less mildly than usual," that it is really none of society's business, being "a question of the feelings of a gentleman." And when pressed, he adds:

> if such feelings [of gratitude, of respect, of admiration, and affection] on the part of this gentleman, induced this gentleman to marry this lady, I think he is the greater gentleman for the action, and makes her the greater lady. I beg to say, that when I use the word, gentleman, I use it in the sense in which the degree may be attained by any man.

The sense in which "the degree may be attained by any man" poses, however, something of a puzzle (as would the related but unposed question of whether there is a similar sense in which any woman can become a "lady.")[1] Comforting though it may be, the logic of Twemlow's thought is puzzling too.

What seems to be going on here is that through Twemlow Dickens is standing up for true love and social equality against arbitrary class divisions, and he is ironically using a gentleman of the old school, so to speak, to stand up for the new. Would that it were so simple. There is actually no reason for a gentleman of the old school under these circumstances to wax egalitarian, however, for a gentleman would under *any* circumstances have raised the woman he married to his rank—however unwise the match might have been from the dynastic point of view— whereas a lady would lower her own station by marrying her inferior.[2] There is also no question in Eugene's case of *his* being anything *but* a gentleman (and of the old school), and indeed he has done hardly anything of merit, being in all things—including his fascination with Lizzie—a classic example of the idleness of the rich. So there is something incongruous and even superfluous in Twemlow's remark.

He nevertheless *expresses* an egalitarianism that assumes that status is something people can achieve, and that assumes in turn a shift from a rank-based model of society in which one's station depends entirely on birth and the "real" property that comes (in theory by inheritance) with it (land, which establishes one's literal stake and ownership in the country itself) to a modern class-based model in which status depends on wealth of any kind (including Wemmick's "guiding-star . . . portable property" [*Great Expectations,* 24] or just plain cash) and the virtue or merit that in theory have been, are, or will be rewarded and signaled by worldly success. That such a shift was occurring and that Victorians of the middle and upper classes, at least, were acutely aware of it—some of them excited, some of them appalled—there can be no doubt, though it hardly began or ended with them, and though both models of society are *merely* models—fictions that have never been more than partially realized. It is a shift that of course has profound consequences for people's experience or subjectivity, that reflects or reverberates with shifts in our largest conceptions of authenticity and authority—religious as well as political and social—and that energizes and informs the tensions we have been tracing throughout this study.

The shift, however, is less radical than the respective theories or ideologies suggest, for the distinction between the arbitrary accident of birth on the one hand and innate individual worth on the other is never neat in practice.[3] Nobles are never as old as the hills in reality, of course, but always have a history that goes back to some act—typically of smashing and grabbing, whether performed on their own behalf or that of someone more highly placed—that got them their rank, which rank they would be most likely to justify not on the basis of their smashing and grabbing, of course, but by claiming some wonderful ancestry and some innately wonderful blood. Thus words like "kindness," "gentleness," and "breeding" that originally denote simply a certain kinship come to assume desirable moral qualities as well, and ones not at all associated with smashing and grabbing, but on the contrary with playing by the rules.

Such words are not really ambiguous or equivocal, but rather they moralize kinship or, in the case of "breeding," assert an identity between nature (birth) and nurture (upbringing), though it is just such an association that the shift from an aristocracy to a meritocracy tries not entirely successfully to break down. Throughout the nineteenth century, and certainly throughout Dickens's career, those on the rise remain enamored of a certain aesthetic and ethos they associate with gentility, even as they may believe themselves to see through such superficialities, like Pip, or, indeed, like Dickens himself, who for all his satire against pretension adopted what he pompously claimed—and without any good reason, it appears—to be "my father's crest: a lion couchant, bearing in his dexter paw a Maltese cross" (Johnson, 1.1). Even that "Bully of humility" Mr. Bounderby (*Hard Times,* 1.4), who boasts about the wretchedness of his own upbringing (entirely falsely, as it happens), is not free of a hankering to attach himself to the genteel, and he employs the poor gentlewoman Mrs. Sparsit as his housekeeper so that, like Magwitch, he can be the owner and exhibitor of such: "Just as it belonged to his boastfulness to depreciate his own extraction, so it belonged to it to exalt Mrs. Sparsit's" (1.7).

G. K. Chesterton notes that the alliance of manners between aristocracy and middle class and their mutual regard for respectability was peculiarly strong in England and that it was a factor in saving England from the more violent class conflicts that occurred on the Continent, for what he called "the Victorian Compromise" extended from manners to politics, and therefore "the most important event in English history was the event that never happened at all—the English Revolution along the lines of the French Revolution."[4] However we judge the rights and wrongs of that compromise, we probably (with Dickens) look down on Joe for his idealization of the blacking factory, and we smile at Pip as he puts his knife in his mouth while eating or tries to stuff his napkin in his glass. We admire Herbert for his (natural?) delicacy in tutoring Pip in table manners ("It is scarcely worth mentioning, only it's as well to do as other people do" [22]), and in uncritical moments like to think, perhaps, that our manners are what they are not merely for conformity's sake, but because they express something about our veritable selves.

There are other aspects of the shift associated with the decline of aristocracy and concomitant rise of the middle class, however, that bespeak
a more genuinely progressive story—or at least a more decided
change—that is important for an understanding of Dickens and the
novel more generally. Aristocracy implies a system of fixed social "sta-
tions" and a hierarchy based on obedience—the so-called "great chain of
being" that has God at its top and the beasts at the bottom. Under this
regime, we obey our betters simply because it is ordained that they *are*
our betters, and likewise we command those below us because they *are*
inferior. Movement up or down the scale is in theory simply not possible, for the difference between a peasant and a noble is as deep as that
between a peasant and his pig; beings at every level are qualitatively different from those above and below—at least in this life, if not the next
(for in Christianity there are certainly sown the seeds of an egalitarianism among souls, even if from the Middle Ages on Christianity comfort-
ably adapted itself to a rank-based hierarchy). Obedience goes hand in
hand with responsibility as well, so that those we command also look to
us for protection and life's necessities. However harsh one's lot, there is
at least the security of knowing one's place, which means having a fixed
and inalienable identity as a birthright, however high or low. Loss of this
security turns out to be an important price paid for entry into the middle class.

    In order for the chain to come undone, there has first of all to be a
skeptical questioning of the authority that defines the order and with it
a questioning of the idea of authority itself. Not for nothing is the rise of
the middle class associated with Protestantism and the great questioning of authority that occurred with the Reformation.[5] While many
Protestants would protest the notion that their beliefs are any less mindful of the absolute authority of the deity than are Roman Catholics'—
indeed, authoritarian strains have evolved in some varieties of Protestantism that can easily compete with any authoritarian shows the
Roman Catholic Church has been able to put on—nevertheless there has
been a clear break in the chain when the most humble are encouraged to
encounter the word of God directly for themselves by reading scripture
in their everyday language without the guidance of the priesthood and
when the unity of the church and power of the church itself to speak
infallibly are denied.[6] Far more subversive questionings of authority and
even of God's existence of course characterize the Enlightenment and
late-eighteenth-century political thought, and we discussed some of
these in chapter 4. They are apparent in the French and American revo-

lutions in varying degrees,[7] as well as in the more gradual and steady decline of royal and aristocratic power in England that had its own dramatic moments nevertheless, for example, in the Civil Wars, the "Glorious Revolution" of 1688, and the passage of the first Reform Bill in 1832. And they are apparent in the questionings of the "natural" superiority of males over females in writers like Bentham and Mary Wollstonecraft in the eighteenth century and a growing band of feminist writers in the nineteenth.

The importance for the novel of the great social shift that we may call for brevity's sake "the rise of the middle class" has long been recognized and can hardly be overemphasized—indeed the birth of the modern novel is now conventionally assumed to depend upon it following the classic account by Ian Watt in *The Rise of the Novel*.[8] The middle class plays a central role in developing new relations between public and private or domestic realms (in which novels are read and largely take place) and in developing new genres of writing that are absorbed by the novel: newspapers, letters and journals, books of travel, legal evidence and forms of testimony, even scientific and philosophical argument. But no less important than these formal developments associated with realism are a few fundamental psychological consequences of the break in the chain that allows in turn for the social mobility upon which the rise of the middle class depends.

In a rank-based society, one's place is in theory fixed. The bad news is that no move up the ladder to a higher rung is (again in theory) possible; the good news is that no real fall is possible either. Once status comes to depend on individual merit and the wealth that merit can earn, however, the ladder becomes scalable. The good news now is the possibility of going from rags to riches; the bad news is the possibility of going from riches to rags. Thus a simple but painful corollary of social mobility is a radical and continual social insecurity. And it is an insecurity not merely about money, of course, for in modern society not just status but even identity is tied to wealth. The shift that makes possible the rise of the middle class makes possible therefore a new kind of self-creation and a new kind of self-annihilation. And an equally far-reaching consequence of the ladder's scalability is that it requires not only that we think about ourselves in a new way but that we think about others in a new way as well.

Under the old hierarchy, beings above and below us are qualitatively different. Thus when Henry VIII looks to the servant bringing him another roast fowl to tear into, he may see merely an animated instrument, one rather less interesting than his upcoming meal. Under the new, when I look to the waiter bringing me my *cappuccino*, it may occur to me to think that here is someone who may be up for an Oscar in another few years. And heaven knows what is going through his mind about me. I do not mean to claim that Henry VIII could not put himself imaginatively in his servant's place, nor pretend that I do a very good job of imagining myself in the place of all the various people I casually encounter. We have already observed that Christianity opens (as, indeed, arguably do all the world's great religions) on some level an ethically egalitarian space for all people—the Golden Rule provides the clearest example—and we have at the same time daily evidence of contemporary humanity's capacity to deny the humanity of others in the most brutal fashion. But I do mean to point out that such imaginative identifications across classes (and genders, which are of course a kind of class) are not called for by anything essential to Henry's worldview, while their contemporary denial is for those of us living under the regime of the middle class just that—a denial: something active and itself transgressive, something we need to work at.

That Dickens was well aware of this feature of the psychology of the middle class is evident in his portrait of Mr. Podsnap (based, it is said, on his friend John Forster), who refuses to acknowledge anything unpleasant on his horizon, whether it be the existence of poor people being starved to death or the existence of foreign nations and other ways of governing; he is in this respect the perfect embodiment of the Victorian middle class's expertise in the art of denial:

> "I don't want to know about it; I don't choose to discuss it; I don't admit it!" Mr Podsnap had even acquired a peculiar flourish of his right arm in often clearing the world of its most difficult problems, by sweeping them behind him (and consequently sheer away) with those words and a flushed face. For they affronted him. (*Our Mutual Friend*, 1.11)

And the fact of such middle-class denial is evident too when the third-person omniscient narrator of *Bleak House* feels the need to invite us to enter the head of Jo the crossing sweeper—or at least to reflect upon what that "must" be like:

> It must be a strange state to be like Jo! To shuffle through the streets, unfamiliar with the shapes, and in utter darkness as to the meaning, of those mysterious symbols, so abundant over the shops, and at the corners of streets, and on the doors, and in the windows! To see people read, and

to see people write, and to see the postmen deliver letters, and not to
have the least idea of all that language—to be, to every scrap of it, stone
blind and dumb! It must be very puzzling to see the good company
going to the churches on Sundays, with their books in their hands, and to
think (for perhaps Jo *does* think, at odd times) what does it all mean, and
if it means anything to anybody, how comes it that it means nothing to
me? To be hustled, and jostled, and moved on; and really to feel that it
would appear to be perfectly true that I have no business, here, or there,
or anywhere; and yet to be perplexed by the consideration that I *am* here,
somehow, too, and everybody overlooked me until I became the creature
that I am! It must be a strange state, not merely to be told that I am
scarcely human . . . , but to feel it of my own knowledge all my life! To
see the horses, dogs, and cattle, go by me, and to know that in ignorance
I belong to them, and not to the superior beings in my shape, whose delicacy I offend! Jo's ideas of a Criminal Trial, or a Judge, or a Bishop, or a
Government, or that inestimable jewel to him (if he only knew it) the
Constitution, should be strange! His whole material and immaterial life
is wonderfully strange; his death, the strangest thing of all. (16)

There but for the grace of God go we; but there, thanks to the narrator,
do we go, at least in imagination. The narrator here in effect subscribes
and invites us to subscribe to Esther Summerson's belief that charity
entails "the art of adapting . . . [one's] mind to minds very differently
situated" (8), even as he acknowledges that such an identification can
only be imaginary, and his gesture reinforces my earlier claim that the
novel itself is designed to be a literal instrument of sympathy. Such a
conception, I am arguing, is essential to the novel's status as a peculiarly
middle-class phenomenon. The narrator here not only follows Esther's
advice, but makes a move natural to, indeed, inevitable in, the ethos of
the middle class.[9]

Compassion (or at least identification) on the one hand, and insecurity on the other. These are twin legacies of the rise of the middle class.
In the case of Jo, insecurity is hardly an issue, however: he has no place
to fall to and no chance of rising; his situation, indeed, defines the
absolute and immobile bottom-most margin. He is immobile not
merely because he is not himself of the middle class, for of course the rise
of the middle class assumes that those beneath can enter the middle
class under the right circumstances. What is wrong about Jo's circumstances, what makes him what we would nowadays call "underclass," is
that he is uneducated, and his immobility (ironic, given the desire of the
police always to move him on) is a function specifically of his illiteracy,

which also cuts him off from the possibility of imaginative identifications of the sort that novels asks us to make, as well, more simply, as
make the literate to him as irredeemably other as he would be to them
without the novelist's help. The omniscient narrator can, after all, without difficulty get into any head *except* the unlettered, whose consciousness is so fundamentally different as to be as alien as that of "the horses,
dogs, and cattle."

This self-conscious stopping short of directly entering Jo's consciousness—while at the same time inviting the reader to imagine it along
with the narrator—is more a strategic move on Dickens's part than a
reflection of any real epistemological difficulty. It may indeed be hard to
imagine what the experiences of people without language "must" be
like, but we can be reminded of what illiteracy *is* like just by having a
glance at texts written in unfamiliar alphabets. Nevertheless, Dickens
significantly puts the crucial barrier to identification at literacy, and this
is appropriate to his conviction that literacy is the ticket to respectability.[10] Education is the *sine qua non* for Lady Dedlock's maid Rosa's marriage to Watt Rouncewell, whose father has educated his own children
so as to be "worthy of any station" (*Bleak House,* 28), and Esther's teaching her maid Charley her letters—or at least trying to—likewise prepares her for a match with a miller who is "well to do" (67). Eugene
Wrayburn's plan to educate Lizzie Hexam and the rival plan of Bradley
Headstone signal their matrimonial intentions (in Eugene's case, long
before he is himself aware of just how respectable they are). Charley
Hexam—"Charley" is with Dickens an obvious choice for names when
literacy is in question—learns to read at his sister's urging and in rebellion against a father who hates and fears learning; his literacy opens up
the possibility of his escaping the life of a "waterside character" (*Our
Mutual Friend,* 1.12) and becoming respectable—and also occasions
Dickens's arresting comment that "No one who can read, ever looks at a
book, even unopened on a shelf, like one who cannot" (1.3), a thought
that, like his excursus on Jo, associates literacy with something far
deeper than merely practical skill or, to use a favorite Victorian phrase,
"useful knowledge."[11]

We may remember that it was the interruption of his education that
was as dispiriting to the young Dickens when he was sent to work at
Warren's Blacking as his having to associate there with working-class
men and boys. Dickens had found it "wonderful" that

> no one had compassion enough on me—a child of singular abilities,
> quick, eager . . . —to suggest that something might have been spared, as

certainly it might have been, to place me at any common school. . . . My
father and mother were quite [as] satisfied . . . [as] if I had been twenty
years of age, distinguished at a grammar-school, and going to Cambridge. (Forster, 1.2)

Already (at least in Dickens's later recollection), learning was here effectively synonymous with respectability. Indeed, Dickens enjoyed "some
station" with his new companions at Warren's because his "conduct and
manners were different enough from theirs to place a space between
them," and perhaps this came about too because he "had made some
efforts to entertain them over our work with the results of some of the
old readings" that he had greedily pored over, "as if for life" (1.1), from
the inexpensive series of novels that was the heart of his father's small
collection of books, and that was among the first of the household goods
to be pawned when John Dickens was imprisoned for debt.

Novels themselves were, however, of dubious respectability in the
early nineteenth century. It is significant that Dickens's own early reading was so heavily invested in the eighteenth-century novelists (especially Defoe, Smollett, Fielding, Goldsmith), for a more genteel gram-
mar school and university education would very likely have served his
later craft less well. His taste in reading, moreover, is connected with his
own class origins, which were especially well suited to a writer destined
to embody and speak to the peculiar instabilities of the Victorian middle
class (and which in turn spoke to corresponding instabilities across the
globe). For Dickens was not born into the middle of the middle class, so
to speak—the solid middle-class world of Pecksniffs, Podsnaps, Gradgrinds, and Dombeys, for example; rather his origins, especially on his
father's side, were at once closer to and further from gentility.

Dickens's paternal grandparents were servants, though of an exalted
and special sort. His grandfather was steward and his mother housekeeper (rather like Mrs. Rouncewell) to Lord Crewe at Crewe Hall in
Cheshire. (His maternal grandfather was of higher status, having been
partner in a firm of musical instrument makers and later a civil servant,
whose son, also a civil servant, worked alongside John Dickens; he
escaped respectability, however, after he was discovered to have embez-
zled over £5,000 and fled to the Continent.)

Servants occupy positions of peculiar intimacy in the households in
which they serve at the same time, especially before the rise of the middle class, they exist across a great divide from those they serve. But as
head servants, stewards and housekeepers in a great eighteenth-century

house enjoyed a peculiar status, for they managed a considerable establishment and were highly trusted by the family. They necessarily understood all the complex protocols of aristocracy, and while of all servants they knew their proper place with exactness, that place put them daily in close contact with master and mistress and gave them unique access to the entire house. They also dealt with local tradesmen who supplied whatever provisions and goods the estate might not be able to produce on its own and had to be always alert to the possibility of their sharp practice. They not only managed but hired, fired, and disciplined the numerous servants under them, the housekeeper being responsible for the females and the steward or butler for the males. They would typically have, too, a measure of delegated authority over younger family members, poor relations, and the governess in any matters that might affect the smooth or economical functioning of the house. When anything went wrong, they would be the first to whom family and servants alike would look for guidance and explanation and to make things right.[12] Thus they were familiar with and comfortable in the company of persons of all classes, were privy to family secrets, were in themselves at the very top of a sort of aristocracy that closely paralleled that of their master and mistress, but had managerial responsibilities of a rather bourgeois flavor and would have on occasion to involve themselves in the doings of lowly scullery maids and stable boys. They necessarily assented absolutely to the traditional hierarchies but earned substantial enough wages (perhaps £50 a year, with no living expenses to worry about) to be able to save substantial sums (Elizabeth Dickens left an estate of £450 [Allen, 92]) and see their children rise through the civil service or such increasingly respectable careers as journalism (like John Dickens) or manufacture (like Mr. Rouncewell the Ironmaster, who winds up a factory owner). It is hardly an exaggeration to say that they performed a far wider range of functions and roles, embracing and penetrating a far broader social spectrum, than persons of almost any other occupation.

Dickens's father's father had been dead for more than 25 years when Dickens was born (indeed, his own father was probably, like David Copperfield, a posthumous child); his father's mother, however, lived until Charles was 12 (she died while Dickens's father was imprisoned for debt), and she spent her last years in London. Charles certainly spent some time in her company, and she was by all accounts a great storyteller,[13] but the influence that his father's parents' lives as servants of this special kind had on him in all likelihood was less direct and impressed upon him more deeply through his father's attitudes towards class, inflected, of course, by the agonies prompted by the pawnbrokers' shops, the debtor's prison, and the blacking factory. Perhaps something of Dickens's peculiar dandified tastes and social cockiness, his fondness for being at once impresario, actor, and spectator—his liking in short for what in chapter 3 we called aggressively "playing all the parts"—may be traced to this source, among many others.

Indeed, Dickens at the height of his career, when he was managing amateur theatricals at the Duke of Devonshire's London mansion, conducting *Household Words,* and superintending Miss Coutts's "Home for Homeless Women," looks a lot like a sort of frenetic steward and housekeeper rolled into one—which suggests yet another way of regarding the double narratives of *Bleak House,* composed at this same time: Esther quite literally *is* a housekeeper, of course, though of a more modest establishment than Mrs. Rouncewell's. Is it going too far to imagine the third-person omniscient narrator as a sort of superior, even supernatural, steward—especially as he guides us through the fashionable world? Earlier we connected the origin of *Bleak House* with the immediacy of Dickens's father's death; we can now see beyond it his more distant origins.

In the great scene in *Our Mutual Friend* that introduces the Veneerings and their circle, we meet a steward dubbed by the narrator "the Analytical Chemist" after his manner of "always seeming to say, after 'Chablis, sir?'—'You wouldn't if you knew what it's made of' " (1.2). About this figure G. K. Chesterton writes, with characteristic acuteness:

> Dickens was never more right than when he made the new people, the Veneerings, employ a butler who despised not only them but all their guests and acquaintances. The admirable person called the Analytical Chemist shows his perfection particularly in the fact that he regards all the sham gentlemen and all the real gentlemen with the same gloomy and incurable contempt. He offers wine to the offensive Podsnap or the shrieking Tippins with a melancholy sincerity and silence; but he offers his letter to the aristocratic and unconscious Mortimer with the same sincerity and with the same silence. It is a great pity that the Analytical Chemist only occurs in two or three scenes of this excellent story. As far as I know, he never really says a word from one end of the book to the other; but he is one of the best characters in Dickens. (Chesterton 1911, 213)

What makes him one of Dickens's best characters, in spite of his silence, is that the narrator does such a convincing job of playing him and speaking for him—or rather speaking what is supposed to be really on his mind. And while I would not want to claim that it is butlers and housekeepers that Dickens plays best, it does seem true that the particular mixture of intimacy and distance enjoyed by these heads of the household staff not only gives them privileged access to the domestic scenes they manage (Chesterton writes in the same place: "Servants, butlers, footmen, are the high priests who have the real dispensation; and even gentlemen are afraid of them"),[14] but that this complex and ambiguous relationship perfectly suits the Dickensian narrator or observer.

The narrator's simultaneous closeness and remoteness may remind us of that figure we met in chapter 1 that Dickens had imagined as the presiding spirit of *Household Words:* "a certain Shadow, which may go into any place, by sunlight, moonlight, starlight, firelight, candlelight, and be in all homes, and all nooks and corners, and be supposed to be cognisant of everything, and go everywhere, without the least difficulty," and that Dickens saw as "a kind of semi-omniscient, omnipresent, intangible creature" (Forster, 6.4). Or it may remind us of Inspector Bucket, who is both a public servant and employed as a private detective and who takes simultaneous deference and mastery to new extremes. Or it may remind us of the "good spirit" wished for by the narrator of *Dombey,* "who would take the house-tops off . . . and show a Christian people what dark shapes issue from amidst their homes . . . where Vice and Fever propagate" (47). Or it may remind us of the various ghosts of Christmas, who shepherd Scrooge through his past, present, and future lives, or, indeed, the narrator of *A Christmas Carol* itself, who disconcertingly explains to the reader just how close Scrooge was to his first ghostly visitor by writing that he was "as close to it as I am now to you, and I am standing in the spirit at your elbow" (2).[15]

Something of this mixture of familiarity and distance finds its way into the very style not just of the narrators but of "Dickensian" prose more generally. David Parker hits upon the happy term *archness,* which conveys a certain knowing and mischievous theatricality, to describe the distinctively *stylized* quality of Dickens's style[16]—or styles, we should say, rather, for it can hardly be said that Dickens possesses a single style, yet there is something distinctively Dickensian in all the many styles he deploys, whether based on the Bible and the Book of Common Prayer, newspapers, fairy tales, popular ballads, Shakespeare and melodrama, advertisements and business circulars, or the jargons of particular trades and professions or the slang of criminals and the streets.[17] And that something is a kind of verbal wink, a calling attention to oneself through some incongruity, exaggeration, or unconventional usage.[18] It is a kind of irony, most broadly conceived, though as is so often the case with Dickens's irony, it can be extraordinarily elusive and ambiguous.

The verbal winks we sense suggest to us perhaps Dickens himself peeking through his creations, with whom he but partially blends. Not only is his narrator in the spirit by our elbows but in the spirit by his characters' elbows as well. Or even closer, while still maintaining a critical distance. A stylistic technique that is typical of the relationship between his characters and his narrative voices has been usefully and extensively analyzed by Mark Lambert. It is what he calls the "suspended quotation," in which a character's words are interrupted by the narrator, who inserts a comment, a bit of mind reading, or a stage direction—as for example in " 'Miss Flite,' said Mr. Woodcourt, in a grave kind of voice, as if he were appealing to her while speaking to us; and laying his hand gently on her arm; 'Miss Flite describes her illness with unusual accuracy' " (*Bleak House*, 14). Lambert provocatively argues that Dickens's extensive use of this technique in fact reflects a general "hostility towards his own characters by an author who resents the special attractiveness those characters have for the audience. It is the resource of a jealous author."[19] This may put the case too boldly, but it does capture well the complexity of Dickens's relationships with his creations in pointing out that these are not purely a matter of love and that his creatures really do have lives of their own and a kind of autonomy or free will. A jealous author is perhaps not unlike a jealous god.

The striking tension between intimacy and distance that we have been discussing in regard to Dickens's relationships with his characters is evident too in the larger relationship of the Dickens narrator to the "world"—not just the world of people but the cosmos, the world of things most generally. When Dickens writes almost offhandedly at the end of the preface to *Bleak House* that he has "purposely dwelt upon the romantic side of familiar things," he places himself in a tradition that includes Wordsworth and Carlyle, each of whom is intent upon presenting "ordinary things . . . to the mind in an unusual aspect" (as Wordsworth puts it in the preface to the second edition of *Lyrical Ballads*). Dickens shares that intention, as well as Carlyle's belief that "Custom . . . doth make dotards of us all" in inuring us to the miraculous in daily life (*Sartor*, 259). As we have seen, Dickens also likes to take us a step further, beyond the wondrous to the positively uncanny, to a space in which we are not really sure if what we are encountering is actually something new and different or something old and familiar. The uncanny marks also a space in which public and private are liable to merge, as in that fascinating tableau we examined in *The Old Curiosity Shop,* in which Little Nell lies sleeping (or dead) surrounded by the grotesque wares of her grandfather's shop (or the gothic religious trappings of the ancient ruin in which she ends her life). Such weird mergings of public and private (I think also of Wemmick's Jekyll-and-Hyde–like transformation as he moves from Walworth to London) perhaps reflect too the impossibility of middle-class attempts to clearly separate public and private spheres.

I noted in chapter 2 that a kind of confusion so strong as itself to constitute an uncanny experience is often elicited by the experience of shame, and I am sure that Dickens's sensitivity to the uncanny was heightened in part by the bewildering psychological effects of his boyhood experiences at Warren's and the Marshalsea. John Dickens's upbringing gave him a keen sense of class, an evident ambition to rise above his parents' station, and—thanks to their prudence—the means to do so. Undoubtedly both that knowledge and that ambition were passed along to young Charles. John Dickens's improvidence, however, threw his family into circumstances very much worse than any his parents had known, circumstances that were shameful and entailed a real fall from respectability. For young Charles they seemed to preclude his ever realizing his "early hopes of growing up to be a learned and distinguished man" (Forster, 1.2). He felt himself almost to have been thrown away in the filthy, rat-infested waterside world of Warren's. The remembered shame of this time remained sufficiently intense to lead him to keep them hidden, as we have seen, from almost everybody, even while he could not himself leave them alone and continually made private reference to them (as well as more public if indirect reference in his conflicts surrounding domesticity and dirt). Respectability, shame, and secrecy are of course deeply connected, for what is respectable is literally what commands regard or can stand looking into, while the shameful is what cannot stand to be looked at, and an uncanny confusion associated with shame arises because what was supposed to have remained hidden is suddenly and newly brought into the open, revealed for all to see.

Thus in the Dickens legacy the ethos of the trusted servants with their privileged views of both the public and private aspects of aristocratic life—with a concomitant knowledge and power that inspire fear even in those whom the servant supposedly serves—degenerates into that of the little factory drudge whose father is in jail and whose identity is thereby radically compromised, even as he is literally put on display in the blacking factory's shop window, only to regenerate in the ambitious young man hungry for respectable, professional status as a writer and a gentleman and eager to display himself before his public while still holding fast to his shameful secret.

Dickens's peculiarly inward relationship with the middle class—which is to say his peculiarly rich understanding of the mobility and insecurity entailed by the rise and potential fallings of the middle class—can perhaps be best appreciated by briefly comparing him with his rival novelists. For if the novel is essentially a middle-class phenomenon, this is of course not to say that all novelists represent the middle class or reflect it in the same way. The novels of George Eliot (whose father was an estate manager and farmer) are very remote from the world of Dombeyism or Podsnappery, even though she is often interested in the solid and stolid as well as characters on the rise or ready for a fall. Her most intimate accounts are of the yeomanry and lesser country gentry, whose world was relatively somewhat more stable than that of the urban middle class. The Brontë sisters were daughters of the curate of a remote church on the Yorkshire moors (son of an Irish peasant farmer, he somehow learned his letters and opened his own little school when he was only 16; he was patronized by a prosperous clergyman who hired him to tutor his sons and then helped him gain admission to Cambridge). Their novels famously grew out of a series of long Byronic romances begun when they were children on which they collaborated with their brother, and they are full of noble and dashing heroes, complicated political intrigues, and a farrago of sensational topics drawn from the newspapers. But Charlotte's novels also reflect her training as a governess, and she fully exploits the figure of the governess in *Jane Eyre* and *Villette* and the ambiguities of the governess's position in ways that wonderfully bring out the kinds of insecurities we have been associating with the rise of the middle class. Thackeray and Trollope were both from any standpoint thoroughgoing gentlemen, though Thackeray's having lost his fortune when still quite a young man brought him into the not-quite-genteel journalistic and artistic circles in which Dickens was moving at the very beginning of his career (Thackeray was among those who applied to Dickens to illustrate *Pickwick* after Seymour shot himself), and *Vanity Fair* presents as good an example of the way in which the insecurities of the middle-class dominate mid-Victorian society as one could hope to find. Trollope is, among the novelists, perhaps uniquely untroubled about class controversies—as Robin Gilmour says, he is "much more at ease . . . with the idea of the gentleman than either Dickens or Thackeray (149)—though his peculiarly self-effacing brand of realism never fails to register the insecurities of his subjects.

Even Elizabeth Gaskell, a novelist much closer to Dickens in the general aims of her art (her *Mary Barton* sets forth a doctrine of sympathy across class lines that surely influenced *Bleak House* as much as *Jane Eyre* did), has a rather different sense than Dickens of not just the middle class, but the working class as well. As the wife of a Unitarian minister in the industrial city of Manchester, she was much better acquainted with the worlds of both the upper-middle-class factory owners (like Mr. Rouncewell or Mr. Bounderby) and the factory hands (like Stephen Blackpool, who may have found life "a' a muddle" chiefly because Dickens knew so little about what went on inside the heads of factory workers that it was easiest to put something of a blank there). She understood at least as well as Dickens the fact of social mobility and its attendant anxieties, and she could portray with rather more verisimilitude the actual details of the life of the poor (see, for example, her description of a workers' tea party in chapter 3 of *Mary Barton* or the death from fever of an impoverished worker in chapter 6) and the stories of those going from rags to riches and riches to rags—she appreciated that risings and fallings were generally made out of much less spectacular providential interventions and crashes than are common in Dickens.

Arguably—and the arguments began already to be made with the contemporary reviewers—each of these novelists commands a more thoughtfully "realistic" view of Victorian society and the interior life of individuals than does Dickens. They were all perfectly conscious of his preeminent popularity with the Victorian public (the earliest of their novels appeared 10 years after Dickens had burst upon the literary scene with *Pickwick*), and they self-consciously aspired to a greater fidelity to life and superior artistry, even if they did not actually declare themselves to be considered rivals (though Thackeray was not afraid to do just that, at least privately, when *Vanity Fair* was appearing simultaneously with *Dombey*). Yet Dickens's continuing popularity has given him, we might say, the last word, for as we noted at the very beginning of this study, he is as much the creator of his age and what we think of today when we think about the Victorian as a reflection or creation of it.

We have to put "realistic" in quotation marks, however, recognizing that language does not have access to the essential nature of things in the ways that the Victorians (and indeed ourselves) may have believed or at least wished for. Language may be true to itself, perhaps, but its representations of the real are, we like nowadays to say, necessarily all constructs. And here too Dickens may be said also to have had the last word, for his work troubles realism in ways that anticipate modernism and postmodernism. Not that he was himself consciously or theoretically troubled about realism, to be sure: his prefaces consistently make what seem today naïve claims for the accuracy of his representations against readers who complained about his exaggerations, and he was very probably unaware of just how transparently present his own personality was in everything he wrote, including the speech even of his most mannered characters. The journalism and public speeches likewise reveal Dickens at his most Podsnappish; he is there unmistakably philistine, and his allegiance to what Watt calls "formal realism" (32) is at the same time culturally conservative and eminently respectable. (How often when parents admonish their children to "be realistic" are they not at the same time urging them to "be respectable"?) Even in exceptional moments, when Dickens privately allows himself a measure of rebellion, the traces of Podsnappery are still apparent. He writes to Forster (15 August 1856) about the peculiar limitations placed upon English writers:

> I have always a fine feeling of the honest state into which we have got, when some smooth gentleman says to me or to some one else when I am by, how odd it is that the hero of an English book is always uninteresting—too good—not natural, &c. I am continually hearing this of Scott from English people here [in France], who pass their lives with Balzac and Sand. But O my smooth friend, what a shining impostor you must think yourself and what an ass you must think me, when you suppose that by putting a brazen face upon it you can blot out of my knowledge the fact that this same unnatural young gentleman (if to be decent is to be necessarily unnatural), whom you meet in those other books and in mine, must be presented to you in that unnatural aspect by reason of your morality, and is not to have, I will not say any of the indecencies you like, but not even any of the experiences, trials, perplexities, and confusions inseparable from the making or unmaking of all men! (Forster, 9.1)

Here Dickens at once accepts the "morality" of his public even as he chafes against it and cannot help but put in a good word for the naturalness of the "decent"—so that there is still room even within realistic fiction for heroes both respectable and "good."

Yet Dickens's fictions themselves do continually trouble the real in ways quite subtle and deep. The schoolmaster Mr. M'Choakumchild believes himself to be an expert in the real in his devotion to "Fact, fact, fact." He asks his class if they would carpet their rooms with "representations of flowers," and then asks Sissy Jupe, who, because she is "very fond of flowers," has answered yes, why she would do such a thing "and have people walking over them with heavy boots?" To which Sissy reasonably replies, "It wouldn't hurt them. . . . They wouldn't crush and wither. . . . They would be the pictures of what was very pretty and pleasant" (*Hard Times,* 1.2). It is the supposed realist here who turns out to have the simpleminded theory. Being a good realist in the Dickens world, as in the real world, requires an understanding of make-believe.

But it is the Dickens narrator who can most reliably be counted on to trouble the real, most characteristically through his uncanny animations of the inanimate. Here, the omniscient narrator prefigures Lady Dedlock's downfall simply through a description of the play of light from the setting sun as it falls upon the family portraits at Chesney Wold:

> Through some of the fiery windows, beautiful from without, and set, at this sunset hour, not in dull grey stone, but in a glorious house of gold, the light excluded at other windows pours in, rich, lavish, overflowing like the summer plenty in the land. Then do the frozen Dedlocks thaw. Strange movements come upon their features, as the shadows of leaves play there. A dense Justice in a corner is beguiled into a wink. A staring Baronet, with a truncheon, gets a dimple in his chin. Down into the bosom of a stony shepherdess there steals a fleck of light and warmth, that would have done it good, a hundred years ago. . . .
>
> But the fire of the sun is dying. Even now the floor is dusky, and shadow slowly mounts the walls, bringing the Dedlocks down like age and death. And now, upon my Lady's picture over the great chimney-piece, a weird shade falls from some old tree, that turns it pale, and flutters it, and looks as if a great arm held a veil or hood, watching an opportunity to draw it over her. Higher and darker rises shadow on the wall—now a red gloom on the ceiling—now the fire is out. (*Bleak House,* 40)

So emotionally charged do the merely natural phenomena of light appear here that this passage may strike us as an extreme example of what John Ruskin called "the pathetic fallacy"—the attributing of human emotions to merely natural phenomena. And yet it may be viewed at the same time as wonderfully realistic, rendered with an extremely clear vision that knows (and lets us, moreover, see perfectly well) the difference between what is really out there and what is purely in the mind's eye. These alternate visions are reflected in the long his-

tory of debate about whether Dickens is essentially a realist, a virtually
hallucinatory illusionist, or some combination of the two. (Critics frequently note how cinematic is the omniscient Dickens narrator, and it is
interesting to imagine this scene as it might be done on film. Apropos of
the debate about realism versus illusion, two versions suggest themselves. In one, the visuals might be straightforwardly realistic and would
be paired with a voice-over reading of the passage quoted; in the second,
there would be no commentary, and the special effects department
would be called on to produce in the portraits unambiguous winks, dim-
ples, and bosomy blushes as well as that great arm holding its veil or
hood. Can we say with assurance which treatment would be the more
faithful?)

We may seem to have drifted far from questions about class to questions
about style and narrative technique. But my (unoriginal) claim is precisely that the concerns and even techniques of the Victorian novel are
functions of the great social shifts associated with the rise of the middle
class. Beyond this I am asserting that the particular qualities we identify
as "Dickensian," moreover, are likewise heavily inflected by Dickens's
own class origins with their compound of intimacy with and distance
from the ways of the great world, as well of course as his famously hard
experiences in boyhood. The compassion and charity for which he is so
celebrated are, I believe, essential and inescapable psychological consequences of the necessary identifications people living under the regime
of the middle class make with one another and its attendant insecurities
about status (just as Marxist critics see the social conditions that cry out
for compassion and charity as equally essential material consequences of
the regime of the middle class). A large part of Dickens's achievement
may have been to understand and realize this more fully than his contemporaries, and in reflecting it so clearly also to realize it for them—
and for us.

Compassion and charity of course also have a clear lineage in Christianity. But Dickens, as I have at several points suggested, is ethically
actually closer to the Utilitarians than to the orthodox religious. This is
the conclusion too of John Ruskin in a famous judgment rendered
shortly after Dickens's death in a letter to Charles Eliot Norton:

> Dickens was a pure modernist—a leader of the steam-whistle party *par
> excellence*—and he had no understanding of any power of antiquity except
> a sort of jackdaw sentiment for cathedral towers. He knew nothing of the

nobler power of superstition—was essentially a stage manager, and used
everything for effect on the pit. His Christmas meant mistletoe and pud-
ding—neither resurrection from dead, nor rising of new stars, nor teaching of wise men, nor shepherds. His hero is essentially the ironmaster.[20]

This surely overstates the case and overlooks the turn in Dickens's later
career precisely towards "resurrection from dead" and spirituality more
broadly that I noted in the last chapter. (It also overlooks the more characteristic and sympathetic appreciations of Dickens's fiction expressed
by Ruskin elsewhere.) It remains true, however, that whatever Dickens
imagines as a good is never far from the comforts or pleasures of ordinary, domestic life. That he was never entirely comfortable himself with
such a homely notion does not so much undermine its truth as point us
once again to the tensions that give it life.

Notes and References

Chapter One

  1. Roland Barthes, "The Death of the Author," in *Image-Music-Text: Essays Selected and Translated by Stephen Heath* (New York: Hill and Wang, 1977); and Michel Foucault, "What Is an Author?" in *Textual Strategies: Perspectives in Post-Structuralist Criticism,* ed. Josué V. Harari (Ithaca, N.Y.: Cornell University Press, 1979); hereafter cited in text.
  2. Roland Barthes, *The Pleasure of the Text,* trans. Richard Miller (New York: Hill and Wang, 1975).
  3. R. H. Horne, "Charles Dickens," in *A New Spirit of the Age,* 2d ed., 2 vols. (London: Smith, Elder, 1844), 1:74.
  4. Robert Garis builds his *The Dickens Theatre: A Reassessment of the Novels* (Oxford: Clarendon Press, 1965) upon his perception of the peculiarly intrusive theatricality of the usual Dickens narrator.
  5. *Times* (London), 10 June 1870, reprinted in Philip Collins, ed., *Charles Dickens: The Critical Heritage* (London: Routledge and Kegan Paul, 1971), 506; hereafter cited in text as Collins 1971.
  6. Forster leaves the impression that he was alone in receiving Dickens's confidences about this period, but there is good evidence from Charles Dickens Jr. in his introduction to an edition of *DC* published in 1892 by Macmillan that his father had read the fragment to his mother sometime between its writing and the writing of *DC*.
  7. There is a great deal of literature dealing with the development of privacy and the particular flavor of Victorian domesticity. Lawrence Stone, *The Family, Sex, and Marriage in England: 1500–1800* (New York: Harper and Row, 1977) is the pioneering work in English. Philippe Ariès and Georges Duby, general eds., *A History of Private Life,* 5 vols. (Cambridge: Harvard University Press, 1987–91) is the most thorough study. Especially relevant to the nineteenth century is volume 4, *From the Fires of Revolution to the Great War,* ed. Michelle Perrot, trans. Arthur Goldhammer. Witold Rybczynski, *Home: A Short History of an Idea* (New York: Penguin Books, 1986) offers a lively and detailed account of how the ideas of home and privacy were realized in actual houses.
  8. Walter Bagehot, *The Works and Life of Walter Bagehot,* ed. Russell Barrington (London: Longmans, Green, 1915), 3:85.
  9. Henry Fielding Dickens, *Memories of My Father* (n.p.: Duffield and Company, 1929), 23–24.

10. In just two paragraphs in *LD*, Dickens manages to uses variants of the word "secret" more than a dozen times. Arthur Clennam is contemplating his mother's house:

> It always affected his imagination as wrathful, mysterious, and sad; and his imagination was sufficiently impressible to see the whole neighbourhood under some dark tinge of its dark shadow. As he went along, upon a dreary night, the dim streets by which he went, seemed all depositories of oppressive secrets. The deserted counting-houses, with their secrets of books and papers locked up in chests and safes; the banking-houses, with their secrets of strong rooms and wells, the keys of which were in a very few secret pockets and a very few secret breasts; the secrets of all the dispersed grinders in the vast mill, among whom there were doubtless plunderers, forgers, and trust-betrayers of many sorts, whom the light of any day that dawned might reveal; he could have fancied that these things, in hiding, imparted a heaviness to the air. The shadow thickening and thickening as he approached its source, he thought of the secrets of the lonely church-vaults, where the people who had hoarded and secreted in iron coffers were in their turn similarly hoarded, not yet at rest from doing harm; and then of the secrets of the river, as it rolled its turbid tide between two frowning wildernesses of secrets, extending, thick and dense, for many miles, and warding off the free air and the free country swept by winds and wings of birds.
>
> The shadow still darkening as he drew near the house, the melancholy room which his father had once occupied, haunted by the appealing face he had himself seen fade away with him when there was no other watcher by the bed, arose before his mind. Its close air was secret. The gloom, and must, and dust of the whole tenement, were secret. At the heart of it his mother presided, inflexible of face, indomitable of will, firmly holding all the secrets of her own and his father's life, and austerely opposing herself, front to front, to the great final secret of all life. (2.10)

11. The most complete study of the subject is Robert L. Patten, *Charles Dickens and His Publishers* (Oxford: Clarendon, 1978).

12. Copies of the novels in original parts are of course rare, though many libraries own them. Michael Slater presents an excellent facsimile of a complete novel in parts, including ads, in his edition of *NN* (London: Scolar Press, 1982).

13. These "memoranda and number plans," as they are called, are reproduced in facsimile in Harry Stone, ed., *Dickens's Working Notes for His Novels* (Chicago: University of Chicago Press, 1987)—hereafter cited in text—and,

where available, are reprinted in all Clarendons and some other modern editions.

14. The original illustrations must be considered part of the novels. Only *HT* and *GE* among the novels lacked illustrations in the first editions. Many modern editions reproduce some or all of the illustrations, though frequently the reproductions are poor to the point of uselessness. (Etchings are especially difficult to reproduce because their lines are not uniformly black; a lightly etched line is thin not only in width but also in depth and will print as a shade of gray. Some novels had woodcuts [*OCS, BR*] and engravings [*MED*], and these fare better in modern reprints.) The Clarendon editions reproduce all original illustrations, usually quite well. Collected editions published in Dickens's lifetime and shortly after by Chapman and Hall (frequently found in college libraries) mostly have plates printed from the original plates, as does the rare Nonesuch Press edition (1937–38), which included one of the 877 surviving actual plates in each set, thereby unfortunately ensuring that no subsequent edition could be printed from them.

15. Collins 1971 (1–26) provides an excellent discussion of the reviews and is the best collection of excerpts from contemporary reviews and criticism.

16. One such letter is quoted in George Ford, *Dickens and His Readers: Aspects of Novel Criticism since 1836* (1955; reprint, New York: W. W. Norton, 1965), 50; hereafter cited in text. See also 52–54 for evidence to the contrary. Ford's book is the most useful study not only of the history of Dickens criticism through the early twentieth century, but also of Dickens's reactions to readers' responses.

17. On one occasion Dickens gave in to the temptation to sue, over a plagiarism of *CC*. Though he won his suit, he lost £700 (Johnson 6.3). He had just the year before antagonized much of the United States press by his scolding about the issue of international copyright on the occasion of his first trip to America.

18. Quoted by J. W. T. Ley in his edition of Forster (2.1 n. 107).

19. James Agee may have been the first writer to connect *CC* with Capra's 1946 film, somewhat dismissively discussed in *The Nation*, 15 February 1947, 193. The most extended recent comparative study is in Paul Davis, *The Life and Times of Ebeneezer Scrooge* (New Haven, Conn.: Yale University Press, 1990), 163–70.

20. All of which points are noted by Steven Marcus in his "Freud and Dora: Story, History, Case History," in *Representations: Essays on Literature and Society* (New York: Basic Books, 1975), 309 n.

21. Edmund Wilson, "Dickens: The Two Scrooges," in *The Wound and the Bow* (1941; reprint, New York: Oxford University Press, 1965), 68–85.

22. Ned Lukacher, "Freud's '*Dickens'scher Styl*,' " in *Primal Scenes: Literature, Philosophy, Psychoanalysis* (Ithaca, N.Y.: Cornell University Press, 1986), 330; hereafter cited in text. We shall return to Dickens and "primal scenes" in the following chapter.

23.   The chief military meaning of the verb "police" is indeed to clean, as in "kitchen police."

Chapter Two

1.   The word identifies the peculiar atmosphere associated with Dickens, but also the people who celebrate him, especially members of The Dickens Fellowship, an organization headquartered in London at the Dickens House Museum (in which building Dickens lived from 1837 to 1839), with branches all over the world, and that publishes *The Dickensian.*

2.   Claire Tomalin, *The Invisible Woman: The Story of Nelly Ternan and Charles Dickens* (London: Viking, 1990), 3; hereafter cited in text.

3.   Michael Allen, *Charles Dickens' Childhood* (London: Macmillan, 1988), 86; hereafter cited in text.

4.   *Speeches,* xxi.

5.   From a letter to Forster (?29 September 1854 and Forster 8.2): "*Restlessness,* you will say. Whatever it is, it is always driving me, and I cannot help it. I have rested nine or ten weeks [on vacation in Boulogne], and sometimes feel as if it had been a year—though I had the strangest nervous miseries before I stopped. If I couldn't walk fast and far, I should just explode and perish."

6.   Mamie Dickens, *Charles Dickens: By His Eldest Daughter,* The World's Workers (London: Cassell, 1885), 100.

7.   In *A Likely Story: Probability and Play in Fiction* (New Brunswick: Rutgers University Press, 1989), I have discussed these topics, not in relation to Dickens but to fiction generally. See especially chapter 3, "Fictional Belief."

8.   All quotations from the fragment occur in Forster, 1.2, and quotations not otherwise cited may be assumed to be derived from thence.

9.   Forster gives his account of the fragment and his being designated Dickens's biographer at 1.1 n. 3. as well as throughout 1.2. The fullest scholarly account is in Nina Burgis's introduction to her Clarendon edition of *DC,* xvii–xix, and see also the Pilgrim letters, 5:xii and 290 n. 3.

10.   Allen, 95, estimates John Dickens's total debts at about £700, a very considerable sum, being twice his annual salary.

11.   In "The Hero's Shame," *Dickens Studies Annual* 11 (1983): 1–24, I treat shame in Dickens at some length.

12.   Steven Marcus, "Who Is Fagin?" in *Dickens: From Pickwick to Dombey* (New York: Basic Books, 1965), 358–78. See also John Bayley, "*Oliver Twist:* 'Things As They Really Are,' " *Dickens and the Twentieth Century,* ed. John Gross and Gabriel Pearson (Toronto: University of Toronto Press, 1962), 53.

13.   In a footnote, Forster writes: "Anything more completely opposed to the Micawber type could hardly be conceived, and yet there were moments (really and truly only moments) when the fancy would arise that if the conditions of his life had been reversed, something of a vagabond existence . . . might have supervened. It would have been an unspeakable misery to him, but it

might have come nevertheless. The question of hereditary transmission had a curious attraction for him, and considerations connected with it were frequently present to his mind" (8.2).

14. The phrase is Forster's, but it echoes Dickens's own language as, for example, when David Copperfield says of one of his evil doubles, Uriah Heep, "I was attracted to him in very repulsion" (25).

15. Gary Wills, "Love in the Lower Depths," *The New York Review of Books* 36, no. 16 (26 October 1989), 60–67, discusses the novel's numerous hints at Fagin's pederasty, which is perhaps relevant in this connection.

16. The article first appeared in *Bentley's* in August 1838. It is included in many collected editions along with other *Bentley's* contributions known as "The Mudfog Papers" and is often found in the volume containing *SB*.

17. Christopher Hibbert in *The Making of Charles Dickens* (New York, Harper and Row, 1967), 53–55, 73–80, usefully discusses the persistence of the blacking factory experiences in Dickens's writings.

18. Alexander Welsh, *From Copyright to Copperfield: The Identity of Dickens* (Cambridge: Harvard University Press, 1987); hereafter cited in text.

Chapter Three

1. Michael Slater's *Dickens and Women* (Stanford: Stanford University Press, 1983)—hereafter cited in the text—is the single extended study of this subject and is scrupulously researched. But there is as well a large body of feminist scholarship, several representative examples of which are listed in the selected bibliography.

2. The scenes that Marcus identifies as primal scenes are unusual in often lacking a clear representation of one of the chief players—the mother—who tends to be present if at all in highly symbolic fashion, for example, as a jewel box (a classic "Freudian symbol").

3. Forster (6.7) implies the identification, and Dickens in a letter to Richard Lane (2 January 1844) writes as though Mrs. Nickleby certainly had an original well known to him ("Mrs. Nickleby herself, sitting bodily before me in a solid chair, once asked me whether I really believed there ever was such a woman.")

4. In providing Dora's original, she thus, if we follow the Lukacher line, earns a significant place for herself in the history of psychoanalysis.

5. Gladys Storey, *Dickens and Daughter* (London: F. Muller, 1939), 164; hereafter cited in text.

6. Facts and quotations in what follows concerning Mary and Christiana Weller may be found in Slater's chapter on Mary, pp. 77–102.

7. Except as otherwise noted, I rely for details about Dickens and the de la Rues on the account of Fred Kaplan, *Dickens and Mesmerism: The Hidden Springs of Fiction* (Princeton: Princeton University Press, 1975), 74–105; hereafter cited in text.

8. No one has been able to offer an explanation of what this trouble might have been. There is a letter to Forster of ?8 March 1838—a couple of days after Mary's birth—with a postscript of four and a half lines that have been so heavily canceled as to be illegible even under infrared and ultraviolet light (Pilgrim Letters, 1:385).

9. In addition to Slater's very thorough account (103–62), Phyllis Rose has written astutely about the marriage in *Parallel Lives: Five Victorian Marriages* (New York: Alfred A. Knopf, 1983). Facts about the breakup not otherwise referenced can be found in Slater.

10. In 1860 Dickens held a great bonfire of all the letters he had accumulated over the years, "shocked by the misuse of the private letters of public men," and a tremendously interesting collection of letters by leading Victorians was thereby lost to scholarship, though it amused his children to have "roasted onions in the ashes of the great" (Johnson, 9.2). It seems likely that Dickens's anxiety about his privacy was heightened by his relationship with Nelly.

11. Slater, 376–79, usefully summarizes the very thin evidentiary record in his appendix B, and Tomalin, 167–82, devotes a chapter to "The Year of the Diary." Important earlier discussions of the evidence are Ada Nisbet, *Dickens and Ellen Ternan* (Berkeley: University of California Press, 1952) (hereafter cited in text), and Felix Aylmer, *Dickens Incognito* (London: Rupert Hart-Davis, 1959) (hereafter cited in text), the first work to decode the daily entries in the diary. Probably the single most important publication dealing with Dickens's relations with Ellen (as well as the mood of the Dickens household during the breakup of the marriage), however, has been Gladys Storey's *Dickens and Daughter,* which relayed reports of many conversations between Storey and Dickens's daughter Kate, though the evidence she presents is necessarily at second hand.

12. Her guess is not entirely original; Slater, 378, reports a similar speculation made by W. J. Carlton in 1966.

13. The authoritative account is in *Readings,* 465–71. Facts and quotations not otherwise documented will be found there.

14. George Dolby, *Charles Dickens As I Knew Him: The Story of the Reading Tours in Great Britain and America, 1866–1870* (London: T. Fisher Unwin, [1912]), 386.

15. Charles Kent, *Charles Dickens as a Reader* (London: Chapman and Hall, 1872), 258.

Chapter Four

1. First appeared in the *Edinburgh Review* for June 1829 and widely reprinted. G. B. Tennyson, ed., *A Carlyle Reader* (Cambridge: Cambridge University Press, 1984), 34, 46.

2. "Bentham" appeared first in the *London and Westminster Review,* August 1838, "Coleridge" in the same journal, March 1840. The essays are widely reprinted, for example in *Mill on Bentham and Coleridge: With an Introduc-*

tion by F. R. Leavis (Cambridge: Cambridge University Press, 1980). My quotations from "Bentham" are from the Leavis edition, 39–40. Mill's claim for the centrality of these two men is sweeping and striking and deserves attention by anyone interested in nineteenth-century intellectual history, especially coming from a writer who is today far more likely to be read or thought of as among the leading Victorian minds: "there is hardly to be found in England an individual of any importance in the world of mind, who (whatever opinions he may afterwards have adopted) did not first learn to think from one of these two; and though their influences have but begun to diffuse themselves through these intermediate channels over society at large, there is already scarcely a publication of any consequence addressed to the educated classes, which, if these persons had not existed, would not have been different from what it is" (40). Coleridge made an important and closely related distinction between the "mechanical" and the "organic" in a lecture printed in 1836, but delivered perhaps before 1810, called "Shakespeare's Judgment Equal to His Genius."

3.   There had been in the late eighteenth century a literary vogue of "sentimentalism"; among writers with whom Dickens was familiar, a notable practitioner was Oliver Goldsmith, whose *Vicar of Wakefield* was very influential for *Pickwick*. Several philosophers in the skeptical or mechanical tradition of British empiricism nevertheless believed human sympathies and compassion to be innate—most important, perhaps, Adam Smith and David Hume. The "sentimentalism" of all these writers held in common with Dickens a belief in the innate goodness of most people as against the harshly pessimistic assumptions about human nature of Calvinism. Thus the division between spirituals and mechanicals was not necessarily neater among Enlightenment thinkers than among Victorians.

4.   In an important essay, Steven Marcus shows how that very spontaneity, however, is balanced by an equally pronounced self-consciousness about language and the law and how the interplay of these signals *PP*'s important place in the history of modern thought about freedom: Steven Marcus, "Language into Structure: Pickwick Revisited," *Daedalus* 101 (1972): 183–202.

5.   "Dickens," *Selected Critical Writings of George Santayana*, ed. Norman Henfrey, 2 vols. (Cambridge: Cambridge University Press), 1:200.

6.   The fullest account is in the introduction to the Clarendon edition of *PP*, ed. James Kinsley (Oxford: Clarendon Press, 1986). I make use of Kinsley in what follows.

7.   The enormous eventual success of *PP* and the fact that it began as rather a collaborative effort, with Dickens's being brought in after some lines had already been laid down, not surprisingly led to some later controversy about how much credit might be due Seymour for the originality of the conception. A similar controversy attended *OT*, which, like *SB*, was illustrated by Cruikshank.

8.   The comparison is perhaps not entirely fair to Scott in that his novels were not available in the more affordable serial format.

9. The first is in "A Christmas Dinner" (*SB*). It is interesting for its introduction of most of Dickens's favorite Christmas themes and also for its relentless secularism. It concludes: "And thus the evening passes, in a strain of rational good-will and cheerfulness, doing more to awaken the sympathies of every member of the party in behalf of his neighbour, and to perpetuate their good feeling during the ensuing year, than half the homilies that have ever been written, by half the Divines that have ever lived." W. H. Auden was, I believe, the first to discuss the mythic qualities of *PP* (as well as to elaborate the novel's Quixotic parallels) in his important essay "Dingley Dell and the Fleet," in *The Dyer's Hand and Other Essays* (New York: Random House, 1962).

10. There is an indispensable account of Dickens's attitudes on these heads throughout his career in Norris Pope's *Dickens and Charity* (New York: Columbia University Press, 1978); see especially the introduction, pp. 1–12, and the chapters "Dickens and Evangelicalism," pp. 13–41; "Defence of the Sabbath," pp. 42–95; and "Missions and Missionaries," pp. 96–151.

11. Forster briefly discusses Dickens's retelling of the Gospels (5.2), which was, after all his children had died, published as *The Life of Our Lord: Written for His Children during the Years 1846 to 1849* (New York: Simon and Schuster, 1934). The anonymous foreword quotes Georgina Hogarth, to whom the manuscript was willed along with all of Dickens's private papers, as saying Dickens begged that it not even be taken outside of the house, much less printed, even privately (6). In the early forties, Dickens for a few years attended Unitarian chapels, but by the end of his life, as Forster (himself a Unitarian) explicitly reports, he died quite reconciled with the doctrines of the Church of England (4.1).

12. John Bowring, ed., *The Works of Jeremy Bentham, Published Under the Superintendence of His Executor,* 11 vols. (1843; reprint, New York: Russel and Russel, 1962), 11:71. Bentham's specifying that "this copy" was written on this date suggests this was a favorite motto written by him many times under similar circumstances.

13. Without invoking sentiment, John Stuart Mill makes the same point more generally about Bentham's thought; in defending Utilitarianism against the kinds of criticism that Dickens appears to make of it in *HT*—that it is all about pursuing one's own interests, especially economic interests—he writes that "In the golden rule of Jesus of Nazareth, we read the complete spirit of the ethics of utility." *Utilitarianism,* ed. Oskar Piest (Indianapolis: Bobbs-Merrill Educational Publishing, 1957), 22.

14. See my "Pickwick in the Utilitarian Sense," *Dickens Studies Annual* 23 (1994): 49–72.

15. I follow here Dickens's 1867 substitutions of "Fagin" for "the Jew."

16. Marcus (65n.) quotes this passage in connection with his discussion of *Oliver's* use of imagistic darkness, but oddly doesn't connect the passage with *OT,* p. 34.

17. Henry James recalled that when he read the novel as a boy, the illustrations of the "nice people and the happy moments . . . frightened me almost as much as the low and the awkward" (quoted in Collins 1971, 614).

18. By "romance" I mean loosely a story full of wonderful incidents that involves a quest or test that establishes the identity of the hero *as* a hero. G. K. Chesterton's essay on *NN* as romance in *Appreciations and Criticisms of the Works of Charles Dickens* (London: J. M. Dent and Sons, 1911)—hereafter cited in text as Chesterton 1911—is masterful.

19. Chapter 6 of *NN* was published May 1838; chapter 34 of *OT* was published in June.

20. "Be a woman," he urges Kate when for a second time their uncle blackmails Nicholas into quitting London, "and do not make me one while *he* looks on"; but no sooner is he alone than "he gave free vent to the emotions he had so long stifled" (20).

21. As also is Shakespeare. In chapter 27 there is a particularly extended comic discussion of Shakespeare that ends with Mrs. Nickleby's story of visiting his birthplace while pregnant with Nicholas, dreaming of the bard the next night, and her subsequent anxieties that Nicholas might have turned out to be "a Shakespeare, and what a dreadful thing that would have been."

22. Edwin M. Eigner's *The Dickens Pantomime* (Berkeley: University of California Press, 1989) provides the richest discussion of Dickens's lifelong debt to this peculiarly British tradition of children's drama that is still an essential part of Christmas celebrations in Britain.

23. *MHC,* 6. In April 1840 Dickens began *MHC,* initially intended to be a miscellany of shorter pieces and imagined as emanating from the elderly Master Humphrey, a deformed eccentric, reclusive except for serving as chair to a club of a half dozen equally strange old men who gather weekly to exchange stories and take their name from an ancient clock that has been Master Humphrey's "comfort and consolation" from his earliest childhood and whose "huge oaken case curiously and richly carved" serves as the depository of the manuscripts of the stories the old men tell (1). *OCS* began in the fourth number as among the "Personal Adventures of Master Humphrey," and when Dickens realized his public's interest was far greater in Nell's story than any others (which included reprises of Mr. Pickwick and his circle), he let it take over the periodical entirely with the eighth number, rather awkwardly abandoning Master Humphrey's first-person narration for that of an omniscient third-person narrator. After its completion, *MHC* continued with *BR,* and Master Humphrey did not reappear until the 87th number in November 1841. For Dickens's original ideas for *MHC,* see Pilgrim letters, 1:563–65.

24. Quoted by Hesketh Pearson, *Oscar Wilde, His Life and Wit* (New York: Harper and Brothers, 1946), 208. It may be worth noting here that Dickens never uses the words "sentimental" or "sentimentality" in *OCS* except ironically or satirically.

25. We are later told that Nell is "nearly fourteen" (6) "and would be a woman soon" (54); together with repeated references to her as a "little girl," this suggests that she is on the verge of puberty.

26. Not least among the word *curious*'s complexities is that it can refer both to subject and object, to the psychological state of being curious as well as the quality that renders someone or something an object of curiosity. It is cognate with "cure" and "care" (both of which are in short supply in *OCS*). Thus "curiosities" once identified things carefully made as well as things rare or strange. *Curiosa* is a book dealers' term for books on unusual subjects, but especially erotica.

27. This passage was added after *OCS*'s appearance in *MHC* for the first volume edition in 1841. Robert M. Polhemus offers illuminating commentary in "Comic and Erotic Faith Meet in the Child: Charles Dickens's *The Old Curiosity Shop* ('The Old Cupiosity Shape')," *Critical Reconstructions,* ed. Robert M. Polhemus and Roger B. Henkle (Stanford: Stanford University Press, 1994).

28. But for some possible rivals see *OT*, 5, a chapter describing Oliver's brief employment by Mr. Sowerberry, the undertaker.

Chapter Five

1. I borrow my phrase from Myron Magnet's *Dickens and the Social Order* (Philadelphia: University of Pennsylvania Press, 1985), which offers an important corrective to the frequently voiced view that the younger Dickens inclined towards political radicalism.

2. By far the best discussion of the countless characters in Dickens who either cannot quite grow up or who grow up prematurely is in Malcolm Andrews, *Dickens and the Grown-Up Child* (Iowa City: University of Iowa Press, 1994). Andrews studies professional infants, cases of arrested development, premature little adults, little mothers and housekeepers, and childlike gentle men.

3. Dorothy Van Ghent, "The Dickens World: A View from Todgers's," *The Sewanee Review* 58 (1950), 419–38.

4. Steven Marcus, "The Self and the World," in *Dickens: From Pickwick to Dombey* (New York: Basic Books, 1965), 220–21.

5. Robert Polhemus in *Comic Faith: The Great Tradition from Austen to Joyce* (Chicago: University of Chicago Press, 1980), 88–123, and Alexander Welsh (16–42) both write astutely about the autobiographical elements in Pecksniff.

6. Hilary Schor in *Dickens and the Daughter of the House* (Cambridge: Cambridge University Press, forthcoming 1999) argues persuasively and more broadly in her introduction that "reading with the daughter in mind makes a necessary difference in 'the Dickens novel.' "

7. Possible exceptions would be Georgina Hogarth's (Dickens's 15-year-old sister-in-law) becoming a permanent member of the household shortly

after Charles and Catherine's return from America (Georgina clearly filled the space left by Mary's death five years before) and the relationship with Madame de la Rue in 1844 discussed in chapter 3. It is hard to imagine, though, how either of these could in themselves have produced so significant and lasting a shift of interest in the fiction.

8. Stone, 49. There are two sheets of number plans for *MC*, in what would become Dickens's usual format, but they are relatively abbreviated.

9. In "Embodying *Dombey:* Whole and in Part," *Dickens Studies Annual* 18 (1990), 197–219, I have detailed the novel's fascination with maintaining wholeness as well as its treatment of gender—material from which I shall draw further along in this chapter.

10. Kathleen Tillotson, *Novels of the Eighteen-Forties* (Oxford: Clarendon Press, 1954), 164 n. 4. And see also her "A Lost Sentence in *Dombey and Son,*" *The Dickensian* 47 (1951), 81–82.

11. My phrase "turn to the feminine" of course may be taken to imply at the same time a turning *from* the masculine as it is being redefined especially in the public world of business and as against older, chivalric definitions important to the concept of the "gentleman" (which I discuss in the final chapter, and from which Dickens never seriously turns). For an excellent study of the various models of masculinity available to the Victorians, see Herbert Sussman, *Victorian Masculinities: Manhood and Masculine Poetics in Early Victorian Literature and Art* (Cambridge: Cambridge University Press, 1995).

12. The *Oxford English Dictionary* records the first use of the word in print to refer to things that "cannot be approached in confidence or intimacy" in *DS*. In chapter 45, Dickens applies the word also to Edith.

13. Welsh's very full discussion ("Dombey as King Lear," in *From Copyright,* 87–103) follows Tillotson (*Novels,* 170–71).

14. [Florence:] "Is there any word that I shall say to him from you?" . . .

> "Tell him I am sorry that we ever met."
>
> "No more?" said Florence after a pause.
>
> "Tell him, if he asks, that I do not repent of what I have done—not yet—for if it were to do again tomorrow, I should do it . . . but that being a changed man, he knows, now, it would never be. Tell him I wish it never had been."
>
> "May I say," said Florence, "that you grieved to hear of the afflictions he has suffered?"
>
> "Not," she replied, "if they have taught him that his daughter is very dear to him. He will not grieve for them himself, one day, if they have brought that lesson, Florence."
>
> "You wish well to him, and would have him happy. I am sure you would!" said Florence. "Oh! let me be able, if I have the occasion at some future time to say so?" (61)

15. Julian Moynahan brilliantly discusses firmness in "Dealings with the Firm of Dombey and Son: Firmness versus Wetness," in *Dickens and the Twentieth Century,* ed. John Gross and Gabriel Pearson (Toronto: University of Toronto Press, 1962), 121–31.

16. About Toots the always worthwhile Chesterton writes: "Lastly, there is the admirable study of Toots, who may be considered as being in some ways the masterpiece of Dickens. Nowhere else did Dickens express with such astonishing insight and truth his main contention, which is that to be good and idiotic is not a poor fate, but, on the contrary, an experience of primeval innocence, which wonders at all things" (Chesterton 1911, 126–27).

17. The name "Gay," it may be noted, carried no association with homosexuality for the Victorians; in addition to referring to innocent joy or mirth, however, it could refer to looseness or immorality, and had come via this sense to be associated specifically with female prostitutes. Dickens's original plan for Walter in fact had been "to show him gradually and naturally trailing away, from that love of adventure and boyish light-heartedness, into negligence, idleness, dissipation, dishonesty, and ruin" (Forster, 6.2).

18. Malcolm Andrews's excellent chapter on *DS* (*Grown-Up Child,* 112–34) aptly notes the "new dimension to Dickens's interest in childhood" here (112). It offers a very interesting and full discussion of little Paul's being "old-fashioned" as against his "new-fashioned" father.

19. Perhaps there is a hint of what is to befall Paul in Smike, who is, after all, Kate's cousin if not her brother and a double for Nicholas as well.

20. "Son and Heir" is also the name of the ship in which Walter sails for Barbados (13).

21. Classic and early expressions of this view can be found in G. H. Lewes's 1872 review of Forster for *Fortnightly Review* (Collins 1971, 574) and E. M. Forster's *Aspects of the Novel* (1927; reprint, New York: Harcourt, Brace and World, 1956), 67–72.

22. In addition to Lukacher's *Primal Scenes,* cited in chapter 1, a notable exception is D. A. Miller's "Secret Subjects, Open Secrets," in *The Novel and the Police* (Berkeley: University of California Press, 1988). Miller takes good advantage of his happening to share David's first name and faces head on the problem of the twin risk of writing about autobiographical subjects with whom we strongly identify: "the embarrassing risk of *being too personal*" against its opposite of "*not being personal enough*" (193).

23. Aunt Betsey does say of her husband, however, that "He had been so cruel to me, that I might have effected a separation on easy terms for myself" (47). See Barbara Bodichon, *A Brief Summary, in Plain Language, of the Most Important Laws Concerning Women* (1854; reprint, in *Barbara Leigh Smith Bodichon and the Langham Place Group,* ed. Candida Ann Lacey [New York: Routledge and Kegan Paul, 1987]), 23–35, for an instructive contemporary account of the relevant law.

24.   Chesterton's disappointment is typical, but also wise and germane to our theme of growing up:

> Bleak House is not certainly Dickens's best book; but perhaps it is his best novel. Such a distinction is not a mere verbal trick; it has to be remembered rather constantly in connection with his work. This particular story represents the highest point of his intellectual maturity. Maturity does not necessarily mean perfection. It is idle to say that a mature potato is perfect; some people like new potatoes. A mature potato is not perfect, but it is a mature potato; the mind of an intelligent epicure may find it less adapted to his particular purpose; but the mind of an intelligent potato would at once admit it as being, beyond all doubt, a genuine, fully developed specimen of his own particular species. The same is in some degree true even of literature. We can say more or less when a human being has come to his full mental growth, even if we go so far as to wish that he had never come to it. Children are very much nicer than grown-up people; but there is such a thing as growing up. When Dickens wrote Bleak House he had grown up. (Chesterton 1911, 148)

25.   But the phrase was by no means a Victorian invention. John Bartlett in his Familiar Quotations, 9th ed. (Boston: Little, Brown, and Company, 1901) notes that the phrase is used by John Wesley in his sermon "On Dress," and in a note to a similar notion expressed by Francis Bacon ("Cleanness of body was ever deemed to proceed from a due reverence to God"), traces the idea to the Hebrew fathers.

26.   She writes, "Dirt offends against order." Mary Douglas, Purity and Danger: An Analysis of Concepts of Pollution and Taboo (New York: Frederick A. Praeger, 1966), 2.

27.   Though it would be almost 10 years before Darwin published the theory of natural selection, already from the mid-forties on there were widely read hypotheses about the evolution of species, as for example in Robert Chambers's 1844 Vestiges of the Natural History of Creation.

28.   The richest compendium of historical information bearing on the novel is in Susan Shatto, The Companion to Bleak House (London: Unwin Hyman, 1988).

29.   J. Hillis Miller, Charles Dickens: The World of His Novels (1958; reprint, Bloomington: Indiana University Press, 1969), 187–90. My Dickens on the Romantic Side of Familiar Things (New York: Columbia University Press, 1977), 20–28, elaborates this circularity and also the novel's related uncanniness (47–92), discussed below. See also Miller's introduction to the Penguin edition of the novel (Harmondsworth: Penguin Books, 1971) and Ian Ousby, "The Broken Glass: Vision and Comprehension in Bleak House," in Nineteenth-Century Fiction 29 (1975): 381–92, for excellent accounts of the novel's peculiar epistemological puzzles.

30. D. A. Miller, "Discipline in Different Voices: Bureaucracy, Police, Family, and *Bleak House,*" in *The Novel and the Police* (Berkeley: University of California Press, 1988), 58.

31. The image of the shadow is poignant given Esther's last name, which is of course a fiction that oddly must have been invented by Miss Barbary in an unguarded moment.

32. The misprint "confessedly" for "confusedly" slips in here after the Cheap Edition (1858).

33. James Broderick and John Grant's "The Identity of Esther Summerson," *Modern Philology* 55 (1958): 252–58, marks the beginning of the shift. Other important defenders are William Axton, "The Trouble with Esther," *Modern Language Quarterly* 26 (1965): 545–57; Martha Rosso, "Dickens and Esther," *The Dickensian* 65 (1969): 90–94; Alex Zwerdling, "Esther Summerson Rehabilitated," *PMLA* 88 (1973): 429–39: and Timothy Peltason, "Esther's Will," *ELH* 59 (1992): 671–91.

34. There is an interesting comparison to be made between Esther and Jane Eyre, whom Ellen Moers notices is a probable precursor in *"Bleak House: The Agitating Women," The Dickensian* 69 (1973): 13–24. In Esther, Dickens may have intended to show the world another governess who succeeds without being so quick to express her own discontent as Jane is. In *"Villette and Bleak House*: Authorizing Women," *Nineteenth-Century Literature* 46 (1991): 54–81, I have elaborated a comparison of Esther with another of Charlotte Brontë's heroines, Lucy Snowe, whose appearance is almost simultaneous with Esther's. Though quick to register their discontents, both Jane and Lucy are practically as obedient as Esther to their respective masters, however.

35. See Bruce Robbins, "Telescopic Philanthropy: Professionalism and Responsibility in *Bleak House,*" in *Nation and Narration,* ed. Homi K. Babba (London: Routledge, 1990), 213–30, for an interesting critical discussion of Esther's "amateurish" (214) ethics and their intersection with politics in the novel.

36. *The Standard Edition of the Complete Psychological Works of Sigmund Freud,* ed. James Strachey, 23 vols. (London: Hogarth Press, 1962–73), 17:219–56.

37. In chapters 25 and 39. Both instances involve Agnes. What is odd is that David writes about *déjà vu* the second time as though he has forgotten his first mention of it, thus evoking for the reader precisely what is essential to *déjà vu*: the "feeling, that comes over us occasionally, of what we are saying and doing having been said and done before" (39).

38. If *Jane Eyre* is a precursor of *BH,* Mlle. Hortense may be seen as an incarnation of Bertha, a double for Esther who represents all the rage she has successfully repressed. She also of course doubles for Lady Dedlock. Both Esther and Lady Dedlock have good reasons for wanting Tulkinghorn dead once he recognizes their relationship, and these doublings thus help integrate Tulkinghorn's murder into the plot, for Hortense's ostensible motive—her failure to

extort money from Tulkinghorn—is rather weakly connected with the secret of Esther's birth.

39. Thomas Carlyle, *Sartor Resartus,* ed. Charles Frederick Harrold (1834; reprint, New York: Odyssey Press, 1937), 196; hereafter cited in text as *Sartor.*

Chapter Six

1. Dickens uses the word "utilitarian" in *HT* only twice (1.15, 2.6) and uses it moreover not in its technical philosophical sense, but rather in the sense that refers to the practical as against the aesthetic—a sense the *Oxford English Dictionary* first records only in 1847 but that predominates today. It is interesting that the OED ascribes one of the first uses of "utilitarianism" to Dickens in *NN* (36), and even there (in spite of what the *OED* claims) the sense has to do with mere practicality and not Bentham's Greatest Happiness Principle. Dickens thus plays a small part in yoking "Utilitarianism" to the sense of "utility" that refers to what is serviceable as against pleasurable (which had been current from the fourteenth century onward).

2. This letter is often misdated 30 January 1855 (Pilgrim letters, 7:492).

3. Wilson's essay is noted above in chapter 1, note 21. Philip Collins writes a fascinating account of the almost total critical silence about the large symbolic work of the prison from its first publication until over 80 years later (*"Little Dorrit:* The Prison and the Critics," *Times Literary Supplement,* 18 April 1980, 445–46), though he fails to notice Chesterton, who writes, "The people of *Little Dorrit* begin in a prison; and it is the whole point of the book the people never get out of prison" (Chesterton 1911, 211).

4. The narrator here echoes a sinister remark made earlier in the chapter by Miss Wade that is even more clearly about Providence: "In our course through life we shall meet the people who are coming to meet us, from many strange places and by many strange roads, . . . and what it is set to us to do to them, and what it is set to them to do to us, will all be done."

5. "Little Dorrit," *The Opposing Self* (1955; reprint, New York: Viking Press, 1959), 58. The essay appeared also in the *Kenyon Review* and in 1953 in slightly different form as the introduction to the Oxford Illustrated Dickens volume of *LD.* Remarkably, the essay barely discusses Little Dorrit herself.

6. Dickens will meet Ellen Ternan only three or four months after writing about Arthur's mother's bitterness about "singers, and players, and such-like children of Evil" whose temptations lead to her husband's fall (2.30). Is Dickens perhaps unconsciously laying the ground for his own fall here?

7. Mrs. Clennam also tells her own story, though she shares its telling with Rigaud (2.30).

8. Esther's love for her "Pet" and "darling" Ada Clare has likewise sometimes been perceived as homosexual; it is difficult however to know whether to characterize such passionate same-sex loves among the Victorians

that so far as we know did not involve conscious or overt "sex" as "sexual" when for them the issues of sexual orientation or identity or an unconscious sexuality were as yet unformed.

9. This is very similar to the charge that Mrs. Reed brings against Jane Eyre and thus suggests that in Miss Wade, as in Esther, Dickens is reworking material he has encountered in Charlotte Brontë.

10. Janice Carlisle, "*Little Dorrit:* Necessary Fictions," *Studies in the Novel* 7 (1975): 195–214.

11. In the early exchanges between Mr. Harthouse and Mr. Bounderby (*HT,* 2.2) there begin to bubble up concerns about pretense that look forward to the much more extended treatment in *LD.*

12. Bulwer Lytton, having read the proofs of the original ending, which unequivocally leaves Pip and Estella to go their separate ways, persuaded Dickens to revise it (and in fact Dickens did so twice: once for the weekly installments and three-volume edition, and once very slightly for the Charles Dickens Edition). Most modern editions print a revised ending but include the original in an appendix or note. See Pilgrim letters, 9:428–29 n.3.

13. In Victorian Britain, a "snob" was a slightly different being than in contemporary usage. We nowadays think of snobs as people of higher status who offensively look down on their inferiors; Victorian snobs, rather, were people of lower status who vulgarly scrambled to affect the airs of the genteel. It is easy to see how the one sense slides into the other, since in all cases snobs are self-conscious and defensive about their actual social standing.

14. Q. D. Leavis, "How We Must Read *Great Expectations,*" in *Dickens the Novelist,* ed. F. R. and Q. D. Leavis (London: Chatto and Windus, 1970), 277–331.

15. As Estella explains, the house's name—literally "Enough House"—was meant to convey that whoever had the house could want nothing more (8), but of course "satisfaction" is the last thing that the now-ruined house suggests.

16. In Victorian usage, the phrase means the kind of wish one sometimes forms when one is ill, not necessarily a wish that is in itself psychologically sick.

17. In " 'If He Should Turn to and Beat Her': Violence, Desire, and the Woman's Story in *Great Expectations,*" in *Great Expectations,* ed. Janice Carlisle (Boston: Bedford Books of St. Martin's Press, 1996), 541–57, Hilary Schor persuasively argues that the groundwork for Pip's attraction to Estella has already been laid in his relationship with Joe and Joe's story about his father's violence against his mother. For Schor, the novel as a whole "posits a self that realizes itself through violence, abusive sexuality, by being 'smitten' and loving the smiter" (547).

18. Among the best studies of the novel's plot is Peter Brooks, "Repetition, Repression, and Return: The Plotting of *Great Expectations,*" in *Reading for the Plot: Design and Intention in Narrative* (New York: Vintage Books, 1985), 113–42.

19. Probably the most often cited essay on the novel is Julian Moynahan's "The Hero's Guilt: The Case of *Great Expectations*," in *Essays in Criticism* 10 (1960): 60–79.

20. Of course it is perhaps easy to forgive her here since she is almost immediately to be horribly burned when her bridal dress catches fire (49), and while Pip heroically rescues her (burning his own hands quite badly in the process), it is only to keep her alive for a few days (57). Since Pip has already once been troubled very early on by a horrible vision of her death, imagining her to have hanged herself (8), it may be argued that her actual death is an instance of magical thinking, or at least of the fulfillment of a long-held wish.

21. The opening paragraphs of the novel immediately thematize language itself, and in good Romantic and post-Romantic fashion they radically link language and death.

22. The term "Resurrection-Man" in *TTC* is applied to Jerry Cruncher and, like "resurrectionist," meant grave robber (2.14). The grim comedy surrounding his nocturnal profession qualifies the novel's more orthodox pieties.

23. Whether this means they marry or simply become best friends is of course a question, and even if they do marry, what the marriage is actually like is also in doubt. Under this reading, I like to think of Pip and Estella as going off somewhere on the Continent, rather like Edith Dombey and Cousin Feenix.

24. Most notably, *MED* leaves us guessing not so much as about how the mystery was to turn out in terms of "whodunit," as how it was actually to be revealed and, it appears from accounts related by various of Dickens's friends, narrated by the murderer himself from his condemned cell in some strange psychological state and "as if told of another" (Forster, 11.2).

25. Odd too is that it really isn't so much a postscript as the novel's end proper, for Dickens's language announces the end of the novel as a whole (and in the Charles Dickens Edition—though not the first edition—the final chapter lacks the conventional closing words, with which all his other novels, excepting of course *MED*, in fact do end). The date of the accident specified by Dickens in the postscript, June 9, is the same as the actual date of his death, which was to occur exactly five years later. It is hard for me to accept this as mere coincidence. I rather suspect that Dickens, always the great stage manager, timed his own sudden demise with some probably-not-quite-conscious care.

26. Two excellent essays on the novel's preoccupation with death and its entanglements with the living are Catherine Gallagher, "The Bio-Economics of *Our Mutual Friend*," in *Subject to History: Ideology, Class, Gender*, ed. David Simpson (Ithaca: Cornell University Press, 1991), 47–64; and Albert D. Hutter, "Dismemberment and Articulation in *Our Mutual Friend*," *Dickens Studies Annual* 11 (1983): 135–75.

27. And they do, as in less obvious ways does *DC*, which inspired *The Metamorphosis*. See Mark Spilka's classic *Dickens and Kafka: A Mutual Interpretation* (Bloomington: Indiana University Press, 1963).

28. And it does, for Eliot's original title was a line from *OMF*, Betty Higden's tribute to her young friend Sloppy, who "do the Police in different voices" (1.16). *OMF*'s influence may also be seen in the recurring interest in death by water in "The Wasteland."

29. Contemporary reviewers of *OMF* had less trouble recognizing this than we. See, for example, the unsigned review "Mr. Dickens's Romance of a Dust-Heap" in the November 1865 *Eclectic and Congregational Review* partially reprinted in Collins 1971, 458–60. There is of course also a critical tradition running all the way back to the Bible that associates money with dirt—as in the phrase "filthy lucre" (Titus 1:7)—that runs forward to the more specific psychoanalytic association of money and feces (and that Dickens seems to be playing with in Mr. Merdle's name in *LD*—*merde* being French for *shit*).

30. Henry Mayhew, *London Labour and the London Poor*, 4 vols. (1860–61; reprint, New York: Dover Publications, 1968), 2:136–80. See also Harland S. Nelson, "Dickens's *Our Mutual Friend* and Henry Mayhew's *London Labour and the London Poor*," *Nineteenth-Century Fiction* 20 (1965): 207–22 for Mayhew as a likely source for *OMF*.

31. Actually his wooden leg has value too, for when the illiterate Mr. Boffin hires Wegg to read to him, he regards that "decoration, as if it greatly enhanced the relish of Mr Wegg's attainments" (1.5).

32. Jenny is the subject of a marvelous chapter in Garrett Stewart, *Dickens and the Trials of Imagination* (Cambridge: Harvard University Press, 1974), which argues that she is "the most complete 'imaginist' in the pages of our most imaginative novelist" (221).

33. Edwin Eigner, *The Metaphysical Novel in England and America: Dickens, Bulwer, Hawthorne, Melville* (Berkeley: University of California Press, 1978), 180, 189, 202–3.

34. In " 'To Scatter Dust': Fancy and Authenticity in *Our Mutual Friend*," *Dickens Studies Annual* 8 (1980): 39–60, I also defend Boffin's pious fraud. For a contrary view, see Audrey Jaffe, "*Our Mutual Friend:* On Taking the Reader by Surprise," in *Vanishing Points: Dickens, Narrative, and the Subject of Omniscience* (Berkeley: University of California Press, 1991), 150–66.

Chapter Seven

1. Robin Gilmour, *The Idea of the Gentleman in the Victorian Novel* (London: George Allen and Unwin, 1981) (hereafter cited in text) is the richest study of the meaning of the gentleman to the Victorians (and includes also a very useful chapter on *GE*).

2. Samuel Richardson's *Pamela* of course shows us a gentleman who makes a lady of a servant by marrying her.

3. I shall for simplicity's sake in what follows fold the gentry into the aristocracy and treat them as one, even though the gentry in England have, arguably, always been a sort of transitional and inherently mobile class—a sort

of proto–middle class. Nevertheless the very concept of the gentleman (and its etymology) depends on kinship and thus is consistent with an aristocratic model.

4. G. K. Chesterton, "The Victorian Compromise and Its Enemies," in *The Victorian Age in Literature* (1913; reprint, London: Oxford University Press, 1946), 13.

5. The most infuential study remains Max Weber's *The Protestant Ethic and the Spirit of Capitalism*, trans. Talcott Parsons (London: G. Allen and Unwin, 1930).

6. There is a fascinating study yet to be done on Dickens's profound ambivalence about Roman Catholicism. It is a theme that runs through his mourning for Mary Hogarth and *OCS, BR* of course, and *BH* (where Chancery carries much of the medieval baggage that popularly—i.e., in bigoted English Protestant opinion—attaches to Catholicism).

7. Of course the religious beliefs and intentions of the founders of the U.S. Constitution are controversial, but the Constitution's insistence on the separation of church and state effectively secularizes the state and gives nonbelievers and believers equal standing.

8. Ian Watt, *The Rise of the Novel* (London: Chatto and Windus, 1957); hereafter cited in text. See also Michael McKeon, *Origins of the English Novel, 1600–1740* (Baltimore: Johns Hopkins University Press, 1987); Homer O. Brown, *Institutions of the English Novel from Defoe to Scott* (Philadelphia: University of Pennsylvania Press, 1997); and Richard Kroll, ed., *The English Novel*, 2 vols., Longman Critical Readers (London: Longman, 1998).

9. For an account of this sympathetic project that also connects it with the middle class, though in a rather less attractive light, see Audrey Jaffe, "Spectacular Sympathy: Visuality and Ideology in Dickens's *A Christmas Carol*," in *Victorian Literature and the Victorian Visual Imagination*, ed. Carol T. Christ and John O. Jordan (Berkeley: University of California Press, 1995), 327–44.

10. We should note, however, that the word *literacy* itself, according to the *Oxford English Dictionary*, first appears only in 1883 and that throughout the nineteenth century the various words formed around "literate" are as apt to refer quite broadly to literary sophistication as to the elementary ability to read.

11. The thought here, quite apart from the fact that Charley's appearance is to fetch Mortimer after the discovery of the body and the note with Mortimer's name upon it, recalls Dickens's musing about the fascination of looking at a dead body in *UT*, where he remarks a crowd viewing a body on display in the Paris Morgue who all shared "the one underlying expression of *looking at something that could not return a look*" ("Some Recollections of Mortality," Dickens's emphasis). The literate by contrast look at books "with an awakened curiosity that went below the binding" (*OMF*, 1.3)—as at a living face or as at something that *might* return a look.

12. The highly successful television series *Upstairs, Downstairs* (London Weekend Television, 1971–76) very effectively dramatizes the central impor-

tance of housekeeper and butler in the Edwardian household of an M.P. and his aristocratic wife. Perhaps significantly, there are no extended accounts in Dickens of such servants except for that of Mrs. Rouncewell.

13. See Allen, 31–34, for evidence of possible recollections of her in Dickens's writings beyond the obvious instance of Mrs. Rouncewell, for example, in "The Holly Tree Inn," CS.

14. The Merdles' Chief Butler, who terrorizes Mr. Dorrit (LD 2.16) and is utterly scornful of Mr. Merdle (2.25), provides another nice example.

15. Mickey's Christmas Carol (Walt Disney Productions, 1983) understands the common thread here by nicely incorporating the housetop-removing good spirit of DS: the Ghost of Christmas Present, played by the giant of Mickey and the Beanstalk (Walt Disney Productions, 1947), literally takes some housetops off and peeks into the rooms beneath when he is trying to locate the Cratchits (after he first appropriates a streetlamp as a flashlight). One doesn't normally look to Disney for Foucauldian insights, but the screams that the giant's action elicits also nicely register the invasion of privacy that would be a necessary consequence should the Dombey narrator's panoptical wishes be realized.

16. David Parker, "Dickens's Archness," The Dickensian 67 (1971): 149–58.

17. In an article on the "style of Dickens" in The Oxford Reader's Companion to Charles Dickens, ed. Paul Schlicke and Michael Slater (Oxford: Oxford University Press, 1999), I treat the styles of Dickens at some length.

18. Not only does Dickens delight in incorporating the linguistic oddities and novelties of every imaginable station and calling into the speech of his characters, but he adopts them himself, makes them his own and makes them the language's own too. In Charles Dickens: Linguistic Innovator (Aarhus: Arkona, 1985), Knud Sørensen has painstakingly compiled a list of more than 300 Dickensian neologisms—words and phrases that first appear in print in his works, and many of which are now common if not quite standard in English (such as "butterfingers," "the creeps," "in the same boat," "an acquired taste," "round the corner," "a good cry," "clap eyes on," "fork out," "unapproachable" (of persons), "take leave of one's senses," "hard-worked"). It is rarely easy to tell if a particular neologism registers an authentic Dickensian coinage or just Dickens's ever-alert ear, but in any case—and as in the case of Shakespeare—he exhibits a marvelous facility for being the first to publicize striking words and phrases.

19. Mark Lambert, Dickens and the Suspended Quotation (New Haven, Conn.: Yale University Press, 1981), 35.

20. Letters of John Ruskin to Charles Eliot Norton, 2 vols. (Boston: Houghton, Mifflin, 1905), 2:5.

Selected Bibliography

The number of works by and about Dickens is overwhelming. I cannot hope to include many works that I find excellent and essential (and I have not included many of the works cited in the notes). Trying to identify the two or three best pieces on individual works is an especially hopeless task, one I have not attempted. I would also be less than honest to pretend that I have been able to keep up with absolutely everything available. Up until about 1980, Dickens scholarship was plentiful but fairly cohesive. One could until then count on secondary literature to have a good sense of its own past and present. The rising interest in theory, however, and the sheer volume of scholarly production on Dickens have increased the number of studies that would or could not keep up with what others were saying or have said, and this has made the task of selecting representative sources quite difficult. (The founding of the University of California's Dickens Project in 1981 has fortunately provided a continuing and indeed global center for work on Dickens that helps offset this trend.) And then too with more recent work it is always harder to predict what will actually best stand the test of time. The proliferation in the last few years of digital resources is an additional complication. The texts of the major works and many of the minor ones are available via the Internet and commercially on disk. A fair amount of secondary work is also coming online. But Web sites and CD-ROMs are often less permanent than paper. Web sites come and go, or merely change addresses; libraries do not purchase software or multimedia at all as reliably as they do books and journals—with some reason, for material available on disk (and on the Internet) is often extremely poor in quality, more often than not having been published or posted without peer review. Except for one bibliographic resource, I have therefore limited listings of electronic resources to a separate section of very few items that have some promise of stability.

Bibliographical and Encyclopedic Resources

Dickens Studies Quarterly includes in every issue a checklist that provides the most complete and prompt listing of new editions and scholarship. The annual *MLA International Bibliography* is available on CD-

ROM and online at many university libraries, and in this form provides probably the most convenient access to almost everything published about Dickens since the early sixties. **Philip Collins's** entry in *The New Cambridge Bibliography of English Literature (NCBEL),* ed. George Watson (Cambridge: Cambridge University Press, 1969) is definitive for primary and secondary sources through 1967. **Ada Nisbet's** chapter on Dickens in *Victorian Fiction: A Guide to Research,* ed. Lionel Stevenson (Cambridge: Harvard University Press, 1966) and **Collins's** chapter in *Victorian Fiction: A Second Guide to Research*, ed. George H. Ford (New York: Modern Language Association, 1978) provide excellent and highly detailed narrative accounts of sources of every kind. *Dickens Studies Annual* supplements these with yearly roundups by distinguished scholars. **The Garland Dickens Bibliographies** provide very full annotated bibliographies on each work; at this writing about a dozen have appeared. **Greenwood Press** is publishing a series of **Dickens Companions** that provide good bibliographic information as well as extensive explanatory notations on individual works. *The Dickens Index,* ed. **Nicolas Bentley, Michael Slater,** and **Nina Burgis** (Oxford: Oxford University Press, 1988) is especially useful for information about individual characters and topographical references. The *Oxford Reader's Companion to Charles Dickens,* ed. **Paul Schlicke** and **Michael Slater** (Oxford: Oxford University Press, 1999) is the fullest encyclopedic reference and includes a select bibliography and a wealth of information on Dickens's friends and the Victorian cultural context as well as individual works and characters. Mention should be made here too of the fine volume about Dickens (Boston: Twayne Publishers, 1981) by my predecessor in this series, **Harland S. Nelson.**

Primary Sources

See "A Note on References and Editions" for editions of the major works and preferred editions of letters, speeches, and readings; see the chronology for dates of first publication of books. **Collins's** *NCBEL* entry is an invaluable source for information about the works, except individual contributions to *HW* and *AYR; The Dickens Index* usefully lists all Dickens's known journalism, and **Harry Stone's** two-volume edition of *Uncollected Writings from "Household Words," 1850–59* (Bloomington: Indiana University Press, 1968) reprints all the pieces from that journal in which Dickens is known to have had a major hand. Several facsimiles are important for an understanding of Dickens's working methods. **Harry Stone**'s edition of *Dickens's Working Notes for His Novels* (Chicago: University of Chicago Press, 1987), **Fred Kaplan**'s *Charles Dickens's Book of Memoranda* (New York: New York Public Library, 1981), **Philip Collins**'s *A Christmas Carol: The Public Reading Version* (New York: New York Public Library, 1971), and *A Christmas Carol: A Facsimile Edition of the Autograph Manuscript in the Pierpont Morgan Library* (New Haven, Conn.: Yale University Press, 1993) are especially well done and informative. **Bernard Darwin**, *The Dickens Advertiser* (London: E. Mathews & Marrot, 1930) offers generous samplings of ads from the original issues in parts. Like Michael Slater's facsimile edition of *NN* in monthly parts (cited in chapter 1), it helps recover the experiences of the first readers. Collections of letters worth mentioning in addition to those discussed in my note on references include **R. C. Lehmann**, ed., *Charles Dickens as Editor, Being Letters Written by Him to William Henry Wills, His Sub-Editor* (London: Smith, Elder, 1912); **Walter Dexter, *Mr. and Mrs. Charles Dickens: His Letters to Her*** (London: Constable, 1935); and **Edgar Johnson, *The Heart of Charles Dickens, as Revealed in His Letters to Angela Burdett-Coutts*** (Boston: Little, Brown, 1952). F. W. **Dupee** produced an intelligent and representative if abbreviated collection of *Selected Letters* (New York: Farrar, Strauss, Giroux, 1960), and **David Paroissien** has put together probably the best single volume—regrettably and unaccountably out of print—under the same title (Boston: Twayne Publishers, 1985). He arranges letters topically under the headings "Personal," "Social and Political," and "Professional" and provides excellent introductions and annotations.

Biographies

Among journals, *The Dickensian*, which began in 1905, continues to produce the most rigorous and useful contributions to Dickens's biography. As "A Note on References and Editions" implies, **John Forster**'s and **Edgar Johnson**'s biographies, both now out of print, are simply inescapable for serious students (and see also notes to chapters 1 through 3 for additional important biographical sources by **Henry Dickens, Mamie Dickens, Aylmer, Kent, Nisbet, Rose, Slater, Storey, Tomalin,** and **Welsh,** among others). Useful shorter biographies that were able to draw upon **Walter Dexter**'s three-volume collection of letters for the **Nonesuch Edition** are **Una Pope-Hennessy**, *Charles Dickens: 1812–1870* (London: Chatto and Windus, 1946) and **Hes-**

keth Pearson, *Dickens: His Character, Comedy, and Career* (London: Methuen, 1949). J. B. Priestley, *Charles Dickens: A Pictorial Biography* (London: Thames and Hudson, 1961) has excellent illustrations, as does Angus Wilson, *The World of Charles Dickens* (New York: The Viking Press, 1970), which is equally notable for its sound text, written by a major novelist who well understands that Dickens's development did not end at Warren's. Other centenary volumes notable for illustrative materials are *Charles Dickens, 1812–1870: An Anthology Chosen and Annotated by Lola L. Szladits from Materials in the Berg Collection* (New York: New York Public Library, 1970), *Charles Dickens: An Exhibition to Commemorate the Centenary of His Death, June–September 1970* (London: Victoria and Albert Museum, 1970), and E. W. F. Tomlin, ed., *Charles Dickens, 1812–1870: A Centenary Volume* (London: Weidenfeld & Nicolson, 1969). More recent biographies of note include Fred Kaplan's extremely professional *Dickens: A Biography* (New York: Morrow, 1988) and Peter Ackroyd's immense and highly idiosyncratic *Dickens* (London: Sinclair-Stevenson, 1990), which, like Wilson's, gains insight from having been written by a practicing novelist.

Dickens's childhood has naturally attracted specialized biographies. The first of these is Robert Langton, *The Childhood and Youth of Charles Dickens* (London: Hutchinson, 1891), which adds a good deal to what Forster knew; the most recent and authoritative, if dry, is Michael Allen, *Charles Dickens' Childhood* (Basingstoke: Macmillan, 1988), which corrects and adds to Johnson's account; in between is the very readable and intelligent Christopher Hibbert, *The Making of Charles Dickens* (New York, Harper and Row, 1967). Albert D. Hutter, "Reconstructive Autobiography: The Experience at Warren's Blacking," *Dickens Studies Annual* 6 (1977): 1–14, is an important psychoanalytic study that deserves to be read alongside Steven Marcus's essay "Who is Fagin?" discussed in chapter 2. Peter Rowland has compiled an interesting and entertaining autobiographical collage as *My Early Times* (London: Aurum Press, 1997). Although necessarily synthetic and in some degree fanciful, it is also scholarly, being scrupulous in identifying its components, which are drawn from all Dickens's writing, including of course the autobiographical fragment.

Dickens's celebrity in his lifetime ensured that there would be a great many published recollections. Philip Collins has gathered the best of these in *Dickens: Interviews and Recollections,* 2 vols. (London: Macmillan, 1981). For Dickens in his last years, George Dolby, *Charles*

Dickens As I Knew Him (London, T. Fisher Unwin, 1912), is worth reading in spite of its 400-plus pages. (Dolby was Dickens's manager for the reading tours after 1866.)

Historical and Background Studies, Literary History

Excellent general background studies of the Victorians especially useful to students of Dickens are **J. B. Schneewind,** *Backgrounds of English Victorian Literature* (New York: Random House, 1970); **Richard D. Altick,** *Victorian People and Ideas* (New York: W. W. Norton, 1973); and **Robin Gilmour,** *The Victorian Period: The Intellectual and Cultural Context of English Literature, 1830–1890,* Longman Literature in English Series (London: Longman, 1993). **Humphry House,** *The Dickens World* (Oxford: Oxford University Press, 1941) inaugurated modern historical scholarship on Dickens. House's account of the political, religious, and more general intellectual ethos in which Dickens wrote becomes more valuable with every year that carries us further from the Victorians. **John Butt** and **Kathleen Tillotson** in *Dickens at Work* (London: Methuen, 1957) study topical influences and demonstrate how deeply involved Dickens was—his apparently universal appeal notwithstanding—in contemporary and local issues. (**Tillotson's** introductory chapter and her chapter on *DS* in her *Novels of the Eighteen-Forties* [Oxford: Clarendon, 1954] show also how mutually influential were Dickens, Charlotte Brontë, Thackeray, and Gaskell.) **Philip Collins,** *Dickens and Crime* (London: St. Martin's, 1962) and **Philip Collins,** *Dickens and Education* (London: Macmillan, 1963) study subjects of great importance for Dickens and are worthy successors to House. So too is **Norris Pope,** *Dickens and Charity* (New York: Columbia University Press, 1978), which provides along the way a better account of Dickens and religion than do many more precisely focused studies—as for that matter does **Alexander Welsh,** *The City of Dickens* (Oxford: Clarendon, 1971), which is as much about the heavenly city as the secular. **Fred Kaplan,** *Sacred Tears: Sentimentality in Victorian Literature* (Princeton, N.J.: Princeton University Press, 1978) discusses the roots especially of Dickens's and Thackeray's responses to sentimentality in eighteenth-century intellectual history. **Robert L. Patten,** *Charles Dickens and His Publishers* (Oxford: Clarendon, 1978) is the definitive study of a subject made especially interesting not only because of Dickens's enormous sales but also because of his frequently contentious business dealings. **Edwin Eigner,** *The Dickens Pantomime*

(Berkeley: University of California Press, 1989) demonstrates the influence throughout Dickens's career of a peculiarly British tradition of children's drama that draws in turn on fairy tales (a subject frequently treated by **Harry Stone**, for example, in *Dickens and the Invisible World: Fairy Tales, Fantasy, Novel-Making* [Bloomington: Indiana University Press, 1979]).

Criticism

Journals

The Dickensian, Dickens Studies Annual (formerly *Dickens Studies*), and *Dickens Quarterly* (formerly *Dickens Studies Newsletter*) are the specialized journals. Several others produce Dickens criticism of consistently high quality—among them, *Nineteenth-Century Literature* (formerly *Nineteenth-Century Fiction*), the interdisciplinary *Victorian Studies, ELH, Novel, Studies in English Literature 1500–1900.*

Early Criticism

Philip Collins's edition *Dickens: The Critical Heritage* (London: Routledge and Kegan Paul, 1971) is invaluable for its almost 170 items published chiefly in Dickens's lifetime (including also reviews of Forster and the first collection of letters). **Stephen Wall**'s volume *Charles Dickens* in the Penguin Critical Anthologies series (Harmondsworth: Penguin, 1970) is also excellent (and includes some criticism through the mid-twentieth century). **George H. Ford**, *Dickens and His Readers* (Princeton, N.J.: Princeton University Press, 1955) is the best history of Dickens's reception to 1950, and his anthology *The Dickens Critics* (Ithaca: Cornell University Press, 1961) is a first-rate companion. **G. K. Chesterton** is for me the most enduringly interesting of the early critics (a group that includes such lights as Edgar Allan Poe, Algernon Charles Swinburne, George Gissing, and George Bernard Shaw) in his *Charles Dickens* (London: Methuen, 1906), which is quasi-biographical, and *Appreciations and Criticisms of the Works of Charles Dickens* (London: J. M. Dent and Sons, 1911), which collects the brilliant individual introductions he supplied for the **Everyman** edition of the works. **George Orwell**'s essay on Dickens in *Inside the Whale* (London: Victor Gollancz, 1940) and **Edmund Wilson**, "Dickens: The Two Scrooges," *The Wound and the Bow* (1941; reprint, New York: Oxford University Press, 1965) were both important to the revival of serious critical interest in

Dickens on both sides of the Atlantic and are still very much worth reading beyond that historical importance.

Criticism since 1950

When literary historians like Tillotson, Welsh, Eigner turn out also to be extraordinary critics, we have reason to rejoice, for nothing is more rewarding than good readings that also convey important historical knowledge. But there are first-rate works more purely devoted to readings, and it is here that the constraints of space are most acutely felt. Two excellent anthologies are **John Gross** and **Gabriel Pearson**, eds., *Dickens and the Twentieth Century* (Toronto: University of Toronto Press, 1962) and **Martin Price**, ed., *Dickens: A Collection of Critical Essays* (Englewood Cliffs, N.J.: Prentice Hall, 1967). **Harold Bloom**, ed., *Charles Dickens,* Modern Critical Views (New York: Chelsea House, 1987) and **Stephen Connor**, ed., *Charles Dickens,* Longman Critical Readers (London: Longman, 1996) are fine and more recent. As noted in chapter 6, **Lionel Trilling**'s essay on *LD* in *The Opposing Self* (1955; reprint, New York: The Viking Press, 1959, and reprinted in both Ford's and Price's collections) may well be the twentieth century's best single essay on Dickens. And **J. Hillis Miller**'s *Charles Dickens: The World of His Novels* (Cambridge: Harvard University Press, 1958) may be the most-often cited book on Dickens of the past 50 years. Miller's phenomenological stance there evolves into a poststructuralist one in his important introduction to *BH* for the Penguin edition, reprinted in Connor's collection. **Steven Marcus**, *Dickens: From Pickwick to Dombey* (New York: Basic Books, 1965) has proved almost as influential and is informed by psychoanalytic and sociological theory; after Marcus's book appeared, it was simply impossible to disregard Dickens any longer as a major nineteenth-century *thinker.* **Steven Marcus**, "Language into Structure: Pickwick Revisited," *Daedalus* 101 (1972): 183–202 (reprinted in Bloom) virtually makes the case for Dickens as a major *twentieth*-century thinker as well in looking at recognizably modernist features even of Dickens's earliest work. **Garrett Stewart**, *Dickens and the Trials of Imagination* (Cambridge: Harvard University Press, 1974) is also valuable on Joycean and Nabokovian anticipations in Dickens's style and is itself admirably stylish. **John Romano**, *Dickens and Reality* (New York: Columbia University Press, 1978) aims to correct Miller's attraction to the idea that reality *is* a fiction—as for example also in **J. Hillis Miller, "The Fiction of Realism: Sketches by Boz, Oliver Twist, and Cruikshank's Illustrations," in**

Dickens Centennial Essays, ed. **Ada Nisbet** and **Blake Nevius** (Berkeley: University of California Press, 1971)—by reminding us, especially through a reading of *OMF*, of Dickens's realistic and referential allegiances. **F. R. Leavis** and **Q. D. Leavis**, *Dickens the Novelist* (London: Chatto and Windus, 1970) signaled a major shift in opinion by F. R. Leavis, England's most important and controversial critic of the mid-twentieth century, who, in his extremely influential *The Great Tradition* (London: Chatto and Windus, 1948) had relegated Dickens to an appendix; here (as in his Clark lectures of 1967) Leavis put Dickens at the very center of his history, not just of the novel but of English literature more generally. **Raymond Williams,** writing out of a Marxist and Welsh working-class background, offered the other most intellectually challenging readings of Dickens in Great Britain at mid-century, especially in his *Culture and Society: 1780–1950* (London: Chatto and Windus, 1958)—a vital book for all Victorianists—and more expansively in his chapter on Dickens in *The English Novel: From Dickens to Lawrence* (London: Chatto and Windus, 1970) and in essays such as "Dickens and Social Ideas," in *Dickens, 1970,* ed. **Michael Slater** (London: Chapman and Hall, 1970). **D. A. Miller'**s essays on *OT, DC,* and especially his Foulcauldian reading of *BH* (reprinted in both Bloom and Connor) in *The Novel and the Police* (Berkeley: University of California Press, 1988) stand out among most recent influential work. Miller has a fine sense for the ways in which the novels collaborate in Victorian culture's "carceral" tendencies while appearing to oppose them.

Important and representative criticism on somewhat more specialized special aspects includes **James R. Kincaid,** *Dickens and the Rhetoric of Laughter* (Oxford: Clarendon, 1971) and **Robert M. Polhemus'**s chapter on *MC* in *Comic Faith* (Chicago: University of Chicago Press, 1980). **Ian Watt,** "Oral Dickens," *Dickens Studies Annual* 3 (1974): 165–81, is a tour de force of thematic criticism that makes one regret that Watt did not publish more about Dickens. **John O. Jordan,** "The Medium of *Great Expectations,"* *Dickens Studies Annual* 11 (1983): 73–88, is very astute in understanding Pip as narrator—in seeing the adult Pip always mediating the experiences of the childish Pip. **Peter Brooks'**s likewise narratological essay on *GE* in *Reading for the Plot* (New York: Alfred A. Knopf, 1984) is an established classic that shows (like the work of Welsh) how to be at once heavily indebted to Freud and original—as well as free of jargon. **Catherine Gallagher,** *The Industrial Reforma-*

tion of English Fiction, 1832–1867 (Chicago: University of Chicago Press, 1985) contains an excellent chapter on the contradictions in domestic ideology apropos *HT* and Gaskell's *North and South*. John Kucich, *Repression in Victorian Fiction: Charlotte Bronte, George Eliot, and Charles Dickens* (Berkeley: University of California Press, 1987) has an important chapter on *OMF* informed by the unclassifiable French precursor of postmodernism, Georges Bataille, and Eve Kosofsky Sedgwick's chapter on the same novel in *Between Men* (New York: Columbia University Press, 1985) gives us the first major reading of "homosocial desire" in Dickens and is interesting as well in its treatment of class. David E. Musselwhite, *Partings Welded Together: Politics and Desire in the Nineteenth-Century English Novel* (London: Methuen, 1987) has a long yet bracing chapter on Dickens in spite of being steeped in some fairly abstruse theory (most notably Gilles Deleuze and Felix Guattari's theory of desire). Ian Duncan, *Modern Romance and Transformations of the Novel* (Cambridge: Cambridge University Press, 1990) discusses Dickens as Scott's heir to the role of "national author." Richard Maxwell, *The Mysteries of Paris and London* (Charlottesville: University Press of Virginia, 1992) studies Dickens's and Victor Hugo's revival of allegory in their epistemologies of the city. Malcolm Andrews, *Dickens and the Grown-Up Child* (Iowa City: University of Iowa Press, 1994) is the best study of Dickens's very complicated thinking about childhood and sets this off against an excellent account of nineteenth-century thought about childhood more generally. Joseph Litvack's chapter on "Dickens and Sensationalism" in *Caught in the Act: Theatricality in the Nineteenth-Century English Novel* (Berkeley: University of California Press, 1992) addresses not only theatricality but the genre of the "Sensation Novel"; he writes in a Foucauldian vein to show how the novel complicates distinctions between spectacle and surveillance. Jeremy Tambling, another heir to Foucault, is interested not just in the state but in class and colonization in *Dickens, Violence, and the Modern State* (London: St. Martin's, 1995). Katherine Cummings in *Telling Tales: The Hysteric's Seduction in Fiction and Theory* (Stanford: Stanford University Press, 1991) offers a more flamboyantly deconstructionist reading of *BH* than Hillis Miller's and is also illuminating about gender.

Feminist criticism and its offspring gender studies have had a profound effect on literary criticism since about 1970, but Dickens before this (and after) has of course been written about with great intelligence by several women whose work is sensitive to issues of gender without necessarily bringing them to the fore—including, for example, **Dorothy Van Ghent, Kathleen Tillotson, Barbara Hardy,** and **Janice Carlisle.** Early classics of feminist criticism naturally tended to focus on writing by women and writers less apparently at ease with patriarchy than Dickens, but as early assumptions about the relationship of male and female writers to "dominant culture" have evolved, feminist and gender studies have produced a growing number of sympathetic (or at least pointedly ambivalent) readings that address Dickens directly. Thus, for example, **Helene Moglen,** whose 1976 book on Charlotte Brontë is a classic of American feminist criticism, eventually turned to Dickens in **"Theorizing Fiction/Fictionalizing Theory: The Case of *Dombey and Son,*"** *Victorian Studies* 35 (1992): 159–84. An important and relatively early feminist work, heavily indebted to Lacanian psychoanalytic theory, is **Dianne F. Sadoff,** *Monsters of Affection: Dickens, Eliot, and Brontë on Fatherhood* (Baltimore: Johns Hopkins University Press, 1982). Other noteworthy and relatively early studies are **Ruth Bernard Yeazell, "Podsnappery, Sexuality, and the English Novel,"** *Critical Inquiry* 9 (1982): 339–50, and **Laurie Langbauer, "Dickens's Streetwalkers: Women and the Form of Romance,"** *ELH* 53 (1986): 411–31. **Judith Newton, "Historicisms New and Old: 'Charles Dickens' Meets Marxism, Feminism, and West Coast Foucault,"** *Feminist Studies* 16 (1990): 449–70, articulates relations between feminism and New Historicism especially through a discussion of D. A. Miller's reading of *BH.* Her essay develops a line of thought begun in her **"History as Usual? Feminism and the 'New Historicism,' "** *Cultural Critique* 9 (1988): 87–122, which helpfully discusses the evolution of a wide range of feminist theory and criticism. **Helena Michie, " 'Who Is This in Pain?': Scarring, Disfigurement, and Female Identity in *Bleak House* and *Our Mutual Friend,"** *Novel* 22 (1989): 199–212, and **Mary Poovey, "Speculation and Virtue in *Our Mutual Friend,"** in *Making a Social Body* (Chicago: Chicago University Press, 1995) are especially insightful about bodies. **Carolyn Dever** has a very worthwhile chapter on *BH* in *Death and the Mother from Dickens to Freud* (Cambridge: Cambridge University Press, 1998). I expect **Hilary Schor,** *Dickens and the Daughter of the House* (Cambridge: Cambridge University Press, forthcoming 1999) to prove itself the most influential and durable of book-length feminist studies, and the most likely too to establish itself in the mainstream of Dickens criticism.

Dickens and His Illustrators

Almost all the fiction was accompanied by numerous illustrations when it first appeared, and as these were executed under Dickens's close supervision, they are considered by most scholars to be integral to the works, even though, except for George Cruikshank and John Leech, the illustrators were not extraordinarily interesting in and of themselves. (I have touched on this topic in chapters 1 and 4.) Unfortunately, because most of the original illustrations were etchings, they generally do not reproduce very well, even in better modern editions, and often they are so badly reproduced (as for example in the reissue of the *Oxford Illustrated Dickens* in 1987) as to be useless. Many libraries and used book stores make accessible editions with illustrations struck from the original plates, however, and to give the illustrations their due, it is important for serious students to make the effort to see them in the state in which they first appeared. Failing this, the first issue of the *Oxford Illustrated Dickens,* completed in 1958, has serviceable and complete reproductions (though reduced), and the **Clarendon editions** have generally very good reproductions, including the wrapper designs and extra illustrations. **Albert Johannsen** in *Phiz Illustrations from the Novels of Dickens* (Chicago: University of Chicago Press, 1956) reproduced quite well many of Hablot Knight Browne's plates in all their variants (for wear to the plates often required the etcher to produce two or even three plates); unfortunately it is itself something of a rarity. *The Dickensian* has from its inception included the illustrations among its interests and presents them well. Important secondary works are **F. G. Kitton,** *Dickens and His Illustrators* (London: G. Redway, 1899); **E. A. Browne,** *Phiz and Dickens* (London: J. Nisbet, 1913); **Arthur Waugh's** essay "Dickens and His Illustrators" and **Thomas Hatton's** "A Bibliographical List of the Original Illustrations to the Works of Dickens" in *Retrospectus and Prospectus: The Nonesuch Dickens* (Bloomsbury: Nonesuch Press, 1937); **J. R. Harvey,** *Victorian Novelists and Their Illustrators* (London: Sidgwick and Jackson, 1970); **John Buchanan-Brown,** ed., *Phiz!: The Book Illustrations of Hablot Knight Browne* (Newton Abbot: David and Charles, 1978); **Michael Steig,** *Dickens and Phiz* (Bloomington: Indiana University Press, 1978); and **Jane R. Cohen,** *Charles Dickens and His Original Illustrators* (Columbus: Ohio State University Press, 1980).

Electronic Resources

I stress again that when consulting electronic sources one should be very cautious, for much material available online has been posted or published without the checks of peer review of any sort. The Internet is as much a highway of misinformation as of information.

Project Gutenberg, currently housed at http://promo.net/pg, is probably the best source for downloadable electronic texts of the novels in the public domain—and much of the shorter fiction as well. *Like the Dickens* (Parsippany, N.J.: Bureau of Electronic Publishing, 1994) is a CD-ROM containing most of the works (including several shorter items mistakenly attributed to Dickens), Forster's *Life,* and a miscellany of secondary sources, including Chesterton's *Appreciations and Criticisms.* Allan Liu of the University of California, Santa Barbara, maintains *The Voice of the Shuttle,* at this writing the most comprehensive collection of Internet links for literary studies; it can be found at http://humanitas.ucsb.edu and is as good a place as any to begin searching for electronic literary resources. Mitsuharu Matsuoka of Nagoya University (Japan) maintains a massive though not very conveniently organized Dickens page at http://lang.nagoya-u.ac.jp/~matsuoka/Dickens.html. The University of California Dickens Project's page is at http://humwww.ucsc.edu/dickens/index.html, and The Dickens House Museum's site is at http://www.rmplc.co.uk/orgs/dickens/DHM/DHMZ/index.html. Since film and video adaptations of the works themselves are an important subject, mention should be made here too of the Internet Movie Database, which can conveniently generate up-to-date and accurate lists of film and video adaptations of Dickens's works. It currently resides at http://us.imdb.com.

Finally, there are two noteworthy electronic discussion lists. DICKNS-L is housed at the University of California, Santa Barbara, and is devoted to Dickens. To subscribe, one should send the e-mail message "Subscribe dickns-l [one's name]" to listserv@ucsbvm.ucsb.edu. VICTORIA is housed at the University of Indiana at Bloomington; it is interdisciplinary and devoted more broadly to things Victorian. To subscribe, one should send the message "SUB VICTORIA [one's name]" to listserv@listserv.indiana.edu.

Index

The Author

Robert Newsom is professor of English at the University of California, Irvine, where he has taught Victorian literature since 1977 and is Associate Dean, Division of Undergraduate Education. He received his undergraduate education at Columbia College and Clare College, Cambridge, and returned to Columbia University for his Ph.D. He has also taught at Columbia and the University of California, Riverside. He is on the faculty of the University of California's Dickens Project and has also served as an associate director and member of its Publications Board. He is a member and former trustee of the Dickens Society of America. In addition to his publications on Dickens—which include a book on *Bleak House, Dickens on the Romantic Side of Familiar Things* (New York: Columbia University Press, 1977)—and other essays and reviews, he has written about the problem of literary probability or verisimilitude in *A Likely Story: Probability and Play in Fiction* (New Brunswick, N.J.: Rutgers University Press, 1988). He is currently working on a book about Dickens and Bentham.

The Editor

Herbert Sussman is professor of English at Northeastern University. His publications in Victorian literature include *Victorian Masculinities: Manhood and Masculine Poetics in Early Victorian Literature and Art; Fact into Figure: Typology in Carlyle, Ruskin, and the Pre-Raphaelite Brotherhood;* and *Victorians and the Machine: The Literary Response to Technology.*